INTRODUCTION TO AMERICAN CRIMINAL JUSTICE

INTRODUCTION TO AMERICAN CRIMINAL JUSTICE

FRANK R. PRASSEL

HARPER & ROW, PUBLISHERS
NEW YORK   EVANSTON   SAN FRANCISCO   LONDON

Sponsoring Editor: Alvin A. Abbott
Project Editor: Pamela Landau
Designer: Howard S. Leiderman
Production Supervisor: Stefania J. Taflinska

Introduction to American Criminal Justice

Copyright © 1975 by Frank R. Prassel

All rights reserved. Printed in the United States of America. No part of this book may be used or reproduced in any manner whatsoever without written permission except in the case of brief quotations embodied in critical articles and reviews. For information address Harper & Row, Publishers, Inc., 10 East 53rd Street, New York, N.Y. 10022.

Library of Congress Cataloging in Publication Data
Prassel, Frank Richard, 1937–
   Introduction to American criminal justice.

   Bibliography: p.
   1. Criminal justice, Administration of—United States.   I. Title.
KF9223.P7   364   74–13947
ISBN 0-06-045255-2

Contents

Preface ix

PART I CRIME

1. **Justice under Law** 4
   The Meaning of Law 4
   How Law Began 7
   Development of Legal Systems 10
   A Hierarchy of Standards 13
   Substance and Procedure 15

2. **Criminal Conduct** 18
   State Punishment 18
   Types of Crimes 21
   Extent of Violations 23
   Victims and Offenders 26

3. **Problem Areas** 31
   Disorder in the City 31
   Juvenile Delinquency 33
   Organized Crime 35
   Drugs 38
   Drunkenness and Firearms 41

4. The Criminal Culture 45
   Minorities 45
   Families 48
   Business 50
   Government 53

PART II THE POLICE

5. Organization 62
   Federal Agencies 62
   State Police 64
   Local Departments 66
   Personnel and Administration 69
   Special Police 71

6. Operations 75
   Patrol 75
   Criminal Investigation 77
   Traffic 80
   Support Functions 82
   Community Relations 84

7. Basic Procedures 88
   Arrest 88
   Search and Seizure 91
   Confessions 94
   Identification 96

8. Constitutional Safeguards 102
   Due Process 102
   Rule of Law 104
   The Exclusionary Rule 106
   Self-Incrimination 108
   First Amendment Freedoms 111

PART III THE COURTS

9. The Aftermath of Arrest 120
   Bail, or Jail? 120
   Adversary Practice 122
   The Prosecution 124
   Defense Counsel 127
   Plea-Bargaining 129

10. Judicial Systems 135
    Accusation 135
    Jurisdiction 137
    Courts 139

Judges 142
Juries 144

11. **Trial** 148
    Preliminaries 148
    Procedures 151
    Sentencing 154
    Problems 156
    Appeal 158

12. **Special Courts** 162
    Administrative Agencies 162
    — Juvenile Courts 164
    — Justice for Youthful Offenders 168
    Courts-Martial 170

PART IV CORRECTIONS

13. **Prevention** 178
    Before the Crime 178
    Agency Reform 181
    Purposes of Punishment 183
    The Correctional System 187

14. **Community Treatment** 192
    Punishment Without Confinement 192
    Agency Supervision 196
    —Juvenile Probation 200
    Adult Probation 202

15. **Imprisonment** 207
    Confinement 207
    —Juvenile Detention 210
    Training Schools 212
    Jails 214
    Prisons 216

16. **Release and Recidivism** 221
    Discharge from Confinement 221
    Aftercare 224
    Parole 226
    The Cycle of Crime 229

    Conclusion 235

    Glossary 238

    Suggested Readings 243

    Index 251

Figure 1. A Simplified Guide to the Criminal Justice System

SOURCE: *State–Local Relations in the Criminal Justice System* (Washington: U.S. Government Printing Office, 1971), p. xvi.

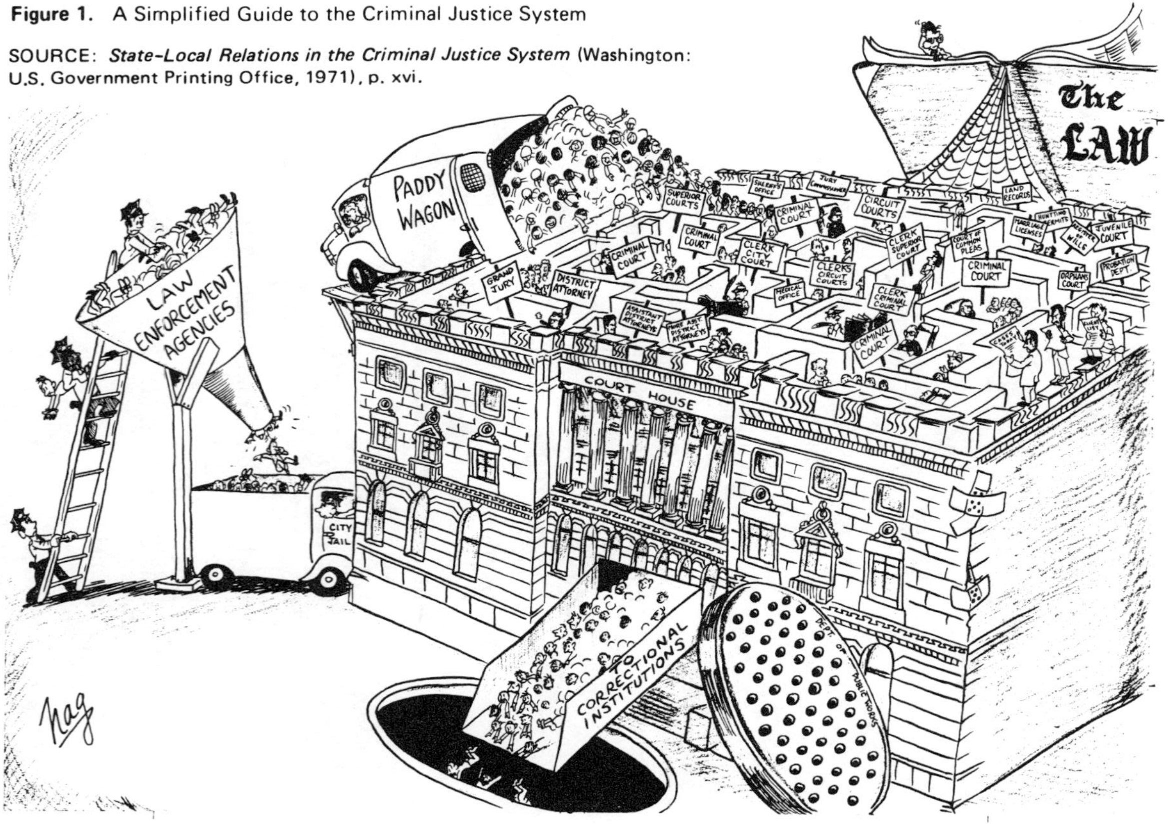

Preface

Introduction to American Criminal Justice is a marked departure from previously existing texts. Within the last decade, a new field of study has appeared in countless colleges and universities throughout the nation. Public alarm and government attention has led to the formation of a discipline devoted to criminal justice.

Even as programs sprout across the country, there remains a critical lack of a common body of knowledge mutually understood and interpreted. This paucity of fundamental information has, in part, occurred because of a continuing dependence on prior academic fields. To a certain degree, criminal justice must naturally rely upon closely related and well-established subjects. Nevertheless, a tendency for overspecialization among disciplines poses major obstacles.

This book is written to provide a preliminary framework for all those academically involved with criminal justice. In the belief that efforts toward interpretation must lie within the concept of interrelated systems rather than isolated functions, four separate areas of attention and content are presented.

First, understanding of American penal justice must start with a grasp of the total crime problem. Traditionally, this aspect has been primarily of concern to sociologists and, today, tends to be treated primarily as a cultural rather than a legal problem. Incredibly enough, this crucial area still rests on limited and frequently unreliable analyses.

Second, criminal justice really originates with those charged with the responsibility of direct enforcement—the police. Here, the emphasis has usually been on technique and administration. Within the academic setting, programs of police science or law enforcement now frequently provide quite specialized education.

Third, the process often continues to involvement with the courts. Both political science departments and law schools have conducted limited inquiries into the subject of justice in formal application. Most attention, however, is directed at conceptual analysis rather than practical interpretation.

Fourth, and finally, criminal justice naturally leads to the area of corrections. Here, those most deeply involved tend to represent the field of social work and welfare. Quite understandably, primary emphasis has been on methods of individual and group counseling for those within or without actual confinement, with principles of treatment replacing those of traditional penology.

The four separate areas of concern tend to be isolated and, to a certain degree, even contradictory. Yet, if analysis and progress are to be anticipated, a limited juncture of interest and mutual foundation of information are required. Those involved with any one of the four basic areas need a far greater understanding of the other three. *Introduction to American Criminal Justice* is designed as a device toward achievement of such objectives.

The book hopefully provides a general background for more advanced and specialized training. Its scope is broad and, admittedly, superficial. Those wishing detailed information on such subjects as juvenile delinquency, police administration, criminal procedure, or parole will find ample opportunity in more specialized texts and courses. *Introduction to American Criminal Justice* must be recognized as a learning device and not just an opportunity for subjective discourse. Attention is directed at present conditions rather than at the past or the future. Reduced to a minimum, the book will hopefully be studied as well as read.

From the standpoint of the instructor, the material herein may be covered in an intensive and fairly short introductory course. It will most often, of course, be supplemented with additional readings, statutory references, or case study. Finally, it can fill the vacuum of background knowledge sometimes encountered even among advanced students.

As a primary suggestion to the reader, criminal justice should be visualized as an ongoing process rather than isolated phases. It may involve at least four major figures: the offender, the policeman, the judge, and the correctional officer. Relations among any two directly affect the others.

Introduction to American Criminal Justice is a portrayal of reality. As such, it may serve to disillusion or even discourage. But those who work in the field soon learn that frustration and disappointment are frequent companions to our nation's system of justice. Too often, there is a wide gap between agency practice and academic theory. Hopefully, this book may also serve as a bridge connecting the two.

FRANK R. PRASSEL

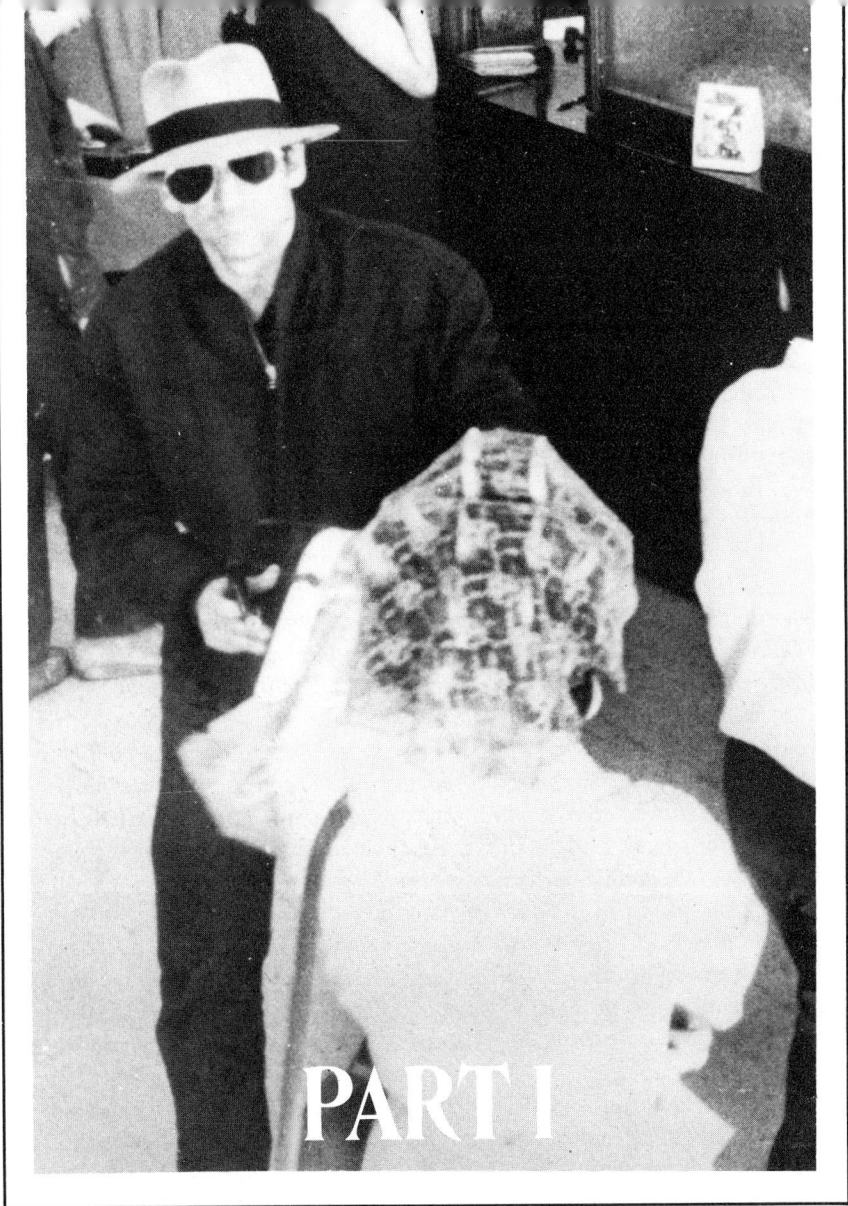

PART I

CRIME

Citizens afraid to walk alone at night, fear of the police, mistrust of judges, and disastrous prison riots are a few of the unpleasant facts of life in modern America. Anyone who regularly watches television or reads the newspapers is probably acquainted with such conditions. These problems are most definitely not new; they existed a century ago and will almost surely remain for generations to come.

Yet, a combination of increased public awareness and political attention has contributed to a marked growth in sincere concern with crime and means for its control during recent years. Greatly increased involvement by the federal government and widespread alarm over trends serve as clear indications of this new regard.

It is possible that a significant shift in attention as well as a recognition of basic social problems are beginning. If so, the United States has reached a critical phase in national development and maturity. For the first time, our society may be really preparing to confront fundamental issues of public order under law. This provides a true and original hope for reform through the efforts of interested citizens and dedicated officials. But, if such changes do occur, we must first learn in some detail about the present situation.

American criminal justice, which has a multitude of parts and aspects, is neither logical nor very efficient (see Fig. 1). Its study may well produce as many questions as answers. Part of the problem exists because almost everyone knows something about crime and justice, but most people have absolutely no concept of overall patterns and trends.

In attempting to gain some insight into the way the pieces and processes go together, one must start with some very basic facts. There really is no clear or simple criminal justice system; instead, we have a complex mixture of tens of thousands of different agencies with varied purposes, practices, and products. At times, these come into contradiction or outright conflict with one another.

Criminal justice depends in many ways upon the existence of law. It is the first major element that must be clearly understood and placed in perspective. Criminal law establishes the rules that put the procedures of justice into operation and then regulates them. This basic pattern extends back in history for hundreds of years and recognizes no national boundaries.

Law is a very complicated and involved matter. It has many systems, levels, and specialized terms. Our laws consist of hundreds of thousands of rules and concepts subject to constant change, evaluation, and interpretation. Yet, these ever shifting doctrines make up the primary reason that police, courts, and correctional agencies exist.

A crime occurs whenever a violation of the law may lead to punishment by the government. This takes place millions of times each year in the United States and has become recognized as a foremost problem in our society. Crimes fall into several categories, depending upon their seriousness, the type of harm inflicted, and which authority is offended. Exact classifications are vitally important in determining subsequent legal processes. Despite the law's literal expectations, we can only estimate the actual extent of crime and, too often, forget the personal suffering it causes.

Law violations disproportionately affect the poor, the black, the male, and the young. These characteristics commonly appear among victims and offenders alike. But crime in America is not limited by geo-

graphic, racial, economic, or other factors. It has become a most unpleasant part of daily life.

While crime in the United States is fundamentally similar to that found throughout the world, we do suffer from several special problems. Inner cities, with their dense populations of minority groups, pose particularly serious difficulties. Juvenile delinquency, while now common throughout America, is especially acute in ghetto areas, a situation closely linked to unsatisfactory family and community conditions.

The United States also faces an unusually strong threat from organized crime. Dominant in the provision of forbidden goods and services, this network of illicit power corrupts government and thrives upon the desires of willing victims. Gambling and narcotics give organized crime its greatest sources of income and create major burdens upon countless agencies of justice.

Life in America is tragically marred by the gross abuse of two very prevalent items: alcohol and firearms. The results include widespread drunkenness and violence, often in fatal combination.

Law, crime, and justice cannot be separated from culture. Each society has its own restrictions and causes for their violation. America's apparent inability to control improper use of alcohol and firearms is only an expression of far deeper problems. The basic reasons for crime are neither simple nor direct; they extend to fundamental moral, economic, and political issues.

Our nation's domestic difficulties tend to be interrelated with one another. Crime is really quite inseparable from prejudice, hypocrisy, abuse of authority, corruption, and the decay of traditional values. While no one has ever proven that any single factor specifically causes delinquent behavior, statistics do indicate that members of disadvantaged racial groups and the children of broken homes have higher rates of arrest and conviction. But such conditions are only part of a broad spectrum of complex social problems.

American culture is rife with dishonesty. Most of it never comes to the attention of the police and the courts, yet the quality of life has nevertheless been undermined. These troublesome aspects reach into routine business practices and the highest offices of government. To what degree this improper and illegal activity has become customary remains questionable, but cumulative damage to public confidence cannot be seriously doubted. To some extent, crime in America is a by-product of personal greed and unethical leadership. The continuation of such conditions may eventually prove an ultimate obstacle to justice under law.

Chapter 1

Justice Under Law

"Law is a bottomless pit."

ARBUTHNOT

The Meaning of Law

The law means different things to different people. In fact, individuals sometimes change their definition to suit the time and context of the situation. We all use the word *law* to indicate a number of things. In the physical sciences it represents an invariable statement of how matter behaves under given conditions. For example: The boiling of water at a certain temperature and pressure can be expressed in absolute terms. However, most of us speak of law not in reference to the ordering of unalterable phenomena but in terms of human beings living in society. The problem of definition then becomes much more difficult.

To the typical man on the street, "the law" probably means the police. This usage is very significant for all concerned. Our ordinary citizen is thinking, quite reasonably, in terms of his actual, daily life. He sees the peace officer as a tangible frame of reference with respect to his personal behavior. His may not be a definition always approved by scholars, but it is nonetheless very real.

The policeman, in turn, ordinarily regards the law as primarily relating to the courts and legislatures. Charged with enforcement of certain standards, he naturally thinks of the means by which regulations are written and interpreted. Quite specifically, the policeman often regards law as being dominated by representatives of the judicial system rather than by theoretical principles.

Attorneys and judges normally define the law in broader and more comprehensive terms. The meaning they might attach to the word involves a vast sea of concepts and rules sometimes incomprehensible to the layman. For them, law consists of a structure in which to work rather than a strange or mysterious set of distant ideals.

We also tend to think of law as being applicable in at least two other related and very important ways. It may be utilized in reference to both moral and social codes. First, one can speak of moral laws, a veritable revelation of the will of God. Second, we frequently think in terms of cultural precepts so widely held that they represent the strongest form of customary behavior. These two definitions revolve around our way of life and intangibly govern the value patterns of every man.

Law, which came to the English language many centuries ago from unknown Scandanavian origins, has in fact taken on so many meanings that any single and simple definition must be incomplete. Apart from the somewhat specialized and scientific usage, however, there exists a tendency to think in general of standards for social conduct. Such a common frame of reference unfortunately only indicates a broad scope of application. A definition for law requires more specific connotation, and that is a problem with which writers have been confronted for many generations.

Hermann Kantorowicz was a noted German legal philosopher who opposed the Nazi movement in the twentieth century. He defined law in complex but meaningful terms as, "a body of rules prescribing external conduct and considered justiciable." For analysis, he broke the definition down into three components. "A body of rules" can be easily understood to include a set of commands or accepted principles. "Prescribing external conduct" means things one must do, leaving out mere thoughts and emphasizing specific physical action rather than general kinds of behavior. The final element, "considered justiciable," refers to a basis for future decisions through some type of court or arbitration. Taken together, it seems that Kantorowicz defined law as rules restricting social behavior and subject to some type of interpretation.[1] The primary difficulty with this explanation occurs when it is applied to criteria for specialized groups and even the ways in which popular games are played. In some situations, the definition appears to fit, yet we would not ordinarily apply the term *law* to such standards as union regulations or football rules. These are the peripheral cases which plague most efforts at formal construction.

A great teacher and long-term member of the U.S. Supreme Court, Oliver Wendell Holmes, Jr., also provided an insight into the meaning of law. He once described it quite simply as, "What the courts will do." Holmes, of course, was a pragmatist and scholar of rare ability, and his definition has much more depth than might at first appear. He thought in terms of cold reality and, being directly concerned with decisions of judges, naturally looked to the courts for ultimate tests of true rules of conduct. Would a statute be a law if magistrates refused to apply the standard? No, it could not be, as judges have demonstrated on many occasions by striking down provisions enacted by legislatures. It is also very significant that Holmes spoke in terms of what courts *will do* instead of what they *have done*. Although a foremost supporter of past decisions (or precedent), he knew they could only be references for future interpretations. In short, Holmes recognized that law only exists in prospective application and can not always be discovered by looking into the past.[2]

Max Weber, a noted social philosopher, defined law as, "That which is enforced by a person in a special status through means that may include the use of force." It is clear that he envisioned order and authority as being directly involved, and this certainly leads to concepts of mandatory observance through sanctions. The utility of Weber's definition suffers, as do most, in application, but it does introduce two very important parts of how most of us really think of law: One is the requirement of abiding by the rules, and the second is the possible punishment we face when deviating from them.[3] Could we conceive of a law which is always ignored if broken? Probably not, since essential elements are missing.

A problem occurs in dealing with groups within larger social systems having conflicting standards. It is possible to have direct opposition between persons of recognized authority, each of whom may be using or threatening force. It is also possible to envision patterns of behavior which are so deeply held as to require no formal need for either enforcement or known sanction. In either situation there are definite problems with Weber's analysis.

Yet another side of law may be seen through the words of William Pitt, a prominent British statesman of the eighteenth century. He once wrote, "Where law ends, there tyranny begins." Pitt's comment illustrates the important but often ignored aspect of liberty and democracy. One can easily relate the element of order to rather obvious freedoms. For example, we speak of conditions as "lawless" when they are characterized by violence or intimidation. Pitt realized the danger of such conditions under both dictatorship and anarchy. To him, law represented a bulwark against despotism and the means by which society guards itself from all types of internal enemies. Such a meaning is by no means alien to modern usage. We tend to view law in somewhat altruistic terms, as representing that which is at least supposed to be fair, impartial, and disconnected from base considerations.

The contributions of Kantorowicz, Holmes, Weber, and Pitt should illustrate the ambiguous nature of the word. *Law* has been adopted by many people as standing for many different things, and no single statement as to its meaning can suffice. Law involves rules, interpretations, enforcement, and protection. At the same time, it means limitations on our behavior imposed, at times, against our personal wishes. In a sense, laws are restrictions imposed upon ourselves but which are so unpopular as to demand enforcement.

How Law Began

What is the ultimate source of law? Of course, we can sometimes trace a particular rule back in time to its origin. But of even greater significance, by what authority did it come about and continue to be? The answer is more difficult than one might guess and has led to the development of schools of legal theory or general groupings of men and ideas dealing with the source of law. For purposes of discussion, they may be classified in somewhat oversimplified form as natural, positive, and cultural.

Natural law followers are often associated with concepts of morality.[4] They claim that reason enables men to understand their own natures and to live by the dictates of a higher order. The source of law, ultimately, is faith in God and inalienable rules of conduct. This is surely the oldest of the three organized schools of legal theory. Aristotle, the famous Greek philosopher who lived more than 300 years before Christ, originated many concepts of natural law. But his ideas were carried on through the Roman Empire to St. Thomas Aquinas. During the thirteenth century, the Italian theologian put forth his views of eternal and human law as an ordinance of reason, and they have continued to be most clearly reflected in attitudes of the Roman Catholic church.[5] Natural law, however, has had many effects beyond religion. Its principles, for example, gave a foundation to the American Revolution by furnishing an explanation for resistance to formally created tyranny.

The second, or positive, school of legal theory developed in England more than a century ago. It probably originated with philosophers of earlier times, but the man most often associated with this particular interpretation was John Austin. He believed that law is based upon power and that natural law thinking would only produce anarchy. Austin felt that the "command of the sovereign" served as the crucial determinant with moral considerations completely apart. Anyone trying to integrate the laws of a dictatorship into a comprehensive definition will have to concern himself with concepts of positive law, for it heavily relies upon the strength of formal decree rather than either ethical or popular considerations.

Finally, a major category of belief falls under what may be termed the cultural school of legal theory.[6] This concept of law began with several European writers in the early eighteenth century. In England, Jeremy Bentham put forth the then revolutionary theory that legal systems had to be directly related to the people living under them and that social reforms might be effected through wise regulations.[7] Not many years later a German scholar named Friedrich Karl von Savigny asserted that law is founded directly upon custom and the historical development of the culture. Both men viewed the legal system as an integral part of the social order. The concept that law both reflects and helps mold cultural patterns has taken on great significance in recent decades, particularly in the United States, as the practical applications of democracy closely mesh with those of legal activity.

It would be a mistake to think that the natural, positive, and cultural schools need always be in conflict with one another. Each has contributed to our present interpretations and retains an independent, if constantly changing, vitality. In modern life, our law apparently demands explanations from all three of these philosophies. Few, for example, would deny that prohibitions against ordinary murder have a basis in fundamental morality. Restrictions on traffic, on the other hand, clearly emit from simple authority. Regulations against misbranding livestock, meanwhile, can be traced to obvious customs. Natural, positive, and cultural law surrounds us in ever shifting and intermixing form. It is now difficult to regard them in isolation for they have taken on practical as well as theoretical aspects.

Schools of legal theory really attempt to provide a reason for the existence of law. They remain somewhat apart from efforts to investigate the actual beginning and development of particular principles and practices. Such inquiries normally lie within the field of legal history. Relatively little is known about the heritage of many doctrines that influence modern law. In many instances, the roots of present rules and and practices extend back hundreds and perhaps thousands of years. To a very great extent the regulations under which men live are the product of history rather than current design.

The actual origin of law remains in doubt. Cavemen had no law as we understand it, but they developed patterns of behavior which eventually required enforcement, with punishment for deviation from accepted conduct. There are at least three plausible theories as to how this occurred.

First, men may have established rules to protect themselves against outsiders. In this view, the earliest laws concerned military functions such as maintaining alert guards for protection of the camp. It might also have been necessary to answer a call to arms in case of attack. Second, laws could have developed as a means of preserving internal social order and domestic security, much as our prevalent regulations attempt to do. Emerging cultures could simply have recognized the need for preventing fights and theft of property. This could logically be accomplished by rules on personal conduct. Third, men might have originated standards for behavior because of supernatural demands. If the culture believed that a superior force required observance of certain rules it would take steps to forestall deviation. Nothing would prevent religion from serving as a reason for punishment.

History appears to lend credence to each of these theories, and elements of all may yet be found in current criminal laws. We have rules against those endangering military security. Our most obvious regulations control interpretation on internal order. And penal laws, such as those against drunkenness, have clear moral roots. Similarly, anthropologists can identify cultures evidencing each of the theories. American Indian tribes, some of which possessed quite advanced legal systems, serve as examples by demonstrating apparent development from all three possible origins. In truth, it appears that different cultures might have formed concepts of law from distinct sources with a blending as social systems expanded and joined together.

Our present forms of law may be traced back to two primary sources. Asian influences, in rudimentary form, originally penetrated westward to what is now the Near East and Europe. Custom, derived from never ending changes in all societies, served as the second major determinant. Introductions from Asia came generally to a conclusion many centuries ago while standards from the culture have never stopped intermixing and developing.

We know that Babylonia possessed a complete set of formal laws by 2000 B.C. There is no reason whatever to suspect this of being the first such system, it merely happens to be the earliest of which modern man has fairly comprehensive knowledge. Portions of the codes from Asia Minor were transported to Europe and have found their way to our present law through Greece. By 600 B.C. the leading Greek city-states had evolved their own legal systems, and these in turn influenced the Romans.

Rome represents a critical point in the development of law. About 450 B.C. the *Decemviri* (or ten learned men) organized customs into what is known as the Code of Twelve Tables modeled along earlier efforts in Greece. The *Decemviri* formalized many important concepts which continue to dominate our law. Roman rules underwent modification, confusion, and increasing complexity for a thousand years. Then, in the sixth century A.D., Justinian, ruler of the related Byzantine Empire centered at Constantinople, caused the entire law to be rewritten in simpler and more coherent order. The *Codex Justinianus*, apart from later supplements, was completed in 529 to constitute the single most significant guidepost in legal development.[8]

As the so called "Dark Ages" began in Europe, much of the carefully organized law of the Byzantine era fell into partial disuse. A great new wave of more rudimentary standards based on custom swept across the fragmenting world of Western man. Germanic tribes brought ideas which ultimately combined with elements of the crumbling Roman codes to form the feudal system. The process, of course, required many generations and took different forms in diverse regions.

Meanwhile, the contributions of Rome were preserved largely through the dedicated efforts of clerics who founded a new set of rules in Canon, or church, law. Roman Catholic writers also relied heavily upon their interpretations of ancient Jewish custom. The inclusion of human concepts, exemplified by the Ten Commandments of Moses, had begun with the decline of Rome. But Canon law principles became interwoven with feudal concepts, despite continued efforts to separate church and secular authority.

Development of Legal Systems

During the Middle Ages, a basic division in systems of law began in Europe. This primary separation of concepts has endured for nearly a thousand years. In Britain, the tribal traditions of Angles, Saxons, Jutes, and Celts were, beginning in 1066, deluged by the Norman conquest. The invaders brought feudal policies which they engrafted upon local custom and established procedures. These formed a foundation for gradual development of a system known as common (or English) law, which places great emphasis upon the precedence established by earlier cases. Geographic and social isolation permitted the concepts to grow for many generations with comparatively little influence from other sources.[9] Within a few hundred years, the common law hammered out basic principles of unique distinction. Under Henry II, who ruled from 1154 to 1189, the centralized court system established many important principles. During the thirteenth century, an English writer named Henry de Bracton compiled a very important set of rules based largely upon the precedent built by prior court decisions. He emphasized restrictions upon the government itself, as exemplified by the Magna Carta of 1215.

On the continent of Europe, meanwhile, development of legal provisions followed a very different course. During the fourteenth century, an energetic young teacher named Bartolus attempted to bring about a more rational and organized approach to law. He turned back to the old Justinian code, and became a founder of the civil (or continental) legal system. Bartolus stressed that the most practical form of law would be based upon direct interpretation and application of written statutes.[10] The newly developing nation-states of Europe relied heavily upon such methods, and produced an inquisitorial approach to cases with the state both discovering the facts and applying appropriate regulations.

Most influential of the national efforts to reorganize law were those of France under Napoleon Bonaparte. The French model spread across the continent and led, eventually, to a relatively uniform system for most of Europe. The principles of the Napoleonic codes were then transmitted throughout the world by empires of many nations. Thus, concepts of civil law came to dominate in areas far removed from their birthplace.

While the continental system developed and expanded, that of England remained closely connected to tradition and precedent.[11] Many writers and judges helped maintain the peculiar majesty of the common law. Then, in the eighteenth century, a British scholar named William Blackstone prepared his very influential *Commentaries on the Laws of England*. This collection of rules spread throughout the English-speaking world and dominated much of common law for several generations. In the United States, Blackstone's interpretations became especially significant because of a temporary shortage of books.[12] Like their civil counterparts, common law principles such as use of juries were exported during the colonial era and took root, by virtue of the English language, in many modern nations.

Today both the English and the continental systems are very much alive. They are, however, not entirely separate. Over the centuries, a considerable degree of exchange between the two approaches occurred; this tendency, especially in regard to criminal matters, continues. Use of the jury, for example, has declined in common law areas while being partially adopted by followers of the civil system. Distinctions today are often of degree. In general, civil law statutes are phrased in broad but concise terms, while reflecting careful organization and craftsmanship of construction. Common law regulations are ordinarily very detailed and numerous; they often demonstrate the contradictory views of many direct contributors at different times in history. The civil system, with its reliance upon judges to interpret and apply statutes, tends to be efficient and expeditious. Common law and the pronounced role of precedent established case by case has uniformity and protection of individual liberty among its attributes.

The mixture of the two legal systems of the Western world, English and continental, may be illustrated in the United States (see Fig. 2). Common law is, without doubt, the primary basis of the American approach, but all jurisdictions have attempted to gather and organize their statutes into codes, reflecting the civil tradition. In fact, it has long been fashionable to recodify such provisions with an unfortunate tendency to promote additional confusion and continued demand for reform. The rules demonstrate remarkable durability; many have endured without significant change for several generations and reflect standards established in England many centuries ago.

Only one state, Louisiana, has a clear civil law history. Its codes may be traced back to the influence of Napoleon and even to the formulations of Justinian's time. Of course, Louisiana's statutes contain many adaptations of the English precedents used elsewhere in the nation. Civil law principles found their way into other parts of the United

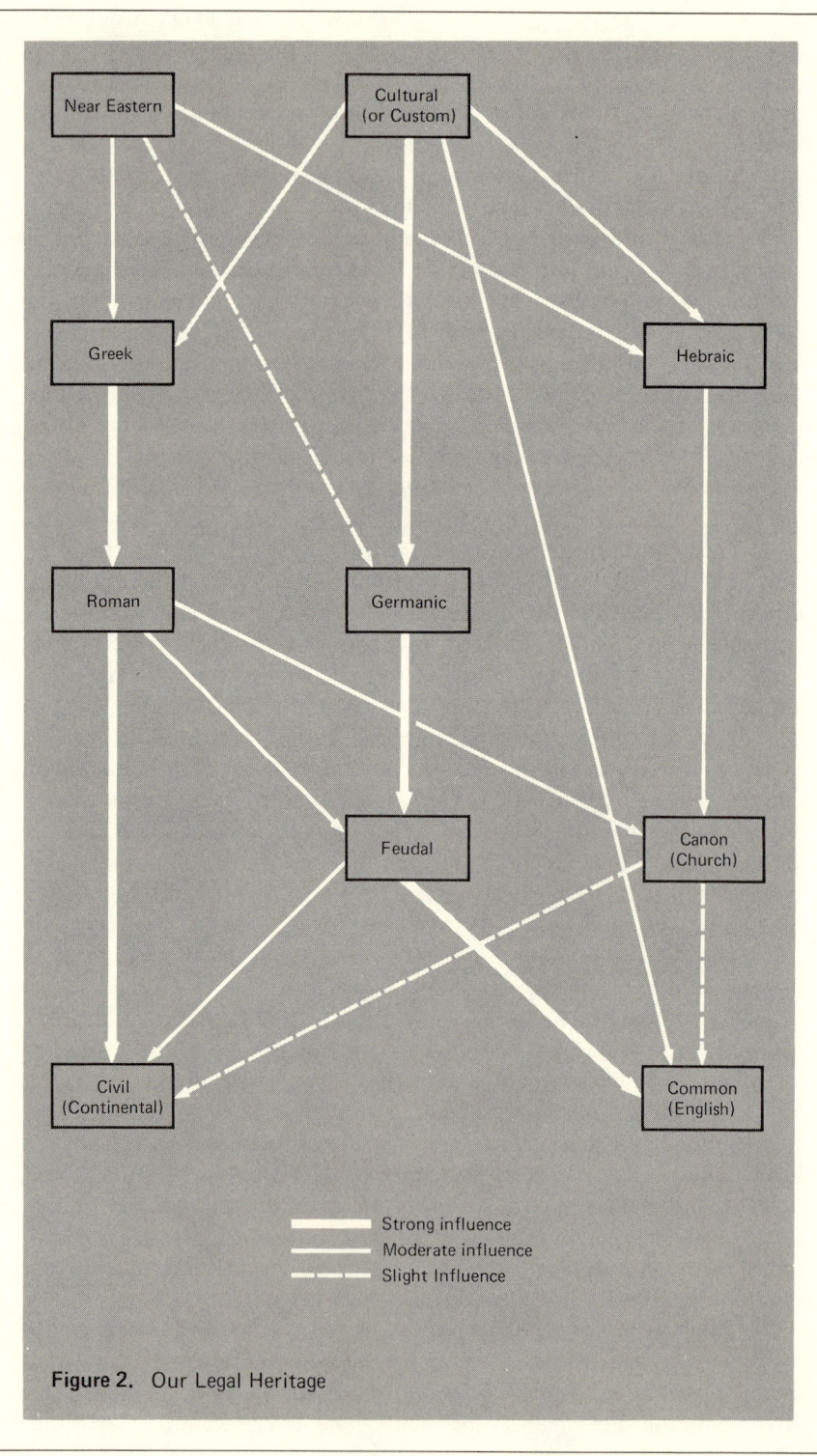

Figure 2. Our Legal Heritage

States in a number of other ways. A few Southwestern jurisdictions continue to show the effect of Spanish influences and, more recently, innovations of the continental system have been adopted in fact, if not with direct knowledge, by expansion of administrative agencies.

A Hierarchy of Standards

Many terms are used interchangeably in daily life but still do not really mean the same thing. Two very frequently confused words are *law* and *justice*. They cannot be entirely separated, for each depends upon the other. Law refers to definite standards, while justice indicates the means by which they are applied. Of course, the two often operate closely together and are mutually complimentary. Justice ordinarily implies fairness, equality, and impartiality. We would naturally like to see these operating with the law, but they do not have to be present. Unfortunately, there is much in law far removed from what is fair, equal, and impartial. Needless to say, justice frequently involves very subjective attitudes.

Regardless of exact meanings attached to particular words, we must recognize an essential doctrine in our legal system. It is most often expressed by the phrase, "justice under law," and it means that established principles rather than individual desires govern the enforcement of standards. This is a vital element in the protection of liberty, for it also recognizes that true justice cannot exist in a dictatorship.

Law is also often confused with custom. The distinction has plagued sociologists for many years without a very satisfactory solution.[13] It is simple to cite customs which are not laws, but where can the line be drawn? In most complex societies the difference is based upon whether or not the government is involved and whether or not the standards are written down. These elements are not, despite their significance, always conclusive. Yet, when the state can take a part in requiring behavior and where the standards have been reduced to some form for future reference, we tend to think that law exists as opposed to mere custom, regardless of the strong personal and group feelings that may exist. As with justice, moreover, there should ideally be a connection. Law works best as an outgrowth of custom, but here again that which might be preferred may be difficult to find. In reality, we have a multitude of regulations that are quite divorced from standards clearly supported by society. When this occurs we may have situations approaching either anarchy or tyranny, and the quality of justice suffers greatly.

While all laws are related to both justice and custom, they are sometimes in opposition or even direct conflict with one another, and definite superiorities exist.[14] Aside from the continuing question of a higher law derived under strict interpretations by natural, positive, or cultural schools, a hierarchy of regulations exists. In a democratic republic such as the United States, this ordering of laws becomes especially complex.

Major societies are today governed under constitutions or general statements of fundamental principles upon which the state should operate. These concepts are ordinarily quite broad and comprehensive, often with included obstacles to change. Such general statements usually represent the highest type of formal, tangibly expressed law. In the United States, of course, a double layer of written constitutions exists (see Fig. 3). The federal version naturally takes precedence over that of a state in cases of conflict.

Beneath the constitution are thousands of statutes enacted by the centralized government. These laws, which differ greatly between individual states and again from those of the federal system, fill dozens of books. Such statutes are ordinarily far more specific and detailed than provisions found within the constitutions, but they frequently contain acts which enable passage of regulations for even smaller and more limited agencies. There are two major forms of these lower types of laws. The first, and more obvious, consists of local ordinances dealing

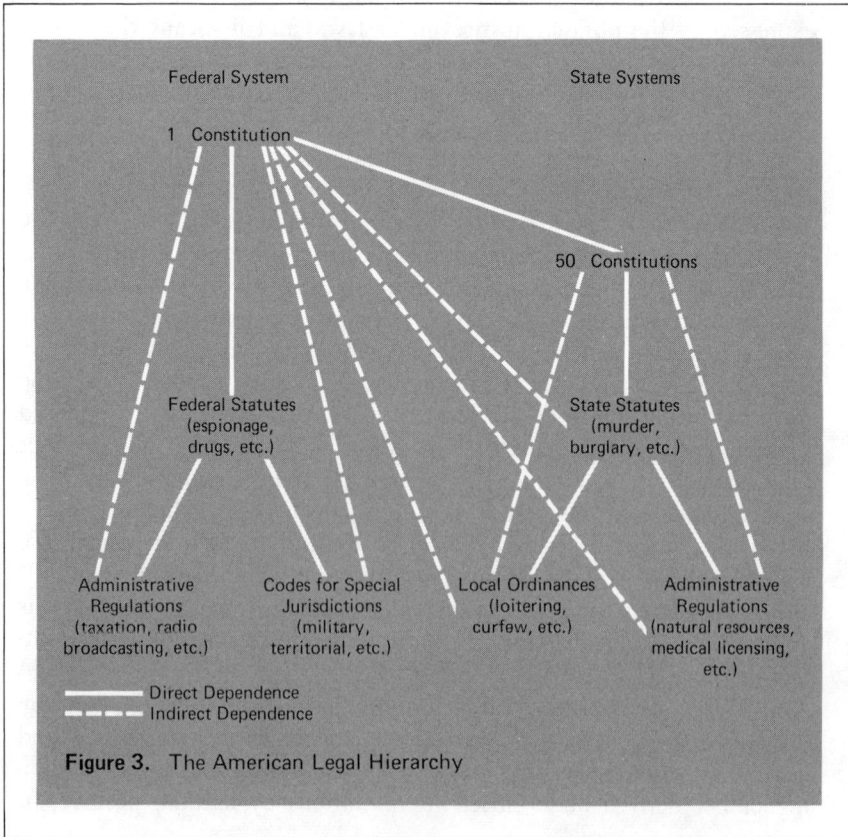

Figure 3. The American Legal Hierarchy

with practical realities of daily living. Second, and of rapidly growing significance, is a multitude of varied rules and guidelines established by administrative agencies. Hundreds of thousands of such standards exist within a society such as the United States, and all could, at least in theory, be tested by the statutes and constitutions under which they have been promulgated.

Substance and Procedure

In practical application, there are several different types of law. A primary but often confusing distinction is drawn between substance and procedure. The first type deals with the actual rules by which everyone is supposed to live. How do you obtain ownership of property, when is killing excusable, what sort of public behavior is forbidden? These are questions which are answered by substantive law. Such regulations ordinarily include the sanctions, or punishments, which may be imposed for deviation. A rule forbidding some particular act and saying what can happen to those breaking it would be a substantive aspect. Exact definitions for violations and interpretations of the various restrictions are very complex and compose the mass of what people frequently think of when they speak of law.

Procedure refers to the application of the standards (substance) imposed by society. When can a matter go to court, how is a jury selected, what is necessary to appeal a decision? These are questions to be answered not by reference to substantive law, but to procedure.[15] Of course, the two sets of rules frequently become very closely intermeshed so that, at times, it is extremely difficult to separate one from another. Procedure is most important to the determination of an actual case. In fact, it sometimes dominates the confused scheme by which society attempts to regulate itself.

Whether or not some particular substantive definition can be imposed often depends upon use of procedural rules. In truth, an unwritten kind of agreement among those within the systems of justice frequently seems more significant than either.[16] Everyone has heard of "deals" whereby the formal requirements are either circumvented or avoided altogether. These arrangements, of course, will be found in neither substance nor procedure. They nevertheless constitute an administrative network of great importance to anyone attempting to understand the complicated working of law. Admission of evidence, which is actually part of procedure and inevitably of crucial importance in the application of substantive rules, is routinely influenced by those people involved in legal questions. Testimony of participants to an event is an obvious illustration of how written and unwritten standards may blur together to determine the outcome, aside from formal rules.

Substantive law tends to change very slowly, with particular portions enduring virtually without modification for hundreds of years.

Procedure, on the other hand, is far more susceptible to innovation and reform. A century old book of substantive interpretations, for example, could probably still be reasonably accurate. But a volume of that age on procedure would surely be very much out of date. It appears that we express more willingness to accept change in the way we apply the rules than in the rules themselves.

Which is more important, substance or procedure? The question cannot be answered since each is dependent upon the other. Formal education tends to divide the two types along quite rigid lines, for purposes of instruction. In practice, such arbitrary separations do not exist. No rules could survive without means of application. Conversely, form without content would be meaningless. A legal system demands both substance and procedure. Lacking either it becomes a shell behind which anarchy or tyranny may lurk.

Despite efforts to maintain separate codes for substance and procedure, the two tend to come together. An original portion of the Constitution of the United States, Article III, Section 3, provides that:

> Treason against the United States, shall consist only in levying War against them, or in adhering to their Enemies, giving them Aid and Comfort. No person shall be convicted of Treason unless on the Testimony of two Witnesses to the same overt Act, or on Confession in open Court.

The first part of the above paragraph defines the crime itself, it is therefore the substantive element. But the second sentence adds very significant procedural safeguards related to the requirements of proof. To be correct, one must read the entire provision; the Constitution clearly blends the regulation and restrictions on its application. Treason against the national government is just one specific instance of substance and procedure combining to form a meaningful rule whereby public security and private liberty may be jointly protected.

American justice is founded upon detailed and complex statutes on substance and procedure. Neither law nor its application can be understood without knowledge of both areas. Some jurisdictions have separate codes covering both aspects; others unite the two. Regardless of arrangement, these constitute the formal basis of regulatory action. Without them, law and justice could not exist.

Summary

Law means many things when viewed in different ways. It can ordinarily be defined in terms of enforceable standards of social behavior, but even this involves complex problems of application.

The three major schools of thought on the ultimate source of law are known as: natural, positive, and cultural. Actual regulation, however, may have begun for military, domestic, or religious reasons.

Our concepts of law developed slowly over many centuries. Two basic legal systems eventually emerged: English (or common) and continental (or civil). Each has endured and found recognition in the United States.

Law is closely related to but different from both justice and custom. Furthermore, it exists in a hierarchy reaching from particular rules to general principles. Law may also be divided into two major types: substantive and procedural.

Questions

1. What does *law* mean?
2. Where and why did law begin?
3. How are the common and civil law systems distinguished?
4. Can justice and custom be related to law?
5. What part of law is substance, and what part procedure?

NOTES

[1] Hermann Kantorowicz, *The Definition of Law* (London: Cambridge University Press, 1958), pp. 11–89.

[2] Oliver Wendell Holmes, "The Path of the Law," *Harvard Law Review* 10 (March, 1897), pp. 457–478.

[3] Edwin M. Schur, *Law and Society* (New York: Random House, 1968), pp. 75–76.

[4] Lon M. Fuller, *The Morality of Law* (New Haven: Yale University Press, 1964), pp. 33–94.

[5] *Law and Society*, pp. 51–58.

[6] E. Adamson Hoebel, *The Law of Primitive Man.* (Cambridge: Harvard University Press, 1954), pp. 3–28.

[7] Jeremy Bentham, *A Fragment on Government and an Introduction to the Principles of Morals and Legislation* (Oxford: Blackwell, 1948), pp. 281–311.

[8] Rene A. Wormser, *The Story of the Law* (New York: Simon and Schuster, 1962), pp. 145–149.

[9] Clarence Ray Jeffrey, "The Development of Crime in Early English Society," *Journal of Criminal Law, Criminology and Police Science* 47 (March–April, 1957), pp. 647–666.

[10] *The Story of the Law*, pp. 193–197.

[11] Roscoe Pound, *The Spirit of the Common Law* (Boston: Marshall Jones, 1921), pp. 1–84.

[12] Daniel J. Boorstin, *The Americans: The Colonial Experience* (New York: Vintage, 1958), pp. 201–202.

[13] Burton M. Leiser, *Custom, Law, and Morality* (New York: Anchor, 1969), pp. 99–133; Bronislaw Malinowski, *Crime and Custom in Savage Society* (London: Routledge and Kegan Paul, 1926), pp. 50–59.

[14] Hans Kelsen, *General Theory of Law and State* (New York: Russell and Russell, 1961), pp. 123–162.

[15] Hazel B. Kerper, *Introduction to the Criminal Justice System* (St. Paul: West, 1972), pp. 25–26.

[16] Richard T. LaPiere, *A Theory of Social Control* (New York: McGraw-Hill, 1954), pp. 318–320.

Chapter 2
Criminal Conduct

"Men will always grow rogues . . . unless they find themselves under a necessity to be honest."

MACHIAVELLI

State Punishment

Of the thousands of laws found in every jurisdiction, only a few deal with crime. Typical contested cases and most statutes are concerned with disputes over the ownership of property, claims of individual damage, rights in regard to contracts, and similar private actions. Yet, the distinction of criminal from other types of law is far more difficult than might at first appear.[1]

A difference exists between the legal treatment of crime and violations of other kinds of enforceable rules for conduct. Suppose a speeding driver strikes and injures a pedestrian. Is this a matter for application of criminal law? Yes, it very well may be, but it is not solely such a situation. The pedestrian can privately sue the driver for compensation of his injury. This suit would not directly involve any question of crime, but there can also be an entirely separate charge against the driver. It would be heard in another court with different rules of procedure and evidence. The dispute between private parties is termed a civil action for damages, the other case becomes a criminal matter.

What is the fundamental contrast between the two proceedings? Both the civil and the criminal actions may result in sanctions against the speeder, and both revolve around a struggle to present the same basic evidence and resolve very similar questions. In the private suit, the injured party is himself bringing the charge and hopes to recover for his suffering. In the criminal case, the state, meaning a governmental unit, is making the accusation and trying to extract some form of punishment. There are, therefore, two crucial and distinguishing characteristics to criminal (or penal) law. The state must itself bring the charge and then demand the punishment directly. Private citizens may, of course, at times initiate the process by complaint.

Such distinctions, in practice, sometimes become blurred. In the matter of the speeding driver, the outcome of the criminal (or state) case may drastically affect the civil (or private) claim. Other situations involve a mixture of the two kinds of law. Certain statutes (for example, those against monopolies) enable an injured party to recover far more than his actual damages. In a sense, the private suit is then performing a clear kind of punishment. Many civil actions also eventually involve government enforcement. If the injured pedestrian receives an award from the court through his damage suit, and the driver refuses to pay, the state will require him to do so.

Civil cases normally are restricted to infliction of closely limited types of sanctions. Ordinarily a private suit can only result in payment of money or performance of certain functions, such as fulfillment of a prior binding agreement. Criminal charges, on the other hand, could produce fine, imprisonment, and even death. In the not too distant past, of course, they could involve physical torture, exile, and mutilation. But suits between private parties may also result in actual confinement, such as in the case of a parent who, though able to do so, continually refuses to pay for the support of a child despite the command of the court. Here the state can be indirectly required to enforce a sanction by infliction of punishment.

The government may itself be involved in cases other than criminal. It is commonly a party in matters of taxes, licenses, and other disputes that involve no specific criminal charge. Here the state is not technically either inflicting or receiving a punishment. Of course, such situations can and sometimes do lead to separate charges concerning the same basic facts.

In criminal matters, the state may begin an action without the complaint of any injured party. In fact, many punishable violations involve neither damage nor danger to anyone. Here again, however, no absolute distinction may be made. In practice, it often is useless, because of problems with evidence, for a criminal charge to be permitted without a willing complainant. It is, for example, usually a total waste for the state to bring a penal charge where the victim and witnesses refuse to give willing testimony. Such situations are far from rare.

Assuming a general meaning for penal law as those regulations made punishable directly by the state, it is relatively easy to define crime. The first merely forms the boundaries for the second. Crime, consequently, simply consists of an act which violates the penal law.[2] Naturally there are different definitions for criminal conduct more closely tied to moral and social concepts; these do not apply in actual cases of governmentally imposed punishment, and that is the ultimate distinction between the two primary kinds of law.

What actually makes something a crime? The fact that the state may impose punishment often provides a rather feeble solution. Most of the time the government does nothing even though a violation has occurred, and often the sanction is not carried out. Could we have a criminal law that never leads to any punishment whatever? Many such regulations have existed for decades, forgotten anachronisms in a transitional society. Despite inherent contradiction, we really could have no crime within a truly permissive state. Penal law is by its very nature repressive and could scarcely operate where violations are totally ignored. Yet, this in turn creates major difficulties for the criminal justice system in a free society.

In a democracy, a logical answer to the question of who determines what shall be crimes would be the people, or at least the electorate. Of course, we almost never enjoy the freedom to directly control which acts will be punished through voting, but we elect officials to make such decisions. The causal relationships between public desire and penal law, however, are very nebulous and indirect. Vast numbers of provisions would undoubtedly be erased if subject to popular referendums. Many crimes are defined to satisfy powerful groups representing special interests or continue to exist simply through official inaction for generations.

Do the elected officials, primarily the legislative element, then make our penal laws? Certainly they play an important part in the process, but their's is by no means an absolute power. A new provision totally unconscionable to the people would, hopefully, be eventually recalled, at least in a truly representative system of government. Far more common, however, is a negative reaction from other officials.

There have been laws that are regarded as administratively unenforceable and simply ignored. They may be phrased in such ways as to render them useless. The obvious enforcement agency, the police, frequently recognizes the absurdity or impossibility of demanding adherence to certain formal standards. If such an attempt would be made, those responsible for actual prosecution can simply reject the case. Particular traffic regulations serve as one example of rules never applied. Are we punished for merely failing to signal the technically required full distance before making a turn? Is it actually possible to always maintain the proper length between vehicles when driving? The literal rules have certainly been violated, but enforcement remains incomprehensible. Those responsible for administration may then exercise discretion in reducing some regulations to insignificance.

Even when enforcement is attempted, penal provisions may be destroyed with interpretation by our courts. Every year acts of the legislatures and administrative bodies are struck down by judges at all levels. Local ordinances conflicting with state or federal statutes cannot be permitted. These statutes may themselves violate parts of various constitutions. And the courts will occasionally neglect to apply regulations that run counter to very strong public sentiments or deeply entrenched legal principles.[3] In this respect, the people's will sometimes surfaces through findings by the grand and petit juries which can, at least in regard to crime, stand as one of the last bastions of real democracy.

The element of punishment sometimes also involves a virtual veto power on penal law. Judges and juries may, when permitted, impose such minimal sanctions as to render the violation almost meaningless. In those situations in which correctional officials enter after determination of an actual crime, the punishment may be further reduced. The overwhelming majority of those persons convicted for very serious offenses, for example, actually receive only a small portion of the sanction which could legally be applied.

The true making of tangible criminal law is not an event but a process. It may involve the voters, legislature, police, courts, juries, correctional officers, and others. No penal statute means anything in isolation. It always involves a multitude of people frequently working in opposition to one another. Whether or not a given act will actually be treated as a crime therefore becomes subject to individual interpretations variously invoking the power of the state.

Types of Crime

The basic references in any practical study of criminal law are the books of statutes containing the rules and punishments which the police and courts apply. Penal codes in the United States are frequently very lengthy and complex. There may be far more than a thousand separate rules for only one state, and the annotated collection of such laws normally runs to several volumes. Efforts to reorganize and restructure these provisions nearly always conclude in frustration and additional confusion. Consequently, the penal codes found in the United States are normally involved, sometimes outdated, occasionally contradictory, and often impractical patchworks. Nevertheless, these varied criminal laws remain bound together by traditions and basic concepts often extending back many centuries.

Penal statutes are routinely classified in two primary but simultaneous ways. The first recognizes the role of the victim in the process of forbidden conduct; the second deals with the seriousness or degree of the offense. In the former scheme, codes usually organize crimes according to type as being against person, property, or the general public.

Most collections of penal statutes therefore contain a section devoted to offenses which may directly involve physical safety, including assault, rape, kidnapping, and homicide. Similarly, the criminal codes often compartmentalize violations committed against property (to include both real estate and personal items), such as larceny, burglary, embezzlement, and arson. It is also possible to find, grouped together, those offenses without an obvious victim. In a sense, these are violations that are deemed to threaten the entire public.

Many violations in the latter category deal with obvious protections of moral principles, including incest, gambling, drunkenness, and prostitution. Others reflect a clear demand to maintain some degree of reasonable public order, such as regulations against possession of certain weapons, counterfeiting, and disturbing the peace. Traffic infractions also fall into this general category, but have become so numerous and detailed as to often now require a separate code apart from the less frequent offenses.

Of course, many violations do not fit neatly into a single classification. Robbery, for example, could logically be considered as offending both person and property. Individual penal codes create many subdivisions of the general types. These may include articles referring to crimes against organized government, public health, commerce, suffrage, reputation, justice, nature, and the family.

The second major way of classifying penal prohibitions refers to the seriousness of the offense. Under English common law, crimes were divided into three major categories: treasons, felonies, and misdemeanors. Treason, of course, referred to violations against the crown and certain other personal allegiances. Modern codes still regard such breaches of responsibility as constituting very serious offenses but usually limit them to levying war against, or giving aid to enemies of, the state. Treason is no longer treated as a separate level of crime, however.

Felonies, the second principal category, numbered only some ten of the most serious offenses known in common law. These included murder, arson, robbery, rape, and burglary—still bearing the same designation after nearly a thousand years. Originally a felony could be punished by forfeiture of property. Upon a conviction, the state would take away the guilty party's land and goods, in addition to more customary punishments. Today felonies, which may easily include over a hundred different crimes, are typically identified by possible confinement within a prison, as distinguished from a jail.

While other distinctions do exist, felonies are still separated from misdemeanors by virtue of the potential punishments that may be imposed by the court. Forfeiture, of course, no longer is permitted. Misdemeanors may usually now be defined as all violations made punishable by the state other than felonies. They would, naturally, then include the vast majority of ordinary and common crimes such as drunkenness, simple assault, and disturbing the peace. The distinction between felony and misdemeanor has become most important in our modern system of criminal justice.[4]

A few jurisdictions have recently created a new category of crimes commonly called infractions. These would ordinarily be the lesser offenses, including most traffic violations, that are not made punishable by confinement in either prison or jail. With ordinary penalties of only fines, they constitute the least serious but most frequent kind of crimes.

The classification scheme is important for several reasons. It often determines the power of arrest, possible penalties, and the type of court and jury which can hear the case. And, classification may influence the apparent crime rate for particular offenses. In the United States, for example, the Federal Bureau of Investigation's designation of willful homicide (including murder and nonnegligent manslaughter), forcible rape, robbery, aggravated assault, burglary, larceny-theft (formerly excluding amounts below $50), and auto theft as *index* crimes is frequently used to determine a general index of lawlessness.[5] This relatively new category of offenses, still based essentially on seriousness, has become of considerable significance in official reports on known crimes. The index violations may generally be thought of as those posing the greatest actual danger, in frequency and damage, to the public at the present time. They also represent those offenses which might be most consistently and reliably reported.

Extent of Violations

Surprisingly, no one really knows how much crime actually occurs. Members of the public do not report all offenses to which they fall victim. Police agencies keep varied records of violations made known to them, while only general and incomplete totals for actual arrests exist. Prosecution and court statistics defy compilation while reflecting great differences in accuracy and interpretation. Records for correctional operations, particularly prisons, are usually more comprehensive but demonstrate considerable variation in form and scope.

It is commonly observed that a rising tide of crime is threatening the safety of our society, and this may in fact be true. Statistical analyses, however, remain subject to so many variables and unknowns that they cannot serve as absolute evidence of such an alarming trend.[6] U.S. history reveals that crime has constituted a significant problem for many generations. One can, nevertheless, deduce a few general tendencies within the last century.

It appears that offenses of all types have been quite common, especially in larger cities, since the later part of the nineteenth century. Violations against the person, property, morality, and public order naturally changed in frequency with different social conditions. But no region or era enjoyed any true freedom from the crime problem. After

1930, more adequate records of known offenses were kept and permit the general conclusion that the United States has indeed been beset by steadily growing numbers of major violations. During the 1960s FBI statistics showed that reports of index crime increased on the average of more than 14 percent annually, adjusted to population growth.[7] Property crimes and robbery demonstrated the sharpest rates of expansion. Figures for the most recent periods, however, indicate that the era of such rapid increases may have ended.

Although figures on violations are always subject to question, primarily since they can never be complete, the grand totals must be regarded as sobering. For 1972, the FBI recorded the following numbers:

	OFFENSES	RATE PER 100,000 PEOPLE
Total Crime Index	5,891,924	2,829.5
Willful Homicide	18,515	8.9
Forcible Rape	46,431	22.3
Robbery	374,555	179.9
Aggravated Assault	388,650	186.6
Burglary	2,344,991	1,126.1
Larceny ($50 and over)	1,837,799	882.6
Auto Theft	880,983	423.1

SOURCE: *Uniform Crime Reports for the United States—1972* (Washington: U.S. Government Printing Office, 1973), p. 61.

Several conclusions may be drawn from these statistics. Property crimes, for example, compose the greatest part of index violations. Acts such as murder, rape, assault, and robbery, while attracting the greatest public alarm, comprise only 14 percent of major offenses. Most serious criminal acts are directed against property through burglary, larceny, and car theft, rather than immediately threatening individual security. Or, expressed in other terms, only about one major offense in every seven involves personal safety.

The scope of America's crime problem is not fully illustrated by reports of index violations. Only a tiny percentage of all offenses fall into the key FBI list. Statistics on other, and frequently far more numerous, crimes are even less complete. Indeed, in regard to such common violations as drunkenness, disorderly conduct, driving while intoxicated, simple assault, and petty theft we have only the most general of estimates. It is probable, however, that minor crimes outnumber the index variety at least ten to one. In short, when simple statistics are regarded, it becomes clear that the real lawlessness in America consists of countless smaller offenses rather than the relatively few violations attracting the most public attention. Minor crime has become so common in the United States that it very rarely is accorded anything but the briefest concern, even from many of the victims. And that, perhaps, is the most serious of all threats posed by these violations. America is quite close to accepting crime as part of life, thereby condoning its existence.

This condition may be illustrated by recognizing that most offenses are never reported at all. Since the FBI's index consists of compilations of police records, a crime not known to law enforcement agencies will not be included in the statistics. And, amazingly enough, the majority of even very serious violations fall into this unrecognized category.[8] It has only been in recent years that the magnitude of unreported crime has been realized.

While estimates vary, it appears that perhaps 70 percent of major offenses, or more than twice the total officially known, are never recorded. They remain hidden from the public and hence never appear in statistics for reported violations. Citizens of the United States probably really suffer some 20 million serious crimes every year.

Recent surveys reveal that four times as many forcible rapes, twice as many aggravated assaults, and three times as many burglaries may actually occur than are noted by official law enforcement reports.[9] Presumably, people are quite reluctant to inform the police about these serious crimes because they feel the effort would be useless, too time consuming, or they do not want the offender arrested. Some victims certainly are afraid or wish to handle the matter privately. Nevertheless, the conclusion must be that official crime rates are highly questionable as a measure of actual occurrences. The situation in regard to lesser offenses, particularly fraud, petty theft, and vandalism, must be even more distorted.

When we speak of crime, it is extremely important to remember that we are frequently dealing only with the tiny fraction of formally recorded violations. In truth, the problem is like an iceberg with the real danger lying hidden and often unrecognized beneath the surface. It is difficult to see how efforts to reduce the true rates of crime can achieve marked success until far more is known about the real number of such occurrences. The facts will be equally difficult to obtain before the public determines that it is worthwhile for them to enlist the aid of the police. This, in turn, requires a new confidence in our entire system of criminal justice.

Aside from the inestimable personal suffering caused individuals, crime costs enormous sums of money. In the United States, the annual economic loss probably exceeded $40 billion in 1974. Such figures are only estimates, for no one can gather detailed data on such a nebulous but critical problem. The loss in dollars includes the expenses of police, insurance, security services, prisons, and other activities necessitated by the very existence of crime. More obvious, of course, and much greater is the economic drain caused by the destruction or the taking of property. It appears that commercial thieves, gambling, fraud, and drunken driving (through accidents and negligent homicides) constitute financial liabilities of enormous but frequently forgotten significance.[10] And, strangely enough, the greatest economic damages may occur by evasion of taxes, malfeasance in public office, and diverse forms of business misconduct which are quite impossible to measure or even estimate.

Victims and Offenders

Crime is not evenly distributed across the nation. Major violations per person are more than four times as common in larger urban areas than in rural sections.[11] In the cities reported crime is primarily concentrated in the inner core of poor but crowded older sections inhabited by members of ethnic and racial minorities. Serious offenses occur everywhere, but a disproportionate number transpire within business and low-income districts. It is, however, likely that certain types of ordinarily unreported crime, such as embezzlement and fraud, take place primarily in sections with comparatively low degrees of violence.

Offenses transpire in all regions, but the rates by type of violation vary considerably in different parts of the country. Major crimes, for example, are generally most frequent in western states, but California, New York, and the District of Columbia ordinarily report the highest rates. Conversely, southern states record the least such offenses overall with North Dakota, West Virginia, and Mississippi having the lowest number in relation to their populations. As may be noted, crime tends to increase with density of population. All heavily urbanized sections show high rates which fall sharply in the suburban fringes, while private homes and public streets are the most common sites for serious offenses.

Those most vulnerable are tragic but likely victims. Persons working and living in deteriorating sections of larger cities endure the highest possibility of violent attack. Individuals with higher incomes stand the least chance of becoming victims of serious crime, apart from some types of larceny and theft. In general, offenses occur most frequently against members of racial and ethnic minority groups, and men are more likely to be victimized than women. A black male, for example, has ten times the statistical likelihood of experiencing an assault than does a white female.[12] In regard to many property crimes it is, naturally, commercial activities which often fall prey. Many retail operations in the United States connect as much as 5 percent of their expenses to various types of theft and robbery.

Persons between their late teen years and middle thirties run the greatest risk of being physically attacked. It is, of course, also true that a disproportionate number of violent crimes occur where intoxicants are consumed.[13] Often, victims are personally acquainted with the offenders in such assaults. We all share a common danger, but it bears most heavily on the poor, the black, and those who live in the ghettos of our big cities. These characteristics, unfortunately, tend to be very closely correlated in American society today.

Logically enough, victims and offenders seem to statistically have much in common. The link may exist simply because we all fall into both categories and jointly share many of the community's problems.

The tendency to divide the population into two clear groups, the criminals and the law-abiding majority, is an unfortunate oversimplification. Everyone is guilty of technical violations, and studies indicate that as much as 90 percent of the general public has knowingly committed offenses for which they could be sentenced to jail or prison. Of course, only a small portion of the population devotes a significant part of their lives to criminal activity, but even they cannot be isolated from the general pattern of daily life.[14] In a complex civilization it is virtually impossible to invariably obey every penal provision, and human nature rarely encourages such ideal behavior. Criminal law, apart from its significant moral connotations, is an involved labeling process that the majority of citizens succeeds in avoiding most of the time.

Victims and offenders are also closely connected by ties surpassing mere circumstance. Both frequently come from the same neighborhood and family. Crimes of violence commonly involve people who know one another. In the United States, about 25 percent of murders transpire within the immediate family. Another 40 percent of such crimes implicate friends or acquaintances rather than true strangers.[15] Meanwhile, a large percentage of serious violations against property occur within walking distance of the offender's home. Crime can thus frequently be seen as a family or community problem, with combative efforts apart from home and neighborhood quite possibly doomed to failure.

Attempts to study characteristics of actual offenders meet insurmountable obstacles. As has been indicated, less than one in three of the serious violations is ever reported, and only a part of these produce convictions. In fact, we possess no detailed knowledge about the nature of all offenders. Perhaps the small minority brought into the processes of formal justice represents only the most inept and disadvantaged of violators. The available statistics on persons actually arrested or convicted may give some valid clues to the bulk of frequent offenders, but they must be approached with the utmost caution to avoid conclusions without sufficient foundation.

Among recognized violators the poor, uneducated, and disadvantaged reach dramatic proportions. Prison inmates in the United States show relatively little schooling, common backgrounds of poverty, and a general lack of the technical skills now required for employment opportunities; they also represent the unmarried, separated, widowed, or divorced. This pathetic yet socially dangerous collection of identified offenders only comprises those criminals who have been caught, tried, and imprisoned; this minority may not reflect the true characteristics of all serious violators.

U.S. arrest statistics also point out some likely attributes of suspected criminals. By sex, it is obvious that males account for a disproportionate share of those placed in custody. The arrest rate for men is about six times that for women. When compared by age, it is youths and young adults who pose the greatest apparent threat to internal social order. Statistics indicate that persons between the ages of 15 and 25 account for more than 40 percent of all arrests; in major crimes, the youthful provide an even higher percentage.[16]

By race, Negroes demonstrate a much higher likelihood of being placed in police custody. The arrest rate for black citizens is fully three times higher than that for whites, evidencing the position of the most obvious minority in regard to criminal justice. Other racial groupings in the United States reflect a variety of social forces. American Indians, for example, have an arrest rate which surpasses that of blacks. Those of Chinese ancestry, meanwhile, appear on police reports to a far lesser degree, in proportion to their numbers, than do whites.[17]

It should be obvious that marked similarities between known victims and offenders exist. Both tend to be youthful, predominately male, and are frequently members of some minority group. Victim and offender often share economic backgrounds of poverty, little education, and poor housing. And, of course, an unusually high number of both groups come from the inner city areas. We tend to think of such backgrounds as closely related to the criminals themselves but forget that the victims quite routinely reflect the same disadvantageous conditions. It is sometimes said that crime is directed against ourselves. So far as comparison between the parties involved may apply, it would seem that such a concept has something more than a superficial basis.

One must realize that information on known offenders does not show causal relationships. No study has ever established that housing, poverty, race, sex, family status, education, or any other characteristic actually produces crime. In fact, pure numbers would tend to disprove any claim of a single cause. The vast majority of persons with any specific attribute is basically law abiding and, so far as records reveal, could no more readily be classified as criminal than those with opposite characteristics. With the very limited information available, only the most general of patterns may be established.

Summary

Criminal law involves acts made punishable directly by the state. It should be distinguished from civil actions between private parties.

The creation of actual criminal law is a lengthy process involving the entire administration of justice.

Our penal laws may be classified according to type of harm or seriousness, but the principal distinction is drawn between felonies and misdemeanors.

No one knows how much crime actually occurs, for much of it is never reported. Perhaps 20 million serious offenses take place annually in the United States, and the economic losses must be measured in billions of dollars.

Crime is concentrated in the low income, inner city sections of the country. Rates rise with density of the population, and blacks, youths, and males are likely victims. Characteristics for offenders, overall, tend to resemble those of persons suffering personal attack and loss of property.

Questions

1. How should crime be defined?
2. What is the difference between felonies and misdemeanors?
3. Which crimes are most common?
4. Who suffers most frequently from crime?

NOTES

[1] Paul W. Tappan, *Crime, Justice and Correction* (New York: McGraw-Hill, 1960), pp. 3–7.

[2] 18 United States Code 1; California Penal Code, sec. 15; Illinois Revised Statutes, chapter 38, sec. 2–12; New York Penal Law, sec. 10.00; Texas Penal Code, sec. 12.01.

[3] H. L. A. Hart, *The Concept of Law* (London: Oxford University Press, 1961), pp. 138–144.

[4] Wayne R. LaFave and Austin M. Scott, *Handbook on Criminal Law* (St. Paul: West, 1972), pp. 26–29; Rollin M. Perkins, *Criminal Law* (Mineola, N.Y.: Foundation, 1969), pp. 9–11.

[5] *Uniform Crime Reports for the United States—1972* (Washington: GPO, 1973), pp. 1–29, 57; "Uniform Crime Reporting Program," *FBI Law Enforcement Bulletin* 42 (March, 1973), p. 33.

[6] *Task Force Report: Crime and Its Impact* (Washington: GPO, 1967), pp. 19–37.

[7] *Uniform Crime Reports for the United States—1972*, p. 61.

[8] *Task Force Report: Crime and Its Impact*, pp. 17–19, 21–25.

[9] *The Challenge of Crime in a Free Society* (Washington: GPO, 1967), pp. 22–24; *Crime in the Nation's Five Largest Cities* (Washington: Law Enforcement Assistance Administration, 1974), pp. 28–29.

[10] *Task Force Report: Crime and Its Impact*, pp. 42–59.

[11] *Uniform Crime Reports for the United States—1972*, pp. 102–103.

[12] *Task Force Report: Crime and Its Impact*, p. 80.

[13] Stephen Schafer, *The Victim and His Criminal* (New York: Random House, 1968), pp. 76–79.

[14] James S. Wallerstein and Clement J. Wyle, "Our Law-Abiding Law-

breakers," *Federal Probation* 25 (March–April, 1947), pp. 107–112; Martin Gold, "Undetected Delinquent Behavior," *Journal of Research in Crime and Delinquency* 3 (January, 1966), pp. 27–46.

[15] Marvin E. Wolfgang, *Patterns in Criminal Homicide* (New York: Wiley, 1966), pp. 203–221.

[16] *Uniform Crime Reports for the United States—1972*, pp. 124, 126–127.

[17] *Ibid.*, p. 131.

Chapter 3
Problem Areas

"The first priority is order and justice for all Americans."
NATIONAL ADVISORY COMMISSION ON CIVIL DISORDERS

Disorder in the City

America's crime problem is like a complex, giant spider web entwining the nation. There are countless lines and junctures blending to form a picture of violence, disorder, and vice. While no single center is apparent, concentrations of crime may yet be noted. And these convergences most frequently occur in the centers of our metropolitan areas. Much of the nation's crime lies behind the boundaries of what is sometimes called the inner city.

Crowded and deteriorating housing, bad health related to inferior sanitation, low income but high unemployment, broken homes with dependent children, and limited education from substandard schools are some of the characteristics of American urban centers. And the problems are greatly compounded by social segregation on racial or ethnic lines. Primarily, of course, the residents are black, poor, and frustrated.

Although crime statistics vary widely among different urban areas, it is clear that inner cities contribute far more known offenses than proportional to their population.[1] Rates for violations against the person may easily be ten times higher in poor black districts than in prosperous white suburbs. The difference for property crimes, while not so extreme, is still commonly twice as great. Most varieties of crimes against the public demonstrate similar tendencies. Inner cities, which contain about 20 percent of our population, may contribute 80 percent of all serious offenses.[2]

With very few variations, American cities have an older central business district with adjoining slums or ghettos. In these tracts, known crime rates and population density are highest. Moving outward, the urban areas include newer and more expensive private homes, with far less frequent reported violations. The general patterns, naturally, are altered by the presence of rivers, mountains, coastlines, major roadways, industrial developments, and suburban shopping centers. Nevertheless, the role of the inner city in the complex picture of crime is quite clear. It is that of a primary source of discontent and disorder within the United States. The crime problem can never be isolated geographically, but the combination of urbanization, poverty, and segregation must be recognized as an explosive social formula.

These conditions became quite obvious during the late 1960s as many inner cities witnessed some of the most dramatic and destructive examples of racial unrest in American history. Los Angeles, New York, Detroit, Atlanta, Washington, and other urban centers suffered major civil disorders that frequently left large areas looted or in flames. In effect, elements of the black inner cities seemed on the verge of a veritable war against the white community. State and national forces had to be rushed to the troubled areas to restore a semblance of order by virtue of military firepower. The riots, in themselves a particular form of crime, involved vast numbers of ordinary offenses against person and property. But, of far greater significance was their demonstration of the deep problems and animosities which continue to seethe beneath a surface of despair and cynicism.

Civil disorders are not new to American history, and they will continue in the future. Studies reveal, however, remarkable similarities between the recent major riots and continuing crime rates near urban centers. In both, the identified offenders are predominantly black, young, single, and male.[3] These characteristics may, of course, also be assigned to a typical known criminal. Furthermore, the victims of rioters and common offenders, alike, come from the same neighborhoods. Here again, the innocent dweller of the city slum suffered the most. An overwhelming majority of those killed during recent urban disorders were black bystanders simply caught in efforts by public officials to restore order.

It is no accident that inner city areas previously marked by high rates of crime became sites for massive and destructive demonstrations. In a sense, these districts are constantly undergoing a repressed form of riot. Vandalism, theft, assault—the very minor crimes that, brought suddenly together, constitute a riot—have become a way of life in the urban ghetto.

There are many possible explanations for these concentrations of crimes, but the most obvious solution is simply to visualize them as legally unjustifiable symptoms of a chronic social problem. The inner city suffers from a multitude of tragic conditions. Its residents are normally poor and uneducated. Their housing tends to be expensive, old, and overcrowded. Schools and health facilities are far below the standards of more prosperous sections. Unemployment and broken homes continue in staggering degree. Perhaps most important, the road out of the inner city is, for most, obstructed by deeply entrenched prejudice on predominantly racial lines. Yet, general society demands the same basic values and conduct from all, regardless of varying life conditions.

Despite the attention drawn to the inner city during the last decade, conditions endure and even worsen. In truth, the gap separating whites and blacks seems to be widening. Not only is the shocking state of urban centers continuing, the population of such districts is also growing steadily. Crime rates rise, discrimination changes in form rather than content, frustration deepens with unfulfilled political promises, and the inner city remains as a primary problem area for American justice.

The vast majority of citizens living within the American metropolitan ghettos is basically law-abiding. But their opportunities and realistic hopes remain sharply restricted despite emergence of new community pride. In view of existing conditions, the continued patience and trust shown by most residents should perhaps be as surprising as the role of the inner city as a focus of diverse crime problems.

Although slum sections of urban areas stand out statistically when comparing rates of offenses, it is a delusion to consider them as the total or only basis. Crime sweeps into every community and neighborhood in the nation. Its causes and effects do seem concentrated, but they are also multiple and complex. The inner city carries the primary burden, and perhaps a major responsibility, while all of society shares the harm and the blame.

Juvenile Delinquency

Perhaps the most dramatic single change in the nature of crime within the last century deals with the age of offenders. There has been an apparent sharp rise in the proportion of violations by young people. Current statistics indicate a marked increase in nearly all indices of juvenile crime. This trend, especially within the last generation, has attracted an unusual amount of noticeably unproductive though generally optimistic study.

The most common term attached to crime by young people is *juvenile delinquency*. Unfortunately, such a popular usage meets grave difficulty in formal application. *Juvenile* means different ages in the varying states, and *delinquency* is far broader in legal terminology than actual crime. Some jurisdictions within the United States treat as adults those reaching the age of 16, many use 18 as a minimum, others may, in effect, extend the distinction to 26.[4] It is also possible for regular courts, especially those for children, to have concurrent powers, usually in felony cases. Consequently, exactly who falls within the special category of juveniles, or youthful offenders, becomes a complex question.

Similarly, one may be declared delinquent while not guilty of any punishable offense. Children running away from home, associating with criminals, or considered as incorrigible can be placed in such a category. In addition, there are numerous violations, such as truancy and infringement of curfew regulations, for which only youths can be held responsible. Obviously, it is an error to regard delinquency as a synonym for crime, at least in the legal sense of such words. In general, however, juvenile delinquency may be used in reference to young people who, by their conduct, become subject to legal action. Technically, this may not involve the full panoply of criminal justice. In practice, the results are much the same and differ primarily in semantics.

A century ago, youthful offenders represented a smaller part of the crime problem; today they threaten to dominate the scene. Juvenile delinquency constitutes a clear threat to public order. Within the last decade, police and court records show violations by young people to have increased at four times the rate of general population growth. Juvenile delinquency appears to be outdistancing the expanding numbers of crimes by adults. Expressed in other terms, agencies of justice are handling approximately two times as many young people today as they did ten years ago.[5] Facilities, of course, have by no means expanded to deal with such a rapid increase in the number of cases and are presently quite unable to function satisfactorily.

Despite soaring numbers of youthful offenders, it would be a serious mistake to equate juvenile delinquency with the current younger generation. The overwhelming majority of all age groups remains essentially law-abiding. Less than 3 percent of young people are accused of actual delinquency in the United States annually. Still, the number of those processed is staggering. Every year, about 2 million people below the age of 18 are arrested by the police; an equal number may be processed informally. Perhaps more disturbing is the fact that about 11 percent of all young people may at some time before their eighteenth birthday be expected to be involved in some variety of juvenile court action.[6] Such a percentage can only reflect on the present state and future condition of American society. It might be worthwhile, however, to note that the problem is international in scope. Virtually every country has experienced a sharp rise in juvenile crime since World War II. In fact, much of the overall increase in known offenses may largely be attributable to growing numbers of young persons. Most varieties of crime recognize no national boundaries.

Offenses by young people are fairly similar to those committed by adults. Property crimes, however, outnumber those involving violence by an even greater percentage. Moreover, the majority of youths taken into custody have only performed acts against public order. Running away from home, curfew and liquor violations, truancy, certain types of loitering, petty larceny, vandalism, and disorderly conduct are the typical offenses of juveniles. Among more serious crimes, willful homicides, forcible rapes, robberies, and aggravated assaults may far more frequently be attributed to persons above the age of 18 than below.[7]

While major juvenile crime normally takes the form of auto theft, grand theft, or burglary, and youth's reputation for violence seems generally exaggerated, it would be wrong to disregard the continuing possibility of physical danger. Young people commit every type of personal offense known to their elders. Rapes and murders may certainly be attributed to some juveniles, and the rate for such violations is rapidly rising.

When compared with adults, youths tend to commit an abnormal percentage of crimes in groups rather than as individuals. This is especially noticeable in large and sometimes extremely well-organized gangs.[8] Such groups may be principally found within the inner city ghettos and barrios of urban areas. Even though statistics indicate a predominance of these juvenile gangs and all varieties of youth crime among slum and ghetto sections, they are by no means limited to the poor, racially segregated, or ill-housed. Many prosperous white suburbs also suffer from large and expanding amounts of youthful delinquency. The problem extends beyond geographic or organizational lines.

Perhaps the most disturbing aspect of juvenile delinquency is, quite reasonably, the age of the offenders. Arrests for major violations are most frequent among those aged 16 and 17 years; for all crimes, the predominant ages are even lower—15 and 16. Expressed in another fashion, those under 18 now apparently account for approximately half of all index offenses, and about 25 percent of lesser violations. Still more sobering are statistics for those under 15 years. They are arrested in approximately 20 percent of cases involving major crime, and perhaps half that proportion of other offenses.[9] Police agencies frequently deal with violators below the age of 12, and it is by no means unusual to find children of eight or nine placed in custody for quite serious acts. In truth, we may be faced with the eventual necessity of creating a new category for *child* delinquency. Projecting these trends into the future only serves as a further source of alarm. It is well established that today's young offender, unfortunately, tends to become tomorrow's major criminal. That is reason enough to label juvenile delinquency as one of the most disturbing features of the domestic scene.

Organized Crime

The problems posed by inner cities and juvenile delinquency may be easily demonstrated by current statistics. Another and extremely serious facet of crime in America lies hidden from ordinary view. It consists of the vast numbers of normally lesser violations regarding forbidden goods and services—the zone dominated by organized crime.

Here, again, a serious problem of definition exists. America's organized crime consists of well-established groups controlling illegal transactions, particularly gambling, loan-sharking, and narcotics. Furthermore, their operations revolve essentially around illicit activities. Ordinary street prostitution might not qualify because it could lack the characteristic of being so thoroughly established; routine business fraud should also be excluded because it operates behind a facade of acceptable commerce; and gangs of professional thieves or robbers would not be included because they do not deal directly in any form of forbidden goods or services. Much carefully arranged or deeply entrenched crime falls outside such a definition. What remains of planned and controlled offenses constitutes the basis of a complex web throughout the nation.

It is most likely that organized crime has no exact center or top. Rather, it should be envisioned as a constantly evolving entity which, though directly dependent and closely related to society as a whole, also maintains a separate and powerful order. No single "mob" or "syndicate" really controls organized crime, and this feature contributes to the remarkable strength demonstrated by a flexible and versatile combine.[10]

No urban area in the United States is entirely free of some type of established and controlled vice. Consequently, there is no region, state, or sizable city that does not possess a variety of organized crime. Of course, the problem is far more obvious and acute in certain areas than in others. Illegal gambling, narcotics, loans, prostitution, and bootleg liquor or tobacco may be easily found throughout the nation, and most of such activity is a direct part of organized crime.

There are many groups involved in providing these illegal goods or services. Some operate relatively independently and others are closely tied to an incredibly powerful and wealthy hierarchy. But all rely upon three related features: public demand, private greed, and an ultimate threat of force.

First, it must be noted that true organized crime exists to profit from providing that which has been forbidden. Only a continuing demand for illicit operations or items makes the entire system function. Organized crime could theoretically be immediately destroyed through legalization of what is normally termed vice. In practice, of course, the moral concepts which would prevent such a plan are not truly followed and, in a peculiar way, contribute to the problem.[11] Control is manifestly difficult where "victims" consent to or even actively desire that which is forbidden.

Second, organized crime could not endure either nationally or locally without corruption in government.[12] The private greed of officials makes possible the great number of forbidden transactions. Because no large area in the nation is truly free of organized crime, it is reasonable to assume that corruption is manifest almost everywhere. In fact, the suppliers of illegal goods and services probably pour half their financial gains into the pockets of willing officials. This greed is by no means limited to any particular level or type of government employee. Policemen, prosecutors, judges, correctional workers, administrators, legislators—the list of those compromised ranges through all phases of criminal justice. From vice bureaus of law enforcement agencies to assemblies of elected representatives, the secret power of organized crime may be detected. In fact, in some instances it dominates.

Third, the position of organized crime relies upon possible use of force. The normally veiled threat of violence is needed to collect from customers and to defend the system against outside competition. Some cities probably experience a murder per week by organized crime. But this brutality is sometimes now replaced by use of official enforcement. Why resort to secret violence if a legal arrest and prosecution may be arranged?

The principal damage attributable to organized crime does not involve present or potential violence; it is financial. Every year Americans pay enormous sums for illegal goods and services. The profit, perhaps 30 percent of the gross, to organized crime may exceed $10 billion annually despite enormous sums flowing outward in the form of bribes. Authorities seem to agree that gambling is, by far, the largest source of illicit revenue.[13] Numbers, craps, card games, slot machines, and betting on sporting events all serve as major contributors. Each transaction may seem quite small, but it must be multiplied by the billions of wagers made yearly. America presently supports some 50,000 large bookmaking operations, most of which are linked loosely together to provide information on odds, permit layoffs of bets to colleagues, and gain rapid results of horse races and similar contests.

Loan-sharking (the charging of usurious interest rates on usually relatively small sums) and narcotics also bring enormous profits to organized crime. Prostitution and bootlegging, while no longer the lucrative sources of yesterday, add still more money. There is, of course, an interrelation in many of these vices. Because organized crime thrives most readily within the inner city, its residents become the willing victims. Thus, the gambler turns to the loan shark to repay his debts, and the female narcotics user resorts to prostitution to maintain her habit.

The enormous profits derived from illegal goods and services have, along with a desire for still more rewards, led organized crime toward several additional fields. Within recent years, a serious invasion into legitimate business and labor unionism has occurred. Organized crime now maintains strong footholds in finance, entertainment, transportation, construction, and diverse retail operations. These incursions remain limited and localized but presently constitute influences of real significance. With vast profits from vice, close connections with corrupt public officials, and ample experience in the use of force, organized crime becomes a most difficult competitor for both labor and management.

In all probability, some expansion into many serious offenses, not directly involved with vice, has also taken place. Organized crime apparently directs and controls certain kinds of theft, robbery, murder, extortion, and sale of stolen property, especially when very large sums of money are at stake.

Much has been written about the existence of a semi-secret hierarchy known as the Mafia or, more recently, the Cosa Nostra. While adding great strength and cohesion, it is but one element in the picture of organized crime. Traditionally limited to those of Italian ancestry and based largely on family relationships, the Mafia appears strongest in a few larger cities. New York, Buffalo, Philadelphia, Detroit, and Chicago are generally believed to be centers of power. But the network of domination extends outward to Florida, Louisiana, Missouri, New Jersey, Massachusetts, California, Nevada, and other states. This structure involves only a few thousand individuals, generally known to one another and divided into changing patterns of power. Despite occasional vicious struggles for position, most matters are handled through compromise rather than violence. This order has no specific chief; its leadership is diverse and subject to evolution. Nevertheless, conduct of members and followers is regulated by a feared and widely understood code of behavior which binds together the many branches.[14]

Organized crime has many parts and aspects. It plays a multitude of roles, and its influence is pervasive. The different groups that direct operations in particular cities deal with similar local and certain specialized structures. Money, gambling, information, and narcotics must be traded across the nation while unified action may be required in major political and economic questions.

Efforts to combat organized crime have, as yet, proven quite unsuccessful. One great difficulty is the power wielded by the network under attack. With enormous influence available in all agencies of justice as well as legislative bodies, attempts at control frequently devolve into words rather than action. There is another major obstacle in the absence of suitable laws directed against organized crime, partly because of necessarily vague and inclusive language. Perhaps most serious, however, are the durable qualities of greed, fear, and personal weakness under which organized crime continues to thrive.

Drugs

Probably no specific element of the crime problem has attracted more interest and attention within recent years than that dealing with drugs. It has become a popular subject of concern by politicians, educators, clergymen, parents, and even industrialists. To some, narcotics apparently serve as a symbol of social and moral decay in addition to involving criminal law.

The scope of illegal drug use is unknown. We have no truly reliable figures on total consumption, but the problem may properly be regarded as large and growing. While drugs are directly involved in only a small fraction (less than 7 percent) of all arrests, the percentage has had an unequaled increase within recent years and could become a major part of the total crime scene.[15] Such cases are already placing a heavy load on courts in some parts of the country.

In law, *narcotics* is rather loosely applied to those drugs which have been grouped together as either forbidden or subject to strict regulation. This normally includes the derivatives of opium, cocaine (a coca plant product sometimes used in the United States), and marijuana. A separate category of *dangerous drugs* has appeared in recent years to include various stimulants, depressants, and hallucinogens.

Among the opium derivatives, heroin certainly attracts the most concern. It is highly addictive, meaning that use will eventually produce a physical dependence. Heroin relieves tension and causes apathy. Addicts normally inject the drug into the bloodstream, and abstinence produces severe aches, cramps, and nausea. Heroin also is generally regarded as extremely destructive to physical well-being through secondary effects.

No one really knows how many actual narcotics addicts live within the United States; estimates of their numbers range from 60,000 to 600,000. But, as many as half of those physically dependent upon heroin are believed to live in the poorer urban sections of New York, while most of the remainder reside within inner cities of Illinois, Michigan, New Jersey, Maryland, Pennsylvania, the District of Columbia, California, and Texas. The majority of known users appear to be either Negro or Puerto Rican, but drugs recognize neither racial nor ethnic lines.[16]

Heroin is extremely costly for the true addict. The desired amounts may require $100 each day, and most of those in need are poor and unemployed. Consequently, heroin is believed to be indirectly the cause of many robberies, thefts, burglaries, and acts of prostitution. In some cities addiction may lead to between 10 and 40 percent of all serious offenses against property, but no exact statistics are available.

Most of the heroin used in the United States is produced from opium poppies grown in the Near Eastern countries. It is generally refined in Southern Europe, particularly in France, and then smuggled to America on commercial ships and planes. The white powder form available on the streets is quite diluted and increases in value by several hundred times after production, yielding enormous profits to various distributors.

Marijuana, not an opium derivative, is crudely produced from the hemp plant which grows wild in parts of the United States. Much of the tobaccolike substance sold in this country, however, is grown in Mexico (which also supplies some heroin), and then smuggled across the border. Marijuana is normally smoked in groups. It may produce a mild euphoria but effects vary with the personality of the user. Use of marijuana can become a habit, while physical addiction is unknown with the quality grown in America. Consumption of this drug has recently become quite widespread, especially among young people. There may be as many as 5 million regular users in the United States.[17]

Control of marijuana has become a hotly debated public issue. Some believe it should be legalized, while others assert that present treatment of offenders is far too lenient. This dichotomy of opinion has become manifest in the divergence of state laws on the subject. In a number of jurisdictions, simple possession of a minute amount of marijuana can be punished by ten or more years in prison; in many others, the same offense is treated as only a minor misdemeanor subject to no more than a few weeks in jail. Probably only this rather ordinary crime presently poses such divergence of opinion and treatment, and consequent difficulty for the criminal justice system.

Dangerous drugs now comprise an additional problem of great scope. Billions of abusive dosages are consumed annually by the American public, again, frequently by the young. Most use consists of stimulants (primarily amphetamines) and depressants (essentially barbiturates). Pep pills and goofballs are not always illegal; they may be properly obtained by medical prescription. But vast quantities of these drugs flow outside official channels. Some are smuggled, much is produced domestically for illegal consumption, and still more comes from legitimate sources through theft or fraud. Most dangerous drugs become such through improper ingestion of unreasonable quantities and combinations. Many deaths occur every year through abuse of stimulants and depressants originally developed for valid medical purposes.[18]

Among the several hallucinogens, the most psychologically dislocating is probably LSD (lysergic acid diethylamide). This powerful synthetic drug may produce extreme mental states within the user; it also has been known to cause serious genetic defects. LSD is potentially far more harmful than any of the other common dangerous drugs. While it leads to no physical dependence, it can result in suicide and permanent psychological disorders.

As yet, America has obviously failed to cope with the problem of improper drug use. Several hundred thousand annual criminal cases, often bitterly contested, serve as proof of the breadth of abuse. Drugs, once largely limited to the inner city, have spilled across the social and geographic spectrum. Part of the difficulty may unquestionably be related to legal classification. Currently, the most destructive drugs are categorized with those of little proven danger. The unfortunate result is that users of the latter often deal with sources of far more dangerous narcotics and thereby also face possible penalties of great severity.

Addiction itself cannot be treated as a crime.[19] But importation, possession, and sale remain very serious offenses. The failure of present methods to combat all aspects of the drug problem, however, may indicate roots beneath the surface. If so, enforcement effort will encounter endless frustration. Such situations develop whenever law fails to generally reflect the actual desires of the people. Should this be or become the case with drugs, regulations will require suitable alteration.

Drunkenness and Firearms

Juvenile delinquency and use of assorted drugs have increased sharply in recent decades. But the most frequent type of reported offense is minor and almost totally unchanged for a century—drunkenness. Disregarding routine traffic offenses, drunkenness accounts for the greatest share of the overall crime picture, and dominance in this regard has withstood war, depression, prohibition, and all other types of American social change. Despite a significant proportional decline in the last few years, drunkenness still occupies approximately the same share of the crime scene as it did three generations ago.

Every year the United States records about 4 million arrests for offenses directly related to alcohol. For all those reported as taken into custody, about 20 percent of the charges are for public drunkenness, over 7 percent for driving while intoxicated, and 3 percent for liquor law violations. Additionally, a total of approximately 10 percent of those arrested are charged with either disorderly conduct or vagrancy, with alcohol playing a very common role in both offenses.[20] All together, about 40 percent of the reported crime in the United States, apart from traffic infractions, must be directly related to intoxicants. Meanwhile, drinking drivers may account for half of all automobile fatalities, a total far exceeding the aggregate of murders.

Those typically placed in custody for drunkenness, disorderly conduct, vagrancy, and similar offenses by no means represent a cross section of the public. A disproportionate number come from skid rows, usually located in or near urban centers. These individuals (virtually all are males) are commonly arrested again and again for the same violation. In no other area is the total failure of the criminal justice system more clearly manifest; some commit the same offense many times a year. Perhaps 20 percent of those charged with drunkenness account for 60 percent of such arrests. Along certain American skid rows, the police know almost exactly when and where a certain drunkard may be found, merely by estimating the time from his latest release. Local judges frequently refer to such men by their first names, as they have appeared in court with identical charges countless times. And jail guards greet their old inmates with casual familiarity.

Obviously alcoholism plays a large role in drunkenness. But the two should not be regarded as synonymous. There are an estimated 9 million alcoholics in the United States, many of whom are never arrested for drinking. They pose a social problem of unquestioned enormity, but the criminal law, which regards neither limited nor private consumption as a violation, touches only the periphery.

Alcoholism is no defense in the case of legal charges, and communities have authority to control public drunkenness by enforcement of appropriate regulations.[21] Yet, treatment seems more suitable than punishment in most instances. At present, the methods of dealing with habitual drunkards can best be termed a disgraceful failure. The police resort to highly discretionary handling of offenders, courts disregard the rights of those accused, and jails serve as temporary holding points along the endless road of despair. Some 50 percent of all confined misdemeanants are serving time (usually 30 days or less) on drunkenness convictions, and many will return within a few weeks of release.[22]

Authorities and a few municipalities now feel that detoxification centers, counseling, supportive housing, or even limited acceptance might prove a better solution than imposition of obviously unsuccessful penal laws.[23] Whatever the possible answer, drunkenness and associated crimes continue to be a tremendous burden on our agencies of justice.

Alcohol, of course, extends to many more serious offenses. Driving while intoxicated, for example, takes far more lives in the United States than does willful homicide. It is also, except for gambling, the most costly crime in America. Alcohol also contributes greatly to the rates of murder, voluntary manslaughter, assault, and other violence. At least 60 percent of willful homicides involve drinking, usually by both victim and offender.[24]

Our pattern of drinking and killing also commonly involves firearms. Nationally, about 65 percent of murders occur through use of firearms (usually handguns). The combination of alcohol and available weapons is a deadly one, and the United States boasts an ample supply of both. About half the homes in America contain at least one privately owned firearm.[25] In the heat of passion, with inhibitions freed through drinking, it becomes a simple matter for a personal quarrel to erupt into aggravated assault or homicide.

Neither alcohol nor weapons, of course, actually causes any crime; crime requires people. While sincere efforts to control subsidiary elements may accomplish some reduction in overall rates (and even that is open to doubt), any major change must involve alteration of social values and public will. The reason for any crime always lies buried in the mind of the offender.

Most murders and a great many robberies in America involve handguns. The degree to which ready availability and relatively low cost of these weapons contribute to our violent criminal tendencies cannot be easily determined. Firearms are, however, much more common and loosely controlled in America than in other technologically advanced societies.[26] In all probability, the United States will eventually be forced to adopt more rigid regulations on the sale and possession of handguns. But the abject failure of alcohol prohibition during the 1920s should serve as an indication of the problems associated with simplistic solutions. Whenever one right is restricted, others become endangered from the actions of citizens and government alike. As with so many other issues, the difficulty becomes one of practical and reasonable balance.

Summary

Inner city districts of urban areas reflect a multitude of major social ills, and they have the highest rates for known offenses. That conditions have become critical is evidenced by massive civil disorders in which many young people participated. Juvenile delinquency accounts for a highly disproportionate number of all violations, and the number of youthful offenders has risen very sharply in recent years.

Organized crime is largely concerned with illegal goods and services. A powerful system bases its strength on public demand, government corruption, and force, with gambling and narcotics its principal sources of revenue. Drug usage, in particular, has attracted much recent public attention. While heroin addiction is substantial and the indirect cause of many property crimes, marijuana poses a widespread but less dangerous threat. Improper use of dangerous drugs is a newer but very common problem.

Drunkenness causes more actual arrests than any other crime. Police, courts, and jails devote much time and effort to habitual violators. Alcohol is also involved in a great many crimes of violence through firearms.

Questions

1. How is crime related to the inner city?
2. To what extent is juvenile delinquency increasing?
3. What is organized crime based upon?
4. How are *narcotics* distinguished from *dangerous drugs*?
5. In what way is alcohol related to crime?

NOTES

[1] *Report of the National Advisory Commission on Civil Disorders* (Washington: GPO, 1968), pp. 133–136.

[2] Ramsey Clark, *Crime in America* (New York: Simon & Schuster, 1970), p. 57.

[3] *Report of the National Advisory Commission on Civil Disorders*, pp. 73–77.

[4] 18 United States Code 4209, 5006, 5031; California Welfare and Institutions Code, sec. 603; Illinois Revised Statutes, chapter 37, sec. 702–2; New York Social Welfare Law, sec. 371.5, Criminal Procedure Law, sec. 720.10; Texas Civil Statutes, art. 2338.

[5] *Juvenile Court Statistics 1971* (Washington: National Center for Social Statistics, 1972), pp. 10–11.

[6] *Task Force Report: Juvenile Delinquency and Youth Crime* (Washington: GPO, 1967), p. 3.

[7] *Ibid.*, pp. 150–152.

[8] Lewis Yablonsky, *The Violent Gang* (Baltimore: Penguin, 1967), pp. 140–163.

[9] *Uniform Crime Reports for the United States—1972* (Washington: GPO, 1973), p. 126.

[10] Donald R. Cressey, *Theft of the Nation* (New York: Harper & Row, 1969), pp. 109–140.

[11] *Not the Law's Business?* (Washington: GPO, 1972), pp. 4–14.

[12] *Crime in America*, p. 74.

[13] *Task Force Report: Crime and Its Impact* (Washington: GPO, 1967), pp. 52–53.

[14] *The Challenge of Crime in a Free Society* (Washington: GPO, 1967), pp. 192–196; *Task Force Report: Organized Crime* (Washington: GPO, 1967), pp. 25–60.

[15] *Uniform Crime Reports for the United States—1972*, p. 119.

[16] *Task Force Report: Narcotics and Drug Abuse* (Washington: GPO, 1967), p. 48; *Estimating Number of Narcotics Addicts* (Washington: Bureau of Narcotics and Dangerous Drugs, 1971), pp. 1–11; *Drug Use in America* (Washington: GPO, 1973), pp. 41–112.

[17] *Marihuana: An Analysis of Use, Distribution and Control* (Washington: Bureau of Narcotics and Dangerous Drugs, 1971), pp. 9–17.

[18] Sidney Cohen, *The Drug Dilemma* (New York: McGraw-Hill, 1969), pp. 83–95.

[19] Robinson v. California, 370 U.S. 660, 82 S.Ct. 1417 (1962).

[20] *Uniform Crime Reports for the United States—1972*, pp. 120–121.

[21] Powell v. Texas, 392 U.S. 514, 88 S.Ct. 2145 (1968).

[22] *The Challenge of Crime in a Free Society* (Washington: GPO, 1967), p. 235.

[23] *Task Force Report: Drunkenness* (Washington: GPO, 1967), pp. 65–67.

[24] Marvin E. Wolfgang, *Patterns in Criminal Homicide* (New York: Wiley, 1966), pp. 134–156.

[25] *Firearms and Violence in American Life* (Washington: GPO, 1969), p. 9.

[26] Alphonso Pinckney, *The American Way of Violence* (New York: Vintage, 1972), pp. 168–171.

Chapter 4
The Criminal Culture

"Society prepares the crime; the criminal commits it."
BUCKLE

Minorities

The United States, like other nations, breeds crime. Police probably apprehend about 25 percent of the total population every year. Of course, the vast majority of these are very brief detentions for minor traffic violations, but the indication of our normal involvement in crime may still be noted. If the truth were known, most Americans could be held responsible for many offenses every year. The countless lesser and usually unreported crimes, including those against licensing and tax regulations, serve as examples of those committed, sometimes without knowledge, by almost everyone. We tend to separate proven offenders without considering the scope and proximity of true guilt.

Varying rates of offenses in diverse countries clearly reflect social characteristics; America demonstrates a marked degree of violence, especially with firearms, and an inability to either accept or control vice offenses. But there are many other ways in which the culture affects crime in the United States, perhaps none more clearly than that involving minorities.

A number of groups in America feel themselves set apart and discriminated against. Indians, those of Mexican or Puerto Rican ancestry, and particularly blacks may be so categorized. Conditions vary widely among such minority groups, but most share a high rate of crime. American Indians and persons of Latin heritage do not loom so large in overall arrests simply because their numbers are relatively few. The black, on the other hand, occupies a very large portion of the total crime picture. To refuse to recognize this aspect of our culture is to deny reality and avoid a principal factor in the general problem of justice.

Negroes constitute a little more than 10 percent of the total United States population, but their contribution to crime far exceeds this proportional number. While it should never be forgotten that the vast majority of blacks are as law-abiding as any other group of Americans and suffer a great many offenses, arrest statistics reveal a disturbing racial imbalance. Across the nation, the total rate of apprehension of blacks is over three times that of whites, and the picture in regard to serious violations shows even more disporportion. Approximately one in three arrests for major property crimes (burglary, larceny of $50 or more, and auto theft) involves a Negro. For crimes of personal violence, blacks are taken into custody about as often as whites, despite their relatively few numbers. Negroes represent 60 percent of those apprehended for murder and for robbery.[1] In short, blacks play a role in crime cleared by arrest far in excess of their numbers. While actual offenses, including those unknown or unsolved, may not be so greatly imbalanced, the system of American justice must clearly be influenced by racial elements.

It is only reasonable to wonder why blacks display so much apparent criminal behavior. On one extreme, some say biology is the cause; on another, you may hear that prejudice on the part of the police is the answer. Neither of these theories can produce any clear proof, and both fail to satisfactorily explain the disproportion of races apparently responsible for crime. Most experts feel the real causes are directly related to our entire society. Basically, they believe that different forms of discrimination and related cultural problems create such hardships among blacks as to bring about many violations.

The heart of the urban crime problem now lies, of course, in the inner city. But many of the same conditions still extend to some rural areas, especially in the South. A common bond running through nearly all predominantly Negro districts is, quite simply, poverty. If the numbers of poor people, black and white, are compared proportionally to crime rates, a similarity appears. Negroes comprise about half of those arrested in our inner cities, they also total about half of those living in poverty there.

Income alone, however, is not the sole characteristic of known offenders. Other factors combine against many black Americans. Poverty may be directly related to two parallel conditions: lack of education and unemployment. Because most young blacks live in poor neighborhoods, they normally attend schools lacking sufficient facilities, personnel, or standards. Reinforced by home attitudes attaching little value to education, the students routinely fail in classroom performance and become academic drop-outs. Afloat in an increasingly technical society, the untrained and uneducated have few opportunities for employment. Consequently, the black, often incapable of competing in a specialized economy, must either find low paying, unskilled work or go without a job. And thus the cycle is complete, with poverty, poor education, and unemployment combining to close the door against progress.[2]

The Negro faces still more obstacles in the form of family conditions, migration, community standards, and prejudice. With considerably more likelihood than whites, blacks are raised in broken and female-based homes. In many instances, no father resides with the family, and frequently the children are illegitimate and dependent upon the state for support. Such conditions also exist among many whites, but racial imbalance is great.

Many black families also suffer dislocation merely because of migration. A shift of great magnitude has occurred from the South and to the city. Within the last thirty years, about 4 million blacks have left the southern states and moved into the urban centers of the North and West. This migration to a new and urban lifestyle frequently ends only in frustration and disorganization. Movement to inner cities involves more than usual problems because of the conditions at the destination.

The migrating black family normally goes to a neighborhood beset with difficulties. It has a high crime rate, of course, but also suffers from dilapidated and overcrowded housing. Inadequate health and welfare facilities result in poor sanitation, infant mortality, and malnutrition. The social setting is also disturbing as young blacks grow up with large numbers of drug addicts, alcoholics, prostitutes, and professional criminals. Local businessmen appear bent on economic exploitation, and the law seems more a means of oppression than of justice.

Black frustrations are naturally increased by the prejudice and discrimination which both cause and continue present conditions. While current legal policies prevent overt racial segregation, attitudes and beliefs demonstrate far more resistance to change. Prejudice may not prevent all movement from the urban ghetto and the cycle of despair, but it does create major obstacles to significant economic and social progress. Given these conditions, it is not difficult to imagine why a greater percentage of blacks than whites might turn to crime. Exposed to the same basic values and ambitions of all Americans, yet deprived of most opportunities toward fulfillment, many youthful Negroes become bitter and resentful, later turning to violence and disorder.[3]

With certain variations, the black experience is shared by members of other minorities. Set apart and prevented from easily joining the main society, they are subjected to conditions of poverty and still expected to sustain traditional American values. Negroes, Indians, and Latins share the frustrations and despair of relatively powerless minorities. Those unaccustomed to such conditions should not doubt a resulting tendency toward escapism (often through drugs or alcohol) and crime. Many other ethnic groups, including the Irish and Italians, have in time overcome similar obstacles, but problems built on obvious color lines seem to endure and even worsen with increased tension.

Such conditions may provide an explanation for frequent known offenses among minorities. They do not, at least in law, amount to an excuse or justification. It is quite possible that no major improvements can be expected in the control of crime without significant alteration of the social system. Yet, justice recognizes little in the way of cultural causation, and this aspect certainly involves more than the plight of our minorities.

Families

Many experts believe that the roots of crime are usually detected within the family. They suspect that conditions in the home can greatly affect the psychological development of children and, perhaps, indirectly lead to delinquency. This is not, of course, to suggest that parents actually raise their offspring to be offenders; the results can occur despite best intentions and efforts.

If crime can be related to the family, the key is surely one of omission instead of design. Within the United States dramatic social changes have transpired, and important stabilizing factors no longer successfully operate. The fragmentation of the American family is only one such element, but one closely associated with public disorder.

Personality is formed at a very early age, molded during primary school years, and largely finished in adolescence. During this period the family serves as a basic influence for determining individual character. Parents either properly providing or failing to give affection, security, and values become both conscious and unconscious models for their children. Psychologists have little doubt that development of personality depends largely upon a satisfactory presence by mother and father. Yet, in a very large number of American families this beneficial process fails to occur.

Approximately one in every four children is now raised in a broken home; about 10 percent are illegitimate.[4] Not all such cases, of course, pose serious difficulties, but the likelihood of personal problems increases significantly with absence of either the natural mother or, more typically, father. Families shattered by death, divorce, or separation may reconstitute themselves and serve as a sound basis for young people; normal development, however, becomes more difficult whenever a broken home occurs.

The relationship between crime and the lack of a complete family is clear. Within the United States, approximately 25 percent of all children are presently reared in broken homes; about 50 percent of juvenile delinquents come from such backgrounds. If statistics were available on the number of families divided emotionally, rather than physically, the association might be even more closely correlated.[5] Whether or not broken homes indirectly increase the chances of delinquency, the American family must obviously be regarded as in flux. Values and standards have changed markedly during the last few decades and could show still more flexibility in coming years.

Disintegration of the traditional family probably contributes to the rising tide of juvenile unrest, delinquency, and disorder. Without the stabilizing and cohesive influences of a strong home, many young people resort to socially disapproved varieties of conduct. This may range from participation in civil disobedience to the tragedy of drug abuse. Some naturally follow paths leading to overt criminal behavior and involvement with legal authorities.

At one time, people believed that tendencies toward improper conduct could be biologically inherited. Today the emphasis clearly rests upon the responsibility of society, and, particularly, on the family. Everyone is tempted to commit certain types of crime, but most people develop sufficient resistance to these desires to remain law-abiding in ordinary situations. This behavior may come about because of moral principle, conscience, or simple fear of punishment. For some, however, the ability to resist opportunities in crime is less well-established or almost entirely lacking. At times, the broad terms *sociopath* or *psychopathic personality* may be attached to such individuals, meaning those whose activities conflict, without reason, with cultural standards. In truth, this condition is probably a relative one with respect to all people, and has become more of a general category than a specific condition. Most people demonstrate certain forms of sociopathic behavior at some time or another.

The exact degree to which a psychopathic personality may be related to the home is unknown. Many experts believe that a lack of affection in early childhood might cause a person to fail in developing a normal conscience. At any rate, there is little doubt that bad family influences can contribute to development of criminal tendencies.[6] Of course, a simple definition of good homes becomes quite subjective, but most people would agree that child molesting, brutality, and neglect (all of which are far more common than generally believed) could scarcely contribute to proper upbringing. Aside from such obvious forms of mistreatment, however, a multitude of more subtle influences can be at work.

No one knows the extent to which emotional suffering could unfavorably affect a child. While compensating factors may often alleviate lasting harm, it is reasonable to assume that homes divided by divorce, violence, drugs, alcohol, or simple misunderstanding between parents are less than wholly satisfactory starting points in a complicated and rapidly changing society.

The American family has been greatly altered in the last few decades. It is, for example, much smaller and more isolated from relatives. Homes have also become, literally, mobile; it is quite routine for a childhood to cover several different locations, reaching from coast to coast. Within the family itself, the functions of mother and father are no longer so distinct. The changing role of women and the sharp increase in the numbers of working mothers illustrate such trends. In themselves, these patterns do not contribute to crime, but they are part of the dramatic change in modern society. The roots of increasing delinquency may well lie within such cultural modifications.

Family conditions both reflect and contribute to the fragmentation of responsibility in America. In many cultures, a crime disgraces relatives of an offender, but the emphasis in the United States is far more closely restricted to the individual. Isolated from both support and duty toward the family, members may more readily tend to drift into delinquent behavior. This disruption of unity in the home can also contribute to social disorganization. Stability of a culture must ultimately reside upon smaller supporting units; traditionally, this basis has been provided by the private home where values and standards are instilled in children. It is possible for a society to endure marked changes in such patterns, or perhaps develop wholly new substitutes. In time, the United States may illustrate these very fundamental modifications. But, meanwhile, people are caught between a continuing social flux of great magnitude and necessarily ancient concepts of crime.

Even where family conditions are sound, other factors in the culture can lead to delinquency. America's urbanization, for example, certainly helps isolate the individual and weaken community influences. Ever increasing reliance on technology and government, together with a decline in the significance of traditional religion adds to the difficulties of adjustment in the modern age. There is no single explanation or cause of crime. It may come from a multitude of usually related sources, and everyone is affected. Whatever the reasons may be, it is essential to recognize that delinquency exists in virtually every aspect of American society.

Business

Crime is not always violent, or even obvious. It may hide beneath the surface of perfectly ordinary affairs and rarely be known to myriad victims. Crime can occur around us every day, determining the way we live with virtually no detection or attempted prosecution. This pattern takes many forms but is especially commonplace in connection with business.

Virtually no commercial activity escapes crime, without and within. Retail operations, in particular, suffer greatly from shoplifting, bad checks, and various kinds of theft. Such losses equal total profit in certain businesses. This problem is especially serious in many poorer districts where merchants raise prices to balance other losses. And such practices, in turn, seem discriminatory and increase resentment in the local community.

Business also experiences much internal crime. Very little is known about the true extent of such violations, for they are frequently not detected, reported to authorities, or solved. Some years ago, a distinguished criminologist, Edwin H. Sutherland, coined the phrase "white collar crime" in reference to offenses by ordinarily respectable people in the course of routine employment. In most instances, these are committed by business people, and the extent of such violations is incalculable in modern America.[7] They illustrate the degree to which crime now permeates normal facets of daily life.

Employee theft and embezzlement cost business millions of dollars every day. In some fields, they probably amount to 5 percent of costs, although accurate estimates remain difficult to obtain. Employee crime is usually minor, continued, and hidden. Nonetheless, it constitutes a tremendous total drain upon the economy. Banks, for example, probably lose ten times more money through internal embezzlement than by far more spectacular and publicized robbery.

Crimes by workers seem almost insignificant in statistical analyses of reported offenses and arrests. The reason, of course, is simply that when employers do discover such incidents, they are reluctant to inform authorities. Most businessmen greatly prefer to handle such matters themselves to avoid unpleasant publicity and the inconvenience of prosecutions. Official figures are, therefore, quite unreliable as an indication of actual white collar crime. Surveys reveal that the true extent of violations by workers is very great. No less than 75 percent of chain store employees, for example, have been reported as stealing from their companies; even in banks the proportion reaches 20 percent.[8] Most of these larcenies are fairly small, but, combined, they become highly significant. They lead to additional expenses for security efforts and insurance, and such losses eventually reach the consumer in the form of higher prices or charges for service. While the immediate victim may be the single business concerned, the public finally suffers the ultimate economic burden.

Employers may experience frequent crime from workers, but they are themselves responsible for various offenses. White collar violations include those by executives and extend to a multitude of devious business activities. Ordinary fraud, for example, costs Americans more than all the traditional property crimes. Yet, cases of misrepresentations, deceit, and false pretenses by businessmen are seldom reported and even less often prosecuted. Perhaps the existence of powerful vested interests operates to militate against the enforcement of laws designed to protect the general public against commercial fraud. At any rate, the numberless customers cheated by the unscrupulous must comprise a considerable portion of the entire population.[9]

Many aspects of American business rely upon deceit or, what Senator Everett Dirksen once called, "imbued fraud." It penetrates the routine transactions of retail and financial concerns and extends to operations of giant corporations. Little is known about the magnitude of this aspect of America, but the few incidents made public indicate economic enormity. Certainly the costs must reach billions of dollars every year.

Variations of deliberate corporate crime are numerous, devious, and serious. A single instance of large scale trade restraint, such as price fixing by a combination of electrical manufacturers, can result in vast illegal profit and higher costs for almost all Americans. But such events produce little popular outcry and, when occasional prosecution occurs, minimal sentences compared to those given ordinary offenders.

Large businesses may also act improperly to ruin competitors or purposefully drain a company of its worth against the interests of stockholders. Financial manipulations, sometimes international in effect, may be so complex as to defy all but the most expert auditors and attorneys. Laws do exist against this type of deliberate mismanagement, but enforcement is made most difficult because of the power exercised by principal conspirators and the complexities of formal proof.

Corporate crime spreads across America on a tide of unethical conduct. False advertising, hidden behind a screen of common business exaggeration, may be detected in nearly every variety of both retail and wholesale trade.[10] Illegal contract kickbacks, tie-in sales, and upgrading of products are but a few of the ways in which business is perverted to criminal ends. Patent, trademark, and copyright violations and offenses against the food and drug laws (which can actually endanger personal safety more insidiously than any assault) also pose major problems. Other examples of crime by corporations include industrial espionage and collusion in bidding.

Business crime grows in response to efforts toward close regulation; it becomes most acute when true competition fails. The most obvious examples of commercial misconduct in recent times took place during World War II price administration. Government efforts quickly led to formation of a vast black market, responding to a law of supply and demand more fundamental than any official controls. At various times, 90 percent of certain items, including meat and lumber, moved illegally in the economy (that is, beyond rationing and price fixing). Public response clearly demonstrated the grave difficulties encountered by extended efforts at economic intervention.[11]

Larger businesses sometimes resort to unfair and illegal labor practices. In their efforts to combat union pressure, management utilizes methods ranging from subtle hints of preferential treatment to physical coercion. And, of course, leaders of many unions respond by similar tactics against recalcitrant employees and employers alike. Violence, threats, and bribery may turn the principle of collective bargaining into a thinly veiled war, with occasional interference from government agencies. If management may sometimes be accused of exploiting workers, the same charge can surely be directed against labor leaders. At times, the employee becomes the real victim of the entire struggle, with secret deals between business and union chiefs.

Commerce is only one aspect of American society influenced by crime. Businessmen may indeed inflict damage on the public by illegal conduct, but they are also victimized by customers, suppliers, employees, and even representatives of government. Blame for crime in the United States should never be directed at a single class or isolated source. It must be broadened across the entire social spectrum, from bottom to top. To some degree, we may all share the responsibility as criminals, but we also must truly be regarded as victims. The magnitude of the crime problem has forced a growing realization of the need for cooperative effort. Businessmen and chambers of commerce in many communities are now attempting prevention, assisting police, and increasing public concern.

Government

The very organ of society required to define crime, the state, demonstrates the extent of illegal conduct. Juveniles, members of racial minorities, drug addicts, and gangsters hold no corner on delinquent behavior. America may indeed suffer from what C. Wright Mills termed "structural immorality," a condition in which the entire social system becomes imbued with crime. This reaches into virtually every phase of life; businessmen, attorneys, doctors all have their own unethical and illegal practices. One of the most disturbing extensions of American crime, however, involves the structure of government itself.

Official misconduct is widespread in most nations, including the United States. It may take the obvious form of outright bribery and corruption to become a primary source of strength for organized crime. Policemen, prosecutors, and judges enable vice to flourish in virtually every large city and many smaller communities.[12] These officials duly receive their very considerable portion of illicit gains, but improper conduct in government really goes far beyond those charged with enforcement of traditional criminal laws. The continuing expansion of the state into economic, cultural, and educational fields opens vast new vistas of dishonesty. Few such opportunities fail to be recognized and utilized.

Crime exists at all levels of government. Local school board members occasionally are motivated by bribes or award especially lucrative contracts to relatives; they may also function in collusion with builders, suppliers, and administrators. School superintendents and principals, in turn, sometimes even demand and receive kickback payments from teachers in return for employment. Such tendencies are certainly not limited to educational systems; almost every type of government operation displays similar aspects. Where power exists, corruption follows.

The multitude of formal regulations affecting housing, taxation, licensing, pollution, and countless other fields are by their nature subject to discretionary enforcement. This condition may result in direct bribery of working agents, but even more significant influences on policy application must not be disregarded. Many laws designed to protect the general public promptly fall into disuse; victims may discover that efforts to obtain redress and prosecution meet insurmountable difficulties. The simple absence of sufficient facilities for enforcement sometimes explains such conditions, but the very limitations may come about by design and direction.

Examples of corruption may be discovered in each of our major governmental branches. Legislators at state and federal levels are enmeshed in bribery, extortion, and even homicide. Judges, including representatives of the highest courts in the nation, become involved in dubious schemes for personal profit. Executives, from minor bureaucrats to the highest elected officials, flaunt the law and engage in open graft. The military displays a panoply of illegal conduct ranging from defense spending to murder in foreign lands. Perhaps the opportunities for private gain are greatest for those occupying positions of authority. At any rate, such performances appear throughout the nation and extend to the highest places in government.

Bribery, malfeasance, and false reporting are but the most obvious and notorious ways in which officials may surround themselves with impropriety. Most government misconduct is far more subtle and costly. There is, for example, a massive amount of collusion over the allocation of public monies. Fortunes may be easily made or lost on award of a single federal contract. And, once a foothold is established, the road to expanding costs and personal power can frequently be opened. Few business operations could afford the inefficiency and waste manifest in a typical government agency. The initial objective of such programs may be totally admirable, but practical application sometimes becomes a bureaucratic monolith of political favoritism, disguised nepotism, and personal greed. Many such activities either do not formally violate specific legal provisions, or become impossible to prove; but the public still suffers enormously from misconduct in office.

It is only reasonable to expect that a higher general standard of conduct might be anticipated from those representing the people and charged with formulation, interpretation, enforcement, or administration of the laws. This natural inclination, however, encounters grave disillusion. Both the ultimate strength and most glaring weakness of our government is that of political involvement. The demand for election or appointment to office controls the entire system, and while this affords an irreplaceable opportunity for final public authority, it also serves as a cause of corruption. Votes, in practice, require money; thus, a dangerous combination begins.

Politicians utilize the power of appointment both to reward and to guarantee support. They also depend upon diverse sources of financial aid in campaigning, and many interest groups provide assistance to all plausible candidates for purposes of protection. This may, in time, elevate to a condition of virtual governmental extortion, as experiences with certain state legislative and licensing bodies illustrate. In the same regard, much of the money consumed by major political campaigns is raised through illegal means, in violation of the laws against lobbying, reporting, and spending.[13]

If the leaders of government set poor examples for society (a condition by no means unique to the United States), public workers must share the blame. In most jurisdictions, it is technically a crime for employees of the state to strike. Yet within recent years, the United States has witnessed many blatant violations of these provisions and, because of obvious political pressure, such means have achieved notable success. The pattern has extended from local to federal levels and has even involved agencies directly responsible for law enforcement. It is difficult to see how respect for authority can ever be engendered in an atmosphere of overt hypocrisy and deceit.

Government may set something of a criminal example, but it also contributes to violations in a number of indirect ways. The very multiplication of laws and formal regulations adds to the difficulties of justice.[14] In a highly complex society, it becomes impossible for the average citizen to avoid committing lesser crimes. Perhaps the mere existence of so many rules makes misconduct more acceptable to the majority of citizens.

Unpopular regulations surely place many citizens in the category of violators. Rigid limitations on drugs, prohibition of intoxicants, and heavy taxation (evasion of which probably totals more in dollar costs than all ordinary property offenses combined)[15] serve as examples of where criminal laws do not seem to coincide with personal demand. Perhaps still more disturbing is the prosecution of offenders such as

Criminal Justice Expenditures

Local	62%	Police	59%
State	25%	Courts	19%
Federal	13%	Corrections	21%
		Other	1%
	100%		100%

SOURCE: *Expenditure and Employment Data for the Criminal Justice System 1971–1972* (Washington: U.S. Government Printing Office, 1974), p. 11.

drug addicts who actually constitute a social problem requiring rehabilitation rather than punishment. Unfortunately, the mere process of labeling someone as a criminal poses major obstacles to reform.[16] Thus, the state may create still more offenders by its very efforts at control.

Perhaps the final contribution to crime made by government consists of the general failure of formal justice. Certainly, the high odds against detection, arrest, prosecution, or punishment must add to the total number of offenses. Under present conditions, it is difficult to demonstrate that crime actually does not pay and that this situation is surely related to deficiencies within government. About $15 billion is now spent annually on crime control, including police, courts, and corrections. This figure fails to match the sum Americans spend every year on alcohol and amounts to an almost negligible part of local, state, and national budgets.

Simply allocating additional monies to law enforcement can, alone, accomplish little beyond increasing the likelihood of waste and corruption. The overall problems of American society, including those of criminal justice, require sincerity and dedication more than rhetoric and bureaucracy. Any true reform demands modification of existing social conditions; crime cannot be isolated from the culture in which it thrives.

Nevertheless, the agencies of justice remain the only obvious and direct means of control. Their operations are the only immediate answer to handling crime. And, in practical terms, that often becomes a matter of money.

Summary

The rate of known crime is more than three times higher among blacks than among whites. This condition may be explained in part by poverty and prejudice.

Crime seems closely related to family conditions, for delinquency appears to flourish in broken homes. Attitudes and actions by parents may cause sociopathic tendencies or other emotional disturbances to develop in their children.

White collar crime includes offenses by ordinary people in the course of employment. Such violations by workers and businessmen reach dramatic proportions in America.

Much crime exists within government itself. Legislative, judicial, and executive branches, as well as the military, contain a great deal of misconduct and set a grim example for the nation.

Questions

1. How is crime related to prejudice?
2. Why may family conditions contribute to delinquency?
3. What is the significance of white collar crime?
4. Could government cause crime?

NOTES

[1] *Uniform Crime Reports for the United States—1972* (Washington: GPO, 1973), p. 131.
[2] *To Establish Justice, To Insure Domestic Tranquility* (Washington: GPO, 1969), pp. 27–37.
[3] Richard A. Cloward and Lloyd E. Ohlin, *Delinquency and Opportunity* (New York: Free Press, 1960), pp. 121–124, 150–152.
[4] DHEW, Public Health Service, Vital Statistics of the United States, 1968 (annual report).
[5] Sheldon and Eleanor Glueck, *Unraveling Juvenile Delinquency* (Cambridge: Harvard University Press, 1950), pp. 108–133; Hermann Mannheim, *Comparative Criminology* (Boston: Houghton Mifflin, 1965), pp. 618–624.
[6] David Abrahamsen, *The Psychology of Crime* (New York: Wiley, 1964), pp. 42–55.
[7] *Task Force Report: Crime and Its Impact* (Washington: GPO, 1967), pp. 104–109.
[8] Edwin H. Sutherland, *White Collar Crime* (New York: Holt, Rinehart & Winston, 1961), p. 11.
[9] *The Nature, Impact and Prevention of White-Collar Crime* (Washington: GPO, 1970), pp. 5–11.
[10] *White Collar Crime*, pp. 111–127; *Comparative Criminology*, pp. 469–498.
[11] Marshall B. Clinard, *The Black Market* (New York: Holt, Rinehart & Winston, 1952), pp. 16–48.
[12] Donald R. Cressey, *Theft of the Nation* (New York: Harper & Row, 1969), pp. 248–289.
[13] Ramsey Clark, *Crime in America* (New York: Simon & Schuster, 1970), pp. 41–42.
[14] Sanford H. Kadish, "The Crisis of Overcriminalization," *Annals of the American Academy of Political and Social Science* 374 (November, 1967), pp. 158–170.
[15] *Task Force Report: Crime and Its Impact* (Washington: GPO, 1967), pp. 51–52, 113–115.
[16] Howard S. Becker, *Outsiders: Studies in the Sociology of Deviance* (New York: Free Press, 1963), pp. 31–34; David Matza, *Becoming Deviant* (Englewood Cliffs, N.J.: Prentice-Hall, 1969), p. 181.

PART II

THE POLICE

Once a crime occurs, it becomes, at least in theory, the immediate concern of the police. Regardless of causation, an act has violated the penal law, and agencies of justice are empowered to intervene. In daily practice, of course, the police may either actually witness an offense or receive a report of one having been committed. Resulting action depends upon written statutes, court decisions, departmental rules, and individual discretion.

It is possible to view the police role in two very different ways.

Citizens and peace officers often think first of the need for crime control. But the police should also be regarded as performing a social welfare function. They are, after all, essentially created by society to help people. The fact that legislatures grant peace officers certain privileges in connection with carrying weapons and assign to them duties of making arrests should never be considered as their only reason for existence. Our police are the first governmental recourse against crime, but they should also provide a multitude of services to people in need. Their primary responsibility is to preserve order and tranquility, a task which only begins with fair enforcement of the law.

Understanding of the American police role must begin with the realization that such a regular governmental function does not really extend far back in history. It has only been in relatively recent generations that concepts of formal forces for protection of the public against crime have existed. Of course, certain police responsibilities go back many centuries, but such duties were actually for the welfare of rulers rather than the people. Gradually, as ideas of a democratic state replaced those of regal authority, law enforcement expanded to include defense of person and property. The police have been regarded as representatives of the entire public for little more than a century.

To some extent, the responsibilities of government agencies, particularly at the higher levels, still involve defense of the state itself. For thousands of years, however, the security of simple citizens was no direct concern of formal police forces. In early England, people relied upon the "hue and cry" to summon each other's assistance in times of need. Later, the government required citizens to become members of the "watch and ward" to guard city streets and gates at night and in the day. By the thirteenth century, English kings had established offices of sheriff, constable, and ranger, but their duties were specialized and still largely concerned with the monarch's property. Such a rather confused system of law enforcement, buttressed by small units maintained by businesses, courts, and churches, did not suffice to insure public safety. They became, nevertheless, the only means available in colonial America.

The history of disciplined, full-time, publicly employed officers with the duty of protecting all citizens did not begin until early in the nineteenth century. In 1829, Home Secretary Robert Peel finally succeeded in getting the British Parliament to pass the Metropolitan Police Act for Greater London. Under the enlightened leadership of Sir Charles Rowan, the new uniformed force became a model for England and America.

By the Civil War, larger cities throughout the United States had established police departments along the lines pioneered in London. Federal and state law enforcement agencies have long and distinguished histories, but their rapid expansion did not occur until the growth of central political power in the twentieth century. Meanwhile, the tradition of citizens acting in special capacities to preserve order has endured throughout the nation.

America has thousands of independent police forces, with the vast majority operating on the local level. A typical urban department has "line" or primary field operations, and several supporting functions. Patrol, criminal investigation, and traffic duties take up perhaps 90% of time and manpower. A relatively small number of people work in vital juvenile, records, communications, laboratory, and community relations units.

As far as practical law enforcement is concerned, peace officers rely upon several old and basic procedures. Arrest, search, seizure of evidence, questioning, and identification of suspects are the routine practices by which the police attempt to control crime. Authorized by statute, and recognized as necessary by judges, these common measures constitute the way in which an ordinary criminal case begins.

Three centuries ago, a concept of immense importance developed in connection with the emergence of democratic societies. It held that the government was bound to justice under law. Consequently, the police must operate within the confines of legality, and their actions can be indirectly regulated by the courts. This has led, in recent years, to several significant restrictions by interpretation of constitutional protections.

In the United States, everyone, including those obviously guilty of serious crimes, is entitled to constantly evolving rights of "due process." With rule of law, rather than raw force or administrative decree, the major elements of justice come under rather close and continuing scrutiny by the courts of the land. Today, the police are forbidden the use of evidence obtained by illegal means. Similarly, suspects may not be compelled to give testimony which may be turned against themselves. Such rules do not come about at the whim of judges, they are firmly rooted in the Bill of Rights.

The police have an ultimate responsibility that goes far beyond that of catching criminals. They must protect the rights of all citizens, including those who violate the laws as well as their victims. Such a difficult and essential task leads to many problems, perhaps most obviously in connection with rights of free speech and assembly. The maintenance of a free society is a challenging and sometimes frustrating duty, and it falls heavily upon the police.

Chapter 5
Organization

"Policemen are soldiers who act alone."
HERBERT SPENCER

Federal Agencies

American police fall into a variety of organizational schemes and categories. Perhaps the most obvious classification is based upon scope of jurisdiction. Basically, the United States has agencies operating at federal, state, and local levels. Exact powers and responsibilities differ according to law and administrative regulations. While all law enforcement officers have much in common, their actual authorities and functions depend primarily upon the organization for which they work. Duty, pay, policy, and a host of other factors can be determined only through and by the agency concerned.

Apart from the military, there are approximately 60,000 federal employees with essentially law enforcement responsibilities.[1] This number does not include those with authority derived indirectly through the central government, such as policemen for the District of Columbia, among Indian tribes, or in overseas territories. A great multitude of federal workers have duties to enforce specific laws or orders; U.S. Marshals and their deputies, Post Office Inspectors, Protective Service guards, National Park Rangers, and agents from the Alcohol, Tobacco, and Firearms and Intelligence Divisions of the Internal Revenue Service stand together with others in this broad and general category. Most ordinary law enforcement functions of the central government are, however, concentrated in five agencies located within the Departments of Justice and Treasury.

Easily the most famous, and the largest, of the units directly involved in U.S. police work is the Federal Bureau of Investigation. Since 1908, duties of the FBI have steadily expanded to now include responsibility for such diverse matters as kidnapping, espionage, bank robbery, theft of government property, interstate flight by wanted fugitives or transport of stolen motor vehicles, and large gambling operations. The generally enviable reputation of this investigatory body was founded upon high standards for personnel, avoidance of political involvement, and an ambitious public relations program under the direction of J. Edgar Hoover.

The Border Patrol of the Immigration and Naturalization Service has, since 1924, protected American boundaries against those attempting to enter the nation illegally. Its uniformed members are largely concentrated in the Southwest and constitute an elite and independent force of well-trained men accustomed to potentially hazardous duty. They frequently receive assignments to rather isolated posts near the Mexican border.

Newest and among the smaller of the major federal police agencies is the Drug Enforcement Administration. This unit enforces U.S. laws against misuse of heroin, marijuana, LSD, and similar items. A good number of DEA agents must assume dangerous undercover or foreign assignments, but much work concerns checking the records of those legally entitled to possess and sell regulated drugs.

The relatively small Secret Service has long protected the President and other leading political figures. Its primary mission, however, is actually the investigation of offenses against the currency, negotiable instruments (including checks), and certain financial operations of the federal government. Probably the best publicized of Secret Service investigations concern counterfeiters and those suspected of endangering the President or other high executives.

Finally, the Bureau of Customs enforces numerous restrictions and collects duties on items imported to the United States. It is the oldest and next to the largest among the federal police agencies. Most employees work near the country's major land, sea, and airports, for primary operations concern shipments and travelers. This force, naturally, combats both professional and amateur smugglers attempting to import forbidden items or escape barriers to international trade.

None of the five principal agencies has general police power; their authority is strictly limited by law to specific violations. Generally, federal units deal with crimes that the states either cannot or wish not to enforce. These include offenses against the United States itself (including matters of national security), violations of the basic rights guaranteed citizens, or major transgressions on Indian and military reservations.

In all law enforcement operations, there are frequent overlaps of interest and attention. The Border Patrol, for example, often makes arrests of smugglers and those in illegal possession of narcotics. By the same token, federal agencies routinely come in contact with state and local police. These relationships are normally cooperative and mutually beneficial, although some jealousy and a common tendency toward protection of self-interest exists.

Federal law enforcement is widely regarded as offering the best job opportunities among the three levels of government. Employment by the United States offers prestige, security, and good working conditions in comparison to other police agencies. Standards for recruits are among the highest within the nation, and both training and chances of promotion appear better than average. While initial assignment may not be the most desirable, the federal units have good equipment and adequate facilities and demand high levels of competence and dedication.

With strongly entrenched pay scales and opportunity for increases, federal service appears quite attractive from the standpoint of salary and eventual retirement. As in all bureaucratic systems, discrepancies exist, but those directly employed for enforcement of national laws generally receive benefits superior to those available in state or local organizations. These factors contribute directly, of course, to the significant element of prestige.

Despite public attention and respect, federal agencies constitute a small portion of overall American law enforcement. The government of the United States provides only a small fraction of the manpower and money used annually for police activity, although the figures have risen in recent years.[2] Responsibility for everyday law enforcement still rests primarily upon local and state units of government.

State Police

State governments, on an average, assign less than 3 percent of their employees to law enforcement duties. All together, 70,000 people work in about 200 separate agencies at this level. It might reasonably be wondered how fifty states support four times their number in police organizations. The answer lies in decentralization of functions among different offices. A typical state, for example, could support a highway patrol, a unit for the enforcement of liquor laws, a bureau assigned to drug control, and a team to conduct special investigations for the attorney general. In some areas, the functions are still more diversified, while others maintain a single central law enforcement agency.

Overall, the states devote about 1 percent of their total general expenditures to police activity. The figure may appear small, but it is many times the proportion so spent in the federal system. Maryland expends the largest share for law enforcement purposes, and Hawaii, which alone among the fifty states has no actual central police system, the least. The picture of financial support, however, is becoming more complex with assistance grants between levels of government.[3]

The concept of a state police force really originated in frontier Texas, but considerable expansion in the number of units occurred during early twentieth century labor strife. Involvement in economic and political affairs eventually led to restrictions upon legal powers and possible assignments for these officers. The majority of states formed forces in response to the rapidly growing system of highways and auto travel between World Wars I and II.[4]

About 70 percent of state police expense is in connection with traffic law enforcement. A few forces possess authority only over crimes involving autos and highways or under specific statutory conditions. In truth, the state units devote an overwhelming portion of their time and effort to road safety and related infractions. Some highway patrols have the additional responsibility of licensing of drivers, inspections for automobile standards, and weight and measure limitations for trucks. These functions can become quite technical and require specialized and highly trained divisions within the larger force.

Although the vast majority of state law enforcement duties occur upon the expanding highway networks beyond urban centers, they are by no means restricted to such daily routines. Actual responsibilities vary according to statute and policy. In many states, a basic function is performed largely through assistance to local agencies. County sheriffs often cannot insure routine enforcement in rural areas; they also need to call for aid in case of serious crime or disorder. These circumstances frequently lead to intervention by state officers. Some forces include detachments specially trained to provide help under unusual circumstances.

Despite exceptions, the majority of state police organizations maintain remarkable efficiency and morale. Their normal independence of politics, concentration on highway safety, and separation from close community involvement permit high standards of performance. Because of wide geographic distribution a paramilitary structure can still permit individual responsibility. Major drawbacks of state service include repetitious work, little early choice of location, only fair salaries, and a growing likelihood of encountering dangerous situations.

Central police services have become quite significant within recent decades. California devotes about $150 million a year to employ 10,000 law enforcement personnel (including about 5,500 officers in the Highway Patrol). While this is the nation's largest state police system, New York and Pennsylvania could also be singled out for expense and size. At the other extreme, several less populated jurisdictions, such as Nevada, North Dakota, and Wyoming, maintain units of approximately 100 men with comparatively low budgets. And, as mentioned earlier,

Hawaii completely avoids the need for such a force relying instead on strong island systems.[5]

In addition to large uniformed traffic patrols and small specialized investigating groups, many states have established centralized agencies for assistance and coordination of local police. Aid may, for example, be available in the form of crime laboratories and technical experts. As most rural police departments cannot maintain the equipment and personnel necessary for fingerprint, handwriting, and other analyses, a central state agency often provides an invaluable resource for major investigations.

States also now frequently support a bureau of criminal records. These offices serve as a focus for statistical compilations and comparisons by gathering information on offenses and police forces. In addition, their files now prove useful for centralized suspect and stolen property identification. Modern means of electronic data processing, linked to the National Crime Information Center of the FBI, can greatly expedite detailed record examination.

Within recent years, many states have entered the field of police standards and training. Led by California, legislators throughout the nation created commissions with authority to establish minimum levels for recruits and to specify common educational objectives. Perhaps these measures will eventually produce significant improvements in general police service. At any rate, it is clear that the possible role of the state in requiring unified and professional law enforcement remains largely unfilled.

Local Departments

The majority of American police are under local control and administration. Federal and state governments include no more than 25 percent of the personnel and less than 1 percent of the public agencies assigned to law enforcement in the United States. Obviously, the vast bulk of police activity occurs on the local level in numerous independent departments.

About 450,000 people work in nearly 40,000 decentralized police agencies. About 13 percent of the employees are civilians and cannot function as sworn peace officers.[6] While an incredible number of separate agencies actually exist in America, the majority are extremely small and contribute relatively little to overall problems of crime control.

Individual police authority is legally given to towns, precincts, cities, districts, and counties. Many smaller units have only one or two officers who devote their efforts solely to civil and traffic matters. In fact, some of those with the legal power of policemen in America do not even know or fail to fully understand that they possess such authority.

Most local peace officers work for departments of cities or counties.

Perhaps 7,000 of these consequential agencies, wholly independent of and separate from one another, operate within the United States. These forces include 90 percent of all local police employees; the remainder are primarily elected or appointed officers serving small townships and precincts.

It should be obvious that American law enforcement is extremely decentralized. In fact, so many separate police agencies exist that only general estimates as to their total number may be made. Some authorities for district and borough forces simply lapse into disuse with the passage of time. Offices of precinct constables, for example, may remain vacant because no one runs for the position. Meanwhile, the aggregate and variety of independent police powers serve as ample proof of antiquated legislation and deeply entrenched political interest.

For at least fifty years, informed observers have urged the consolidation of smaller local agencies, but with little success. Many counties contain scores of separate police departments; within one hour's drive, a motorist can easily pass through the jurisdiction of twenty or thirty forces. Of course, there are obvious benefits of close community law enforcement ties, but the plethora of tiny independent agencies seems beyond any reasonable justification. Modern police operations certainly demand 24 hour community service, radio dispatching, available support in time of emergency, and personnel specially trained in handling juveniles and investigating major offenses. At the least, it would appear that a force of no less than twenty, probably including at least one policewoman, would be necessary to fulfill these needs. Yet, more than 80 percent of America's departments contain fewer than five officers![7]

The pressing need for immediate consolidation has led to efforts at cooperation and great overlapping of legal authority. A single location may easily fall in the jurisdiction of city, precinct, county, and state officers, all charged with enforcement of the same primary laws. Consequently, the departments establish informal policies for dividing territories and providing uncertain assistance. Some local patrolmen, as a result, cruise about with up to three radio receivers tuned to frequencies of other jurisdictions. Certain counties or districts have devised stopgap techniques of central dispatching. Nevertheless, the present and continuing lack of consolidation contributes to avoidance of responsibility, inefficiency, and low minimum standards which reflect unfavorably on the entire police system.

A few counties, most notably in California and New York, now support strong central agencies which provide protective service for rural areas and small communities. This may normally be accomplished under a contract scheme which maintains the independence of separate municipal governments. Unfortunately, the facilities of most large jurisdictions do not permit expansion of services into traditionally local functions. Some wealthy suburbs, which, probably possess America's best community forces, naturally react unfavorably to efforts at consolidation. The outcome for such fortunate areas would be higher taxes and lower standards of police service.

Local governments devote a greater proportional share of their total general budgets (currently about 8 percent) to law enforcement than do either state or federal systems.[8] Yet, most departments remain short of funds and personnel. Facilities and equipment sometimes leave much to be desired, and vital functions must be shorted for reasons of economy. In manpower many local agencies stand below authorized strength, while even these higher figures remain under those recommended by law enforcement experts. The problem of force size is frequently compounded by existing pay scales. Local departments offer the lowest regular salaries among the three levels of government, averaging little more than half that offered by federal service. Yet, communities provide an extreme range of starting pay rates. A new local patrolman can earn as little as $200 or up to $1,000 a month, depending on job location and personal qualifications.

The number of actual officers varies widely by city. New York, Chicago, Philadelphia, and Los Angeles maintain the largest forces by far; among all major cities nearly one in every three government workers is assigned to law enforcement. Of course, the typical police department includes a substantial number of civilian employees in technical, clerical, and other capacities. A large portion of those on agencies' payrolls presently possess no authority as actual peace officers. Furthermore, a good number of police workers only serve part-time. With these categories removed, the nation is left an approximate total of 360,000 sworn full-time local policemen.

In general, the biggest cities maintain proportionally larger law enforcement organizations. Expressed by police ratio (the number of employees per 1,000 inhabitants), most urban areas range between 1 and 4, with an average of about 2.4. The highest figures are, reasonably enough, found in such eastern metropolitan centers as New York, Boston, and Washington. Among the cities with the lowest police ratios are San Antonio, Omaha, and San Diego. Communities of populations less than 10,000 actually show the greatest variation in law enforcement strength. In 1972, their ratios ranged from 0.1 to 9.7.[9]

Several years ago, the federal government commenced an ambitious program to provide law enforcement assistance. In theory, agencies of criminal justice were to be restructured into logical systems. Police departments, in particular, might coordinate their operations if not actually consolidate command structures. Despite grandiose titles and planning, practical organizational results remain extremely limited. To a significant degree, the program has become another bureaucratic channel for dispensation of federal money previously taken by taxation.

Personnel and Administration

Within recent years, the total number of police employees has increased sharply. Expansion of agency size may be noted on federal, state, and local levels of government. This substantial growth in law enforcement strength has produced a marked rise in the total police ratio for our cities. In 1971, the figure stood at 2.4, up from 1.7 in only six years. Unfortunately, this rapid increase was matched almost exactly by soaring numbers of known crimes.

The influx of thousands of new officers and retention of established organizations has magnified a number of administrative difficulties. Many problems revolve around the central considerations of personnel so significant in a service organization. Law enforcement, as all of criminal justice, depends solely upon the quality of the people working within the system. Their success or failure delineates order from anarchy and freedom from tyranny.

About 85 percent of all police expenditures go toward salaries. Employee pay is therefore closely tied to overall financial support; high wage scales and low budgets cannot exist simultaneously. While some American policemen receive excellent salaries, the majority are substantially underpaid. In many cities, the pay of new officers remains far below that required for adequate support of a family. As a consequence, large numbers of patrolmen "moonlight," or take part-time jobs in addition to their police duties. More money is spent on pets than on the police in America; combined annual budgets for all public law enforcement agencies in the United States constitute less than is spent in one month for national defense! Perhaps international conditions have led to a situation where public security draws comparatively little economic support. Nevertheless, the limited funds available for police service loom as one basic explanation for current problems of criminal justice.

Law enforcement agencies rarely lack a sufficient number of ready applicants; the difficulty arises in locating those meeting minimum requirements. Only about one in every four of those expressing an interest in police employment meets the standards set for recruits. Applicants most often fail because of educational background, physical condition, or a past record of suspicious activity. It is not single standards beyond those of reasonable expectation but the cumulative effect of different requirements that causes so many rejections.

The majority of police departments require the equivalent of high school graduation, a minimum height of at least 5'8", uncorrected vision of 20/40, age between 21 and 35 years, and no prior arrests for felonies. These basic standards, which may be either more flexible or more rigid in particular agencies, exclude thousands of ready applicants every year; additional individuals are rejected because of psychological, oral, and agility tests. Some observers feel that such formal requirements discriminate against potentially valuable employees and should be adjusted to meet personal abilities, but police agencies tend to resist these efforts.[10]

Larger law enforcement organizations maintain their own independent training systems. Recruits may attend a series of classes and practical exercises ranging from a few hours to several months in length. Some police academies are excellent, others terrible. Only within the last few years have state commissions begun to demand very minimal standards for training; better forces maintain courses far superior to those required by central authorities.

The most glaring weakness of present police schooling is not in that given recruits but in the lack of in-service programs. Even those agencies with adequate academies for new patrolmen seldom provide satisfactory courses for supervisory personnel and specialists. Some departments require officers to occasionally fire a few rounds on the pistol range; almost none have a continuing and mandatory program of advanced training in the techniques of personal defense.

Young patrolmen quickly discover they have entered a unique professional subculture. The police form a strong and defensive enclave based upon special values and customs. In truth, most officers soon learn that common sense and cautious discretion are essential attributes to successful performance.[11] With classroom instruction over, a policeman begins to acquire knowledge about the strange world of power and repression in which he must operate. Arbitrary enforcement of law quickly results in recrimination from superiors and from those he is supposed to both control and protect.

Police work in America has fallen largely under the job patterns of civil service. While smaller departments remain dominated by overt political appointment, larger ones offer security and retirement plans. Realities of government service, unfortunately, also contribute to the substantial number of annual police resignations. A basic problem lies in rigid and traditional patterns for promotion. Police agencies ordinarily demand prior service and utilize formal objective examinations to fill supervisory and administrative positions.[12] As a consequence, officers often feel opportunities for promotion and change are extremely limited.

To some, many police departments appear bound by unsuitable and ineffective practices. Agencies commonly fulfill such unrelated functions as licensing dogs, checking pawnbroker reports, reviewing taxi driver applications, and removing abandoned cars. Such diverse responsibilities seem rather far removed for a law enforcement system which might be described as provincial paramilitary. Yet they require a large part of present police effort and attention.

Reliance upon traditional attitudes blocks many avenues of potential agency reform. Women, for example, continue to hold only 1.5 percent of sworn police positions; this number could reasonably be increased by ten times, but departments commonly show little or no interest in hiring females as regular officers.

Most American law enforcement forces lack good leadership, fail to utilize proven principles of efficient management, and resist significant change. In addition, they seldom rely on trained specialists, do not assign existing personnel efficiently, and ignore many technological advances.[13] These conditions, compounded by the avoidance of important policy decisions, are by no means unique to the police among all the agencies of criminal justice; they nevertheless illustrate the interlocking obstacles to organizational reform.

Improvements generally do not occur by accident.[14] They come about through careful study, planning, implementation, and review. These tasks fall to persons occupying administrative positions. Unfortunately, relatively few of those holding key posts in American police organizations possess the skills required for successful management. While the picture is gradually changing, most departments continue to be administered by men without specialized training, knowledge, or ability. Experience and political connections do not automatically combine to produce a good police chief.

Special Police

Many people fail to comprehend the substantial role of special policemen in the United States. These include a diverse assortment of private, honorary, reserve, and auxiliary officers. Many possess direct powers as policemen while others function in the capacity of citizens with assumed responsibilities for law enforcement. Comparatively little is known about such personnel and their influence on criminal justice.[15]

The approximately 1 million special policemen to be found in the United States can be divided or grouped in several elemental ways. Some are paid, others are not. Some are directly associated with government agencies, and others work under purely private auspices.

Though it may seem difficult to believe, there are probably more unpaid public policemen in America than those receiving regular wages. This situation has developed from a combination of the civilian heritage of law enforcement and desires to promote political interests. More than 500,000 normally unpaid but publicly sponsored policemen are probably scattered about at present. The most obvious form taken is that of membership in a law enforcement reserve or auxiliary. In the main, such supporting forces tend to be found at the county and precinct level, rather than at federal, state, or city levels. While countless variations exist, the typical reserve organization is rather informal and consists of volunteers who occasionally may ride with patrolmen or provide other services without pay. The auxiliary officer sometimes undergoes rudimentary training and, especially in larger forces, is required to work a minimum number of hours every month. In return, the reservist becomes a commissioned peace officer, although his authority may be restricted by state law. Still, the volunteer citizen policeman usually acquires a uniform, badge, identification card, and gun. His authority to utilize these items and act upon his own initiative frequently depends primarily upon local policy.

The value of most police auxiliaries is rather questionable. In a few districts, they provide valuable support for regular forces in time of unusual demand or public emergency. Reserve units rarely attain a marked degree of efficiency and discipline, but they do provide a badly needed means of directly maintaining citizen interest and involvement in local law enforcement. The greatest problems in regard to such units are those of allowing significant numbers of poorly selected and trained individuals to act as lawmen and of permitting a public police force to avoid its responsibility for securing the highest possible standards among all personnel.

In addition to actually functioning reservists, many governmental units permit the issuance of special or honorary commissions. Some sheriffs and constables routinely glean votes by wholesale distribution of these authorizations among supporters. While the honorary policemen (and they exist by the tens of thousands) usually are not actually available as a reserve, they still may acquire much of the fundamental power possessed by full-time, publicly paid peace officers. In many instances, these commissions require no screening or training of applicants. Possible abuses of this system are obvious and pose considerable difficulties in some areas of the country.

Reserve and honorary officers often serve private rather than public interests. Commissioning by a governmental agency may lead to considerably greater authority of arrest and possession of firearms. Consequently, many protective services secure reserve or honorary appointments for employees. Certain types of nonpublic law enforcers are normally licensed by local or state organizations. Private investigators, railroad detectives, and livestock inspectors often fall into this category. Such official recognition facilitates the fulfillment of various employers' specific requirements.

America contains about as many privately paid as publicly employed policemen.[16] Some possess reserve appointments or government licenses while others have neither. The variety of assignment of these law enforcers without government support is incredible. They range from the simplest guard at a neighborhood store, through large security forces maintained by industrial and retail operations, to rather sophisticated private investigators. Equipped with radios, polygraph machines, and firearms these special police units (often available for hire) constitute a significant but often overlooked part of American law enforcement.

Private security is big business, and it relieves official agencies of enormous burdens. Under present conditions, many leading commercial and industrial operations, particularly those connected with national defense, could not function if entirely dependent upon the regular public police. Businesses must rely on their own security operatives for protection against shoplifters, burglars, embezzlers, and many other kinds of criminals. The strange result of having so much economic activity supported by private means of enforcing public laws may seem peculiar, but it has been the system in general use for several generations and shows no indication of immediate change.[17]

Summary

Policemen in the United States operate on three basic governmental levels: federal, state, and local. Law enforcement by national agencies is limited to specific offenses and certain types of crime.

All together, the states maintain 200 separate police units. The majority of actual effort, however, is directed at highway safety. Fully 75 percent of the policemen within the United States work for local governments. They are concentrated in larger urban areas throughout the nation.

The number of policemen has increased sharply in recent years; yet many departments remain under strength. To some extent, the problem of personnel may be connected to lack of administrative initiative and leadership. Most agencies resist change and show little sustained interest in organizational improvements.

America also contains vast numbers of special policemen. These may hold reserve, auxiliary, or honorary commissions issued by regular governmental agencies. In addition, thousands of security personnel work solely for private employers.

Questions

1. What are the basic functions of federal law enforcement?
2. How have state police forces developed?
3. What is the scope of local law enforcement?
4. In what significant ways might police administration be improved?
5. Why does America have special policemen?

NOTES

[1] *Expenditure and Employment Data for the Criminal Justice System, 1970–71* (Washington: GPO, 1973), p. 14.
[2] *Ibid.*, pp. 1–2.

[3] *Ibid.*, pp. 11, 16–22, 36–41.
[4] Frank R. Prassel, *The Western Peace Officer* (Norman: University of Oklahoma Press, 1972), pp. 150–178.
[5] *Uniform Crime Reports for the United States—1972* (Washington: GPO, 1973), p. 174.
[6] *Ibid.*, p. 167.
[7] *State-Local Relationships in the Criminal Justice System* (Washington: GPO, 1971), pp. 14, 305.
[8] *Expenditure and Employment Data for the Criminal Justice System, 1970–71*, pp. 16–22.
[9] *Uniform Crime Reports for the United States—1972*, pp. 39–41, 162–163.
[10] *Who Will Wear the Badge?* (Washington: GPO, 1971), pp. 30–33.
[11] Arthur Niederhoffer, *Behind the Shield* (Garden City, N.Y.: Anchor, 1969), pp. 55–94.
[12] O.W. Wilson and Roy Clinton McLaren, *Police Administration* (New York: McGraw-Hill, 1972), pp. 277–278.
[13] *Task Force Report: The Police* (Washington: GPO, 1967), 42–52, 121–125.
[14] *Innovation in Law Enforcement* (Washington: GPO, 1973), pp. 31–56, 76–114.
[15] *Private Police in the United States* (Washington: GPO, 1972), pp. 10–12.
[16] *The Private Police Industry* (Washington: GPO, 1972), pp. 13–19.
[17] *Ibid.*, pp. 30–54.

Chapter 6

Operations

*"When constabulary duty's to be done,
The policeman's lot is not a happy one."*

W. S. GILBERT

Patrol

The heart of police activity is patrol—long, repetitious hours spent in routine tours through the community. A majority of officers are assigned to this duty; in smaller departments, virtually the entire force may so serve. The patrol unit carries the main burden of the actual police task. Its men are constantly in contact with the public; upon their performance the present system of criminal justice most clearly depends.

Somewhat surprisingly, little of a patrolman's time deals directly with actual crime, and nearly half of that is concerned with automobile infractions. To what, then, are the hours devoted? Simply remaining visible to the community constitutes the greatest portion. The mere presence of uniformed policemen deters crime, preserves order, and maintains a degree of public security and safety. Those on patrol also spend much time investigating suspicious circumstances and persons, receiving complaints from citizens, collecting evidence, and preparing reports. In most communities, the officers also mediate family quarrels, arbitrate neighborhood conflicts, aid the sick and injured, and look for missing children. Such activity may have nothing to do with actual crime, and reflects the catchall nature of police work, but it provides invaluable assistance to the public in time of actual or imagined need.

Distribution of patrolmen by time and place looms as a primary element in departmental management. Generally, assignment depends upon the known crime rates; a concentration of patrol action ordinarily occurs within the inner city during evening hours. Areas are divided into zones and districts, with an effort toward equitable distribution of anticipated work.[1]

In the United States, patrol is primarily accomplished by automobile. Most of the larger urban centers utilize both one and two officer cars, but manpower problems have resulted in a trend toward single assignment. Most police administrators believe that greater coverage and service accrues from maximizing available units.

While automobile patrol is by far the most common type, many departments still rely upon walking beats, particularly in densely populated sections. Some experts believe this traditional means of foot patrol provides contact with the public and interest in neighborhood problems which are sacrificed by dependence on cars. Obvious limitations on the area an officer can cover on foot make the system too expensive for most communities.

Other means of patrol do, of course, exist. Some agencies use motorcycles and aircraft for such purposes. Considerable attention is presently devoted to helicopters specially equipped for low-level police patrol.[2] Unfortunately, the great cost of maintenance and operation militates against practical employment of such measures on a wide scale. At another extreme, a few departments maintain boats and horses for patrol. Where appropriate conditions exist (particularly along waterfronts and in large parks), such traditional measures can be quite effective.

An undue amount of concern has recently been directed toward the use of police dogs. Often assigned to patrol divisions, these animals may be either a great asset or a serious menace, depending upon skill in employment. With proper selection, training, and direction, a police dog can become a significant benefit to the agency and even a means of promoting public interest. On the other hand, widespread acquisition and inadequate supervision of vicious and poorly utilized animals may lead to community resentment and outcry. The evil lies not with the dogs but with their handlers.

Many aspects of patrol are subject to abuse. Both agency custom and poor leadership contribute to occasional violations of individual liberties. Too many patrolmen are prone to utilize their considerable authority along misguided paths. In some instances, this leads to corruption, discretionary enforcement, and illegal violence. The opportunities for a patrolman to take advantage of his unique position for personal gain or to practice racial discrimination, impose individual moral concepts, or apply unnecessary force are very great. Similarly, the police may violate a suspect's constitutional and statutory rights.[3] Frankly, patrolmen sometimes ignore the legal dictates of proper arrest, search, and interrogation. Before denouncing those engaged in police operations, however, it should be kept in mind that abuses exist at all stages of American criminal justice. Furthermore, one should be mindful of the great provocations and temptations encountered daily by those on routine patrol. While conditions may not excuse improper or illegal conduct, they are far more meaningful than citizens may realize.[4]

A significant aspect of patrol is the not inconsiderable danger involved. The number of injuries and deaths of policemen has risen sharply since 1966. Routine activities of lawmen on patrol cause them to accept more than half of these casualties. Many police injuries occur in ordinary accidents involving automobiles, motorcycles, and firearms. Still, the increasing rate of assaults upon and killings of officers deserves careful consideration. About 100 policemen are intentionally slain in the line of duty every year, 95 percent by gunfire; lawmen, in turn, kill five to ten times that number annually. Furthermore, police work remains less dangerous than such occupations as mining or construction.[5]

Most of the officers who are murdered encounter the fatal attack while attempting to make ordinary arrests, responding to disturbance calls, or investigating suspicious persons. The hazards, along with rates of crime, increase with urbanization. Also, statistics reveal that danger of assault upon policemen is highest during the hours when most violent offenses occur, between 9 P.M. and 3 A.M. Increased danger and an excess of reported offenses cause patrol assignments to be concentrated during evening hours. Some departments now resort to a special shift, to make more officers available during periods of greatest criminal activity.

Many patrolmen (accustomed to possibly hazardous conditions) feel their working hours constitute the worst feature of law enforcement. Attempts to equitably distribute assigned hours encounter major obstacles. Some departments resort to rotating shifts, with patrol units regularly exchanging times of work. This pattern permits a sharing of unpopular hours but severely dislocates personal life. Other agencies use a system of fixed shift assignment, with the unfortunate result that newer and less experienced patrolmen are nearly always grouped in the least desirable time periods. Internal influence and disputes frequently manifest themselves over issues of patrol assignment.

Criminal Investigation

Except in limited experiments, patrolmen do not investigate major crimes. They may conduct initial questioning or searches, but the continuing task of discovering, gathering, and preparing evidence is the responsibility of detectives. These investigators are assigned to a separate division within the city force, apart from ordinary patrol activities.

Organization of a criminal investigation unit varies with departmental size and purpose. Larger communities naturally require greater specialization on the part of detectives. Investigators are typically divided into separate squads or bureaus by type of crime. For example, a large force could maintain individual units to handle such matters as: homicide, bad checks, burglary, auto theft, confidence games, vice, and narcotics. In sprawling urban areas, where the city is divided into police precincts, detectives may also be assigned by district.

Criminal investigation normally has separate leadership, procedures, and offices; it sometimes even possesses a special budget and communications network. Detective work demands careful training and considerable experience to be effective. Many patrolmen strive toward eventual assignment within the criminal investigation division because it offers fixed working hours, relative independence, and an opportunity to wear civilian clothes. Increased recognition of the vital role played by uniformed divisions may, however, be reducing this tendency.

Some departments have a special rank of detective that ordinarily requires several years of prior police experience. Others assign some patrolmen to criminal investigation but grant an extra increment of pay for such duty. Generally, detectives may expect opportunities for continuing responsibility and promotion without heavy supervisory responsibilities.

The investigative subdivisions frequently operate in relative autonomy. Most are quite specialized and often have only limited contact with other sections. Detectives usually receive case assignments and work in pairs. In time, some teams develop considerable experience and expertise in solving particular types of crimes. Desired, but rarely obtained, clearance rates depend on many factors: By offense, they range from about 95 percent for homicides to only 25 percent for larcenies. But some bureaus and squads cannot realistically be evaluated statistically.[6] Larger forces maintain separate units solely to conduct investigations of internal police problems, carry out long-term intelligence activities against organized crime, or concentrate on wide-ranging inquiries of suspected racketeers and gangsters. Such investigations may require months or years to show tangible results. The actual degree of specialization naturally varies with department size. Smaller agencies may simply assign investigative functions to overworked patrolmen; larger cities can afford hundreds of carefully selected detective teams.

Frankly, a great proportion of a criminal investigator's time and effort is devoted to routine and unromantic tasks. Countless reports (in multiple copies) must be made and filed; endless unproductive inquiries and interviews are necessary; and numerous forms and records always need revision or updating. Today, a good detective should be a typist and clerk, in addition to possessing the traditional values of intelligence, patience, and imagination.

Most of the crimes concluded by arrest are not solved by brilliant deduction or sophisticated scientific examination. The single most significant factor in satisfactory clearance is simply identification of the offender by a victim.[7] Thoroughness and care have become of utmost value to the modern police detective. Most criminals actually apprehended display little of the craft and cunning beloved by mystery writers. Investigators begin by realizing that most crimes defy solution and that efforts must, by simple necessity, be first directed toward incidents offering obvious evidence.

Substantial numbers of suspects are identified largely by accident. A patrolman happens to discover stolen property in a routine search, an angry wife reports an assault by her husband, the defendant in one case confesses to other offenses—these are ways in which the strange process of justice often begins. Also, investigators frequently solve crimes merely by checking their files and records. They can occasionally establish strong evidence without ever leaving the police station.

Practical criminal investigation relies to a great extent upon informers. These special agents may work for favors, money, friendship, hatred, or fear, but they aid in the solution of many offenses. Where departments do not provide money for good information, detectives have to make personal rewards. In many instances, the identity of those working with the police must remain among the agency's best kept secrets.[8]

Many investigative problems occur in connection with vice crimes such as prostitution, gambling, liquor laws, and narcotics. Detectives assigned to these violations encounter major obstacles, for they are called upon to enforce laws against the desires of many people. Without a victim to provide willing assistance, the case becomes vastly more difficult, and the investigators must resort to extraordinary means. Often they turn to active encouragement of the particular offense. The officers, or their decoys, may actually influence the commission of a crime. Courts generally allow police to engage in limited deception and even initiate an illegal transaction. However, should the officers go so far as to actually implant an intention to commit the violation, it is held to constitute entrapment, a valid defense to any resulting charges. The line of demarcation varies by court interpretation and sometimes seems quite vague.

Vice investigations are frustrating and frequently wasteful of time. Because the actual causes of such crime lie buried amidst social problems and the public itself is divided in its support of repressive measures, cases invoke ill feeling and discretionary treatment by authorities. These conditions may combine with the substantial sums of money often involved to create a likelihood of bribery. Police corruption is largely limited to enforcement of vice regulations, although the problem extends far beyond the confines of detective divisions.[9]

Traffic

Most actual law enforcement concerns automobiles. Moving and stationary motor vehicle violations number ten times the total of all other known crimes. A great many police agencies look upon traffic supervision as their primary mission, and nearly all devote a significant portion of their energy to this task.

Attention to automobile safety seems both reasonable and justified; every year about 55,000 Americans die in motor vehicle accidents (many times the number killed by willful homicide). It would seem that public safety might constitute one area in which police activity would be widely welcomed and praised. Because of both cultural and administrative reasons, however, such is not the case. A traditional American resentment of authority and a distortion of law enforcement purposes combine to make traffic control an unfortunate basis for mistrust.

An obvious difficulty in public relations involves the traffic ticket. Under a facade of road safety, many jurisdictions utilize traffic enforcement as a lucrative source of revenue. Some local governments derive a substantial portion of their operating expenses from "speed traps," and pay officers on a fee basis dependent upon the number of fines collected! Police organizations have discovered that, in wage disputes, they may exercise considerable leverage upon cities and states merely by writing fewer tickets. In truth, the traffic officer is sometimes used not to protect the public but to provide an extra source of revenue at the citizen's expense.

The public realizes the consequences of hypocritical enforcement, and distrust or fear may result. Few people accept the personal trauma of a routine traffic fine with real equanimity, yet it is the most frequent contact between citizens and criminal justice. A step toward improvement of police and community relations would be taken upon abolition of the routine traffic fine (to remove it as a source of revenue) and substitution of an outright system designed to remove the dangerous driver from the road. If the true goal is protection, surely no repetitive imposition of lucrative penalties will suffice.

Patrolmen often dislike apprehending minor traffic violators but must do so because of agency policy. Most departments have no strict "quota" of tickets, but they do maintain an understood standard or norm of performance for officers. As far as traffic duty goes, this means that too few (or, in some cases, too many) apprehensions may be regarded as a sign of unsatisfactory performance.[10]

Smaller police agencies assign responsibilities for motor vehicle law enforcement to regular patrolmen. In larger departments, a special traffic division frequently exists; these relatively independent commands may be efficient, well trained, and capable of lending support to other units. To some policemen traffic assignments seem most attractive; to others, they appear boring and without personal challenge. Such duty has the advantage of specialization, relatively normal working hours, and escape from many departmental pressures.

Traffic policing normally involves three primary roles: direction, enforcement, and investigation. The most obvious of these concerns the supervision of pedestrian and moving vehicles by lights, arm signals, and other means. In view of the magnitude of auto use, this function is more significant than is usually recognized. It can become quite technical, as application of computers to traffic flow demonstrates.

The enforcement phase deals logically enough with potential and actual violators. Unfortunately, the supposed purpose of deterrence often becomes secondary to apprehension as reliance upon unmarked and hidden cars, radar, and similar practices may indicate. Road safety most definitely demands enforcement of clear and reasonable laws, but the best means of control has been long recognized as the presence of officers with the goal of protection rather than repression.[11]

Traffic investigation refers primarily to accidents. The detailed recording of collisions involving motor vehicles has become remarkably complex. Particularly in cases of serious personal injury, officers may devote hours to interviewing witnesses, locating and preserving physical evidence, measuring distances, testing drivers, and preparing extensive reports. Here again, however, a tendency exists for the apparent purpose of such work to mislead.

Accident investigation may provide proof of guilt or information for improvements in road and auto design. But these admirable goals rarely require exhaustive police records; the true purpose is to supply a reservoir of information for subsequent civil suits among the private parties involved. To some degree, the police are presently performing the work of insurance companies, although the citizen may indirectly benefit. Still, the emphasis on accident investigation seems somewhat unreasonable. Traffic policing has emerged as a very significant and complex problem in America. Unfortunately, it often continues to be regarded almost as an incidental part of criminal justice instead of a primary and essential concern for innumerable state and local agencies.

In a few nations, responsibility for ordinary traffic control has been entirely removed from the regular police. Special government employees handle the vast majority of enforcement duties relating to automobiles, permitting peace officers to concentrate their activities against more serious crime. Such measures in the United States might not only contribute to more effective police assignment but also improve public relations.

Support Functions

While patrol, investigation, and traffic occupy the largest portions of police work, they are dependent upon a variety of auxiliary or staff functions. Large departments maintain separate units for general administration, planning, personnel, training, jail operations, and a host of additional tasks. Of essential interest, however, are those concerning juveniles, communication, records, and criminalistics. No agency for general law enforcement can exist without reliance upon these essential services.

Because the typical police department so frequently deals with juveniles, much attention has been devoted to creation of special bureaus for handling young people. Larger local agencies usually now include a small group of officers who concentrate upon youth work. They often carry responsibility for cases of child abuse and neglect as well as for actual crimes by juveniles. These men and women (for this is one field in which females are fairly frequently employed) may receive additional duties relating to missing persons or public relations. Such added tasks and the frequency of youth crime cause most juvenile units to be understaffed and overworked.

Officers assigned to patrol, investigation, or traffic usually refer young offenders to the department's bureau specializing in such cases. Because of particular needs for understanding and discretion, work with young people requires a degree of sympathy and dedication beyond even that of the ordinary policeman. Those assigned to juvenile units presently handle about half of all cases themselves, without sending the child to court or to other agencies.[12] This creates a heavy responsibility best met with careful selection, special training, and long experience.

Most juvenile officers are still required to perform the duties of social worker and policeman. This condition exists because of a failure to provide centers for coordinating community services. Officers must currently attempt to fulfill a need for extensive counseling, welfare, and referral—tasks for which they rarely possess sufficient knowledge or ability.

Another police support function of major significance is that of communications. We seldom realize the astonishing number of messages and pieces of information, most having no specific relation to crime, that are utilized daily by a law enforcement agency. In reality, the entire police operation depends upon a communications system providing speed, accuracy, clarity, and dependability. Security in our complex urban culture demands no less.

Obvious police communications occur by telephone and radio. Both of these common means have serious problems. It would, for example, seem that law enforcement agencies and public utilities might cooperate to the extent of establishing a standard emergency telephone number for metropolitan areas or, better still, the entire nation. Except in a few progressive cities, a desperate call for aid may now inexcusably result in confusion and delay. Overcrowded police radio channels suffer similar difficulties. Many areas would benefit greatly from central dispatching whereby operations in small connected jurisdictions might be coordinated.

Considerable progress in the technical capabilities of communications equipment has occurred in recent years. Small but powerful radio transmitters for foot patrolmen, versatile television cameras for surveillance, and equipment for rapid transfers of electronically processed data or pictorial facsimiles are but a few examples of scientific advancements. Application of these devices involves expense and imaginative administrators, but the demands made upon law enforcement make such innovations of enormous potential value.

The police could scarcely function without vast record systems. The incredible flow of information over long periods of time makes necessary extensive and detailed files. Arrest, personal identification, property, evidence, and accident records are merely the more essential of the score of systems demanded by a large police agency. Entries must be accurate, complete, and current; this requires considerable cost and effort. Unlike some business operations, law enforcement files should be available 24 hours of every day. Public safety cannot wait until Monday morning.

As with communications, the related field of police records seems quite suitable for centralization, but many agencies strongly resist such suggestions. There is, however, increasing reliance upon cooperation between different departments for the exchange of recorded information. With the growing use of electronic data processing, police records may now be consulted and transmitted automatically and almost instantaneously. While consequent opportunities for improved service are vast, grave dangers of misuse also exist. One difficulty lies in control over disclosure of confidential information. On the one hand, the police must protect their records from improper use; on the other, the public has a right to prompt reports especially in times of natural emergency or social disorder.

A significant function required by modern law enforcement is that provided by criminalistics. Examination of evidence and identification of persons and items has become a highly specialized and demanding field. Few police departments can afford to maintain the laboratory equipment and experts required for extensive work in the emerging science of criminalistics. Nevertheless, many smaller agencies attempt to investigate major offenses with untrained personnel and inadequate facilities.

The crime laboratory may be called upon to examine foot and fingerprints; hand, typewriting, soil, or blood samples; hairs; firearms and bullets; bits of paint; and various other kinds of evidence. In addition, it frequently possesses trained polygraph (lie detector) operators and facilities for sophisticated photographic work. These operations and resulting analyses require evidence technicians and scientists that only a large and usually centralized crime laboratory can provide.[13] Scientific developments, along with legal restrictions on traditional methods of investigation, assure a rapid increase in this field of police activity.

Community Relations

The majority of Americans is satisfied that the police do a good job. Community relations constitute a major problem for law enforcement. This apparent paradox exists because those displeased tend to be drawn from groups most often connected with crime: minorities, the poor, and youth.[14] Dissatisfaction with the police is frequently expressed and, more seriously, may directly contribute to unrest and disorder. Realization of these difficulties has prompted considerable attention to public attitudes.

Most concern has beeen directed at problems of law enforcement within the black community. Already strained relations erupted in the numerous urban disorders of the 1960s. The police role was critical in the general dissatisfaction of blacks and the events which triggered massive racial conflict. Countless encounters with Negroes surely contribute to feelings of resentment or even hatred in many inner cities. If the majority of law enforcement officers are somewhat prejudiced, such opinions only reflect those of the general public and, from an already biased viewpoint, seem to find support in rates of known misconduct.

Community relations are made far more difficult because of a clear need for black policemen.[15] Nationally, Negroes compose only about 4 percent of all officers; to bring the proportion in line with the overall population would require three times the number now on duty; and to equal the rate of arrests, that figure should be tripled yet again. Frankly, efforts to recruit qualified Negroes have not been notably successful; suspected discrimination in promotion and assignment provide major obstacles. Washington, D.C., and a few other cities increased their proportions of black police officers in the aftermath of large civil disorders. But many urban areas are experiencing so rapid an increase in Negro population that attempts to improve the ratio in law enforcement have achieved little progress. At present, no state or metropolitan area has a black police representation equivalent to its citizenry; most do not even approach the figure. The situation is quite serious, especially where crime rates are highest. White agencies cannot indefinitely continue to enforce law or preserve the image of justice inside the black ghetto.

The most obvious development from adverse attitudes toward the police has been the creation of special community relations units.[16] These are, unfortunately, at times products of failure and often become little more than a palliative for deep operational problems. Community relations are the concern of every officer interested in the maintenance of order in a democracy.

Crucial encounters between police and citizens occur on the streets; there, attitudes both begin and find expression. Individual officers in large cities does not routinely maintain the close community ties and confidences essential to practical law enforcement. The result, tragically, can easily become a combination of rudeness and force that breeds contempt of the police and the entire system of justice. Sincere efforts to build better public relations must commence with reestablishment of personal contact between officer and citizen, concentration on courtesy so lacking in typical American service organizations, avoidance of force whenever possible, and unqualified demand for integrity.

Larger agencies maintain procedures and personnel to investigate complaints against policemen. The fairness and dependability of these methods, rather than their form, are essential to adequate community relations. Debate over the use of civilian review boards and civil service commissions often ignores the need for fundamental community confidence in the force's own system of internal discipline. Only careful and complete attention to complaints can serve as a foundation for public support and the directly related benefits of high agency morale.

Good relations between citizens and agencies of justice require trust and dependability, for they are directly connected to the efficiency not of a single department but of the entire system by which law is created, enforced, interpreted, and applied. For the police, who sometimes appear to restrict rather than assist the public, the problem is essentially one of changing attitudes and images. The emphases can be altered from repression to service and from fear to respect.[17] Many progressive departments already devote much attention to achievement of these worthy goals.

Efficient community relations units carry out a variety of responsibilities. Officers may provide public information, maintain contact with the press, give tours, and assist in recruitment and training of employees. Moreover, community relations involve efforts to break down the usual wall of misunderstanding separating the police and ordinary citizens. This can lead to the establishment of neighborhood offices and committees, advisory councils, and a host of other potentially worthwhile projects.

Summary

The majority of police work is devoted to patrol. It provides the greatest variety, public contact, and danger in law enforcement. Investigations of major crimes are assigned not to patrolmen but to separate detective units. Usually organized by type of offense, these bureaus have responsibility for discovering, gathering, and preparing evidence.

Many police agencies devote much time and effort to automobile traffic. Such duty involves direction, enforcement, and investigation. Modern police work relies heavily upon separate juvenile units, communications systems, extensive records, and the new science of criminalistics.

While most Americans seem reasonably satisfied with their police agencies, substantial numbers of the poor, black, or young people feel otherwise. The solution lies not with contrived public relations but demand for the highest possible standards of conduct from all officers.

Questions

1. How could the police function without patrol?
2. In what ways are most crimes solved?
3. What does traffic control involve?
4. Which police support functions are least important?
5. Why does law enforcement require public support?

NOTES

[1] *The Use of Probability Theory in the Assignment of Police Patrol Areas* (Washington: GPO, 1970), pp. 4–11, 29–32; O. W. Wilson and Roy Clinton McLaren, *Police Administration* (New York: McGraw-Hill, 1972), pp. 364–368.

[2] *The Utilization of Helicopters for Police Air Mobility* (Washington: GPO, 1971), pp. 12–32.

[3] Paul Chevigny, *Police Power* (New York: Vintage, 1969), pp. 136–146.

[4] William A. Westley, "Violence and the Police," *American Journal of Sociology* 59 (July, 1953), pp. 34–41; Albert J. Reiss, "Police Brutality, Answers to Key Questions," *Transaction* 5 (July–August, 1968), pp. 10–19.

[5] *Uniform Crime Reports for the United States—1972* (Washington: GPO, 1973), pp. 42–50; *Police Community Relations in Philadelphia* (N.p., U.S. Commission on Civil Rights, 1972), pp. 94–98; *Task Force Report: The Police* (Washington: GPO, 1967), pp. 189–190; Ed Cray, *The Enemy in the Streets* (Garden City, New York: Anchor, 1972), pp. 237–254.

[6] Jerome H. Skolnick, *Justice Without Trial* (New York: Wiley, 1966), pp. 164–181.

[7] *Task Force Report: The Police*, pp. 96–97.

[8] Charles E. O'Hara, *Fundamentals of Criminal Investigation* (Springfield, Ill., C. C. Thomas, 1970), pp. 149–156; Hoffa v. United States, 385 U.S. 293, 87 S.Ct. 408 (1966).

[9] *Justice Without Trial*, pp. 207–208, 257–258.

[10] *Ibid.*, pp. 55–56; James Q. Wilson, *Varieties of Police Behavior* (New York: Atheneum, 1970), pp. 95–99.

[11] *Police Administration*, pp. 457–460.

[12] *Task Force Report: Juvenile Delinquency and Youth Crime* (Washington: GPO, 1967), pp. 12–14; Paul H. Hahn, *The Juvenile Offender and the Law* (Cincinnati: W. H. Anderson, 1971), pp. 231–235.

[13] *Criminal Investigation and Physical Evidence Handbook* (N.p., Crime Laboratory Division, State of Wisconsin, 1968), pp. 3–4.

[14] *Supplemental Studies for the National Advisory Commission on Civil Disorders* (Washington: GPO, 1968), pp. 42–43.

[15] Nicholas Alex, *Back in Blue* (New York: Appleton, 1969), pp. 25–34; James D. Bannon and G. Marie Wilt, "Black Policemen: A Study of Self-Image," *Journal of Police Science and Administration* 1 (March, 1973), pp. 21–29.

[16] *A National Survey of Police and Community Relations* (Washington: GPO, 1967), pp. 32–127.

[17] Albert J. Reiss, *The Police and the Public* (New Haven: Yale University Press, 1971), pp. 173–221; *Improving Police/Community Relations* (Washington: GPO, 1973), pp. 60–63.

Chapter 7

Basic Procedures

"The right of the people to be secure . . . against unreasonable searches and seizures, shall not be violated. . . ."
UNITED STATES CONSTITUTION, AMENDMENT IV

Arrest

The practical authority of the police rests upon the power of arrest. That and accompanying elements of legal force both distinguish and permit the actual routines of law enforcement. In America, all citizens technically possess a restricted power of arrest, but its exercise is relatively rare and usually limited to instances when the victim, or his agent, manages to apprehend an offender. For good reasons, this practice has become quite unusual except in situations involving private officers. Arrest is primarily left to the policeman, and society grants him special but limited privileges to aid in the task. He may, for example, carry firearms and call upon citizens for assistance. Actual apprehensions usually occur on the streets, involve little or no violence, take place in the evening hours, and require necessarily hurried decisions based on emotion as well as reason.

Arrest is defined in technical terms as taking a person into custody under color of law; it deprives the individual of his liberty through legal authority. Courts determine whether an apprehension has transpired through reference either to the restraining party's intention or to the suspect's interpretation, and the two views frequently differ widely. While exact powers vary considerably by jurisdiction, a peace officer normally may arrest whenever he has "probable cause" to believe that any crime (regardless of type) is occurring in his presence or that a felony has been committed (even outside his presence) by someone who might escape. He also may take a person into custody on the written or verbal order of a neutral and properly authorized official, normally a magistrate.[1] This warrant of arrest could cover any variety of offense and can be issued in civil as well as criminal matters.

A vast majority of the approximately 9 million annual official arrests (excluding those for automobile infractions) are made by patrolmen, frequently acting without clear departmental instructions, who simply come across crime. They discover drunks, disorderly persons, and vast numbers of ordinary traffic violators. In all such instances, the legality of the arrest depends upon probable cause, a very strong and reasonable suspicion on the part of the apprehending officer. He is normally permitted to use all necessary force to take a party into custody, although homicide would not be justified except in more serious offenses and where life is threatened.

Although many millions of arrests occur each year, care must be taken in the evaluation of statistics. It should not be presumed, for example, that the total of apprehensions reported for a particular crime indicates the actual number of different persons taken into custody for such an offense.[2] Many drunkenness arrests may be compiled by one individual in the course of a year. Similarly, the police may record clearances for several specific violations with just one apprehension where the suspect is associated with an entire series of separate illegal acts. On the other hand, a group of arrests, made perhaps on a gang, can lead to the clearance of only one recorded offense. The extent to which these variations affect overall rates cannot be determined from present statistics.

According to legal definition, even an ordinary traffic citation involves an arrest since a citizen's liberty is briefly restricted. In practice, of course, neither the police nor the public regards it as such. Law enforcement officers and, probably, most people equate an arrest with completion of the "booking slip" most agencies use as a basis for jailing and reporting. The majority of legal apprehensions are probably never actually recorded; patrolmen release many suspects after short and informal periods of questioning.

Arrest statistics reveal uneven distribution by person and by crime. Many of those apprehended are male (85 percent), below the age of 21 (40 percent), and black (25 percent).[3] Furthermore, arrests tend to occur in poor, densely populated districts such as the inner cities. How well the characteristics of those who become involved with the police actually reflect all criminals remains open to question; agency policy and personal attitudes may certainly affect the composite portrait of people apprehended, whether they be guilty or innocent.

Typically, people are taken into custody for lesser offenses against

Arrests

TYPE OF OFFENSE (OVERALL RANK 1–20)	RATE PER 100,000 POPULATION, 1972
Acts Against the Public	66%
Drunkenness (1)	863.2
Driving While Intoxicated (3)	376.7
Disorderly Conduct (4)	363.1
Narcotic Drug Laws (5)	269.1
Liquor Laws (8)	129.5
Runaway (9)	124.2
Weapons (13)	74.6
Curfew and Loitering (14)	72.4
Gambling (18)	43.7
Vagrancy (19)	34.7
Offense Against the Family (20)	33.0
Acts Against Property	24%
Larceny-Theft (Grand and Petty) (2)	423.1
Burglary (6)	196.0
Vandalism (11)	80.9
Auto Theft (12)	76.0
Fraud (16)	60.3
Receipt of Stolen Property (17)	44.7
Acts Against the Person	10%
Simple Assault (7)	191.8
Aggravated Assault (10)	97.0
Robbery (15)	68.1

SOURCE: *Uniform Crime Reports for the United States—1972* (Washington: U.S. Government Printing Office, 1973), pp. 120–121.

public peace, order, and concepts of morality. The twenty violations most frequently listed as cause for arrest, other than traffic infractions, reveal the general pattern shown in the table when arranged by type.

The above list (which would normally encompass 85 percent of all reported arrests, excluding routine traffic violations) is interesting for a number of reasons. Personal offenses are almost incidental in the total picture. Serious violations obviously play a minor statistical part, and some acts resulting in apprehension are not even crimes. No one is convicted for being a runaway, although it may lead to action in a juvenile court. Such notorious crimes as homicide, rape, arson, embezzlement, forgery, and even prostitution result in relatively few arrests—none are included among the twenty most frequent causes. The improper practice of booking on an open charge (suspicion) continues but no longer holds a position of great prominence.

Major offenses, probably most frequently reported by the public, produce relatively few arrests compared to minor violations encountered by patrolmen. Investigations of such serious crimes as robbery, burglary, grand larceny, and auto theft are typically futile and infrequently result in someone being placed in custody. Police statistics indicate that less than half of the known offenses against the person even end in an apprehension; the proportion for recorded major property crimes is far lower, approximately 16 percent. Overall, the odds of a reported, serious violation leading to an arrest stand at only one in five.[4] When one recalls that 70 percent of such offenses are never known by the police, the conclusion must be that only about 6 percent of all major crimes really result in someone being taken into custody, and many of them are never convicted.

As the police are responsible for the apprehension of suspects, they also carry out the function of releasing a great number from custody. Among persons arrested for serious offenses, adults and juveniles, only 60 percent ever face formal charges. Of those apprehended for lesser violations the percentage is much higher, but for all varieties of crime, law enforcement agencies release large numbers after booking. Every year about a million Americans are arrested and discharged from custody without any form of prosecution. In some instances investigation reveals their innocence; more frequently, it is determined that the police have insufficient evidence upon which to proceed, and the matter is summarily dropped.

In the context of modern American criminal justice, arrest cannot be taken as evidence of guilt. The police mistakenly place in custody and charge thousands of persons every year. While this occurs most often through perfectly understandable error, it also occasionally transpires through abuse of authority. Far more common than illegal arrest is that performed on grounds which prove insufficient for subsequent prosecution or conviction. Unfortunately, policemen sometimes detain suspects for purposes of personal correction.[5] Ideally, arrest should take place only on the basis of probable cause, without any imposition of differential treatment or enforcement. It is not the duty of the police to determine guilt or to impose punishment, these are functions purely for the courts. However, such desirable separations of functions often do not fit the practical realities of present American life and law enforcement.

Search and Seizure

Closely related to, but distinct from, arrest are the problems of search and seizure. In theory, the apprehension of a suspect would come before any detailed examination of his person or property, but in practice, the procedure is often reversed. The police frequently conduct limited searches before making a formal arrest, and a majority of such investigations probably never conclude with someone in custody.

Typical street encounters between patrolmen and suspects involve immediate reactions rather than legal deliberations. They are the product of chance and circumstance as well as knowledge and common sense. Both arrest and search must be based upon the existence of probable cause, a concept that goes beyond simple suspicion but need not extend to certainty of guilt. This can only be determined through reference to all the existing circumstances and facts. The police do not have authority to search or arrest at will; their actions must be founded on identifiable knowledge or understanding which would lead an ordinary citizen to believe that a crime had occurred or was in progress. Without probable cause, the courts will rule invasions of privacy to be improper, unreasonable, and illegal.

Searches and seizures of evidence may, under Amendment IV of the U.S. Constitution, be conducted under authority of a duly issued and signed warrant. These orders must be based upon a sworn showing of probable cause by a law enforcement officer. A search warrant must be specific as to place and purpose, and it is limited in duration, usually to ten days. Some jurisdictions restrict the court's order to daylight hours, unless a judge specifically permits service at night.[6]

A problem concerning the use of search warrants sometimes arises over the need for warnings and use of force by police. Traditionally, an announcement was required before a proper entry through violent means. This creates major difficulties where a warning could cause grave danger to policemen or lead to destruction of evidence, as is quite routine in narcotics and gambling raids. Consequently, officers resort to subterfuge to permit sudden entry; some jurisdictions have passed controversial "no knock" statutes allowing the police to break in without warning under particular circumstances.

Whether or not a search is conducted by warrant, it must be limited in scope. The courts do not permit exploratory investigations designed simply to locate some indication of crime. Arrests, which carry with them a clear right of search, are also restricted. Any incidental seizures cannot extend beyond the suspect's person and the area within his immediate control.[7] Application of this rule becomes especially complex, and difficult for the police, in reference to automobiles. Generally, car searches tend to be scrutinized by judges to an extent between that of homes (which traditionally provide the most security from official invasion) and of individuals in public areas. Automobiles should either be impounded by police or be the subject of a warrant prior to search.

Within recent years, the old police practice of stopping suspicious parties and subjecting them to questioning and a cursory search, or frisk of outer clothing, has attracted much attention. It is now established that officers may, upon reasonable grounds, briefly detain and investigate persons. Furthermore, these street encounters may include a frisking of the suspect in order to protect the policeman from the danger of a sudden armed attack. As the justification for such a search is quite limited, it must be confined to intrusions that would lead directly to the discovery of hidden weapons. Again, authority to stop, question, and frisk cannot serve as an excuse for conducting an exploratory search.[8]

A great deal often depends upon the legality of seizing incriminating items. Unless the search is justified under the circumstances, the evidence obtained cannot be used in court against an accused person, regardless of his guilt. This rule, unique to America, places unusual responsibility upon the police. Not only must they discover the proof, but it must be done in a proper manner.

If the police have made a legal arrest, with or without a warrant, they can and should conduct a limited search and seize any evidence of crime. When officers become suspicious, with sound reason, they may frisk a suspect to protect themselves from a possible attack. And, of course, the law specifically requires searches on proper written orders of magistrates. In the direct course of any of these justifiable intrusions, should the police discover evidence of an offense (although perhaps quite different from the one under investigation), it can be used against the responsible party. But, if the officers conduct an illegal and unjustified search to seize proof of guilt, the situation is totally different. Such evidence will be held to be the product of an unauthorized invasion of privacy and may be treated as "fruit of the poisonous tree" since it resulted from illegal activity by officials.[9] Under this doctrine, illegal actions on the part of police can make subsequent prosecution an impossibility, although guilt is clearly established.

Within the last decade, a new kind of invasion of privacy, related to searches and seizures, has come into prominence. Through the use of electronic devices, it is now possible to easily eavesdrop on private conversations. Police, as well as ordinary citizens, can secretly listen on telephone lines and utilize incriminating words against the speaker. Technical advances have made possible pocket tape recorders, small radio transmitters, and microphones capable of penetrating considerable distances, through windows and even walls. With effort and expense, almost any conversation can be detected and noted by outside parties through use of these sophisticated electronic devices.

Until quite recently, such invasions of privacy were subject to varying and confusing degrees of legal control. Now, however, electronic eavesdropping falls under the same basic restrictions as do searches of homes. Under law, citizens who conduct these activities (and they are believed to be widespread) are subject to prosecution by state and federal authorities. The police cannot, ordinarily, invade privacy in an attempt to gather information relating to crime. However, it is possible for them to request an authorization for electronic eavesdropping from a judge. In effect, the police must demonstrate probable cause and specifically identify the place, person, and need to obtain permission. Under a judicial order, evidence of crime can be gathered by interception of telephone conversations or through the use of hidden microphones and radio transmitters.[10]

The operation of these electronic devices is quite expensive, often unproductive, and should be limited to certain types of investigations. While no comprehensive analysis of use exists, it seems that official eavesdropping has been employed primarily in cases involving national security and, more recently, gambling and narcotics. Although many people believe that such invasions of privacy pose grave social and political dangers, most law enforcement officers remain convinced of their value in gathering intelligence, information, and evidence of crime.

Confessions

The Constitution of the United States, in Amendment V, provides that, "No person . . . shall be compelled in any criminal case to be a witness against himself. . . ." These simple words establish a fundamental protection in the American system of justice. In many parts of the world, people may be forced to confess actual or imagined crimes through mental or physical torture. But many generations ago, the system of justice derived from English common law determined such a process to be barbaric and a severe imposition on personal liberty. Over a period of years, it became accepted that an accused person could not be required to testify against himself. This concept has been greatly expanded, especially in America, and has brought about highly significant limitations on the use of confessions. Important protections against such self-incrimination have forced major modifications in police procedure and the entire system of justice.

Within the last decade, a revolution has occurred in regard to the use of confessions in criminal cases. Courts now closely examine statements supposedly made by suspects which tend to indicate their guilt. For many generations, American police relied upon questioning to gather admissions of responsibility.[11] The practice still continues, but restrictive rules now make use of confessions in court considerably more difficult.

At present, interrogation designed to produce acceptable evidence of guilt must be preceded by four specific and clear warnings. The investigating officer should inform the suspect that: (1) he may remain silent and refuse to answer questions, (2) any statement he makes may be used against him, (3) he has a right to have an attorney present during questioning, and (4) if he is unable to afford a lawyer, one can be appointed for him.[12] While the language of these warnings need not be exact, the meaning should be clear and complete. Any significant deviation or omission can invalidate a subsequent confession although it may definitely establish guilt. In practice, police organizations provide officers with a list of written warnings for use prior to questioning.

A suspect may, of course, waive his rights and make any statement he wishes. But the confession will only be acceptable if he clearly understands the warnings and their implications. This sometimes requires the interrogator to explain the warnings in some detail and perhaps interpret them to the subject. It is certain that any waiver of rights by a person under questioning must be affirmative and knowing; mere silence cannot substitute for a willingness to answer. Should a suspect expressly waive his rights after the warnings and then indicate a desire to either remain silent or have an attorney, the interrogation must end. It is significant to note that the need for warnings applies only to the police; confessions made to ordinary citizens do not fall under the same strict rules of judicial interpretation.

For several decades, U.S. courts have rejected statements obtained by physical torture, force, and overt coercion. Now the zone of conduct forbidden to police extends to promises, deception, tricks, and cajolery. These methods, if designed to elicit incriminating statements, will invalidate resulting admissions of guilt and often destroy the basis of an entire case.

The basic test of a confession remains one of voluntariness, but today the warnings have become a judicial requirement to insure that a suspect fully understands his rights before answering questions. Controversy over possible effects of this concept has led to legislative intervention designed to free the police from close restrictions and return the test to one of simple willingness to give evidence.

Application of the warnings can sometimes be quite difficult. Because the police are not required to give detailed instructions prior to merely trying to obtain information, a line is arbitrarily drawn at what is termed the *accusatory stage*. In effect, an officer may *interview* witnesses before giving any special warnings. But when *interrogating* suspects and the investigator begins attempting to obtain some type of incriminating admission, full disclosure of rights to remain silent and to have an attorney become essential.

It is possible for a confession to be acceptable as a spontaneous admission or voluntary declaration without previous warnings. For example, the police may not have an opportunity to speak before a damaging disclosure occurs. Offenders sometimes admit to a crime immediately upon apprehension, prior to any questioning; others may surrender themselves and speak quite voluntarily. In such situations (usually involving crimes of violence), the police operate under no compulsion to interrupt just to give warnings.

The protection against self-incrimination may be relaxed in somewhat unusual circumstances. For example, if a suspect voluntarily testifies in court, a prior confession obtained without proper warnings may be introduced by the prosecutor to show discrepancies. Also, many jurisdictions now have special immunity statutes under which a defendant can be required to testify in return for a promise that his statements will not be used against him.

One might assume that the protection against confessions would cause enormous problems for police and prosecutors, but such is not the situation. Most actual criminal charges have little need for admissions from suspects. A normal arrest for drunkenness or disorderly conduct involves no questioning, and police seldom bother with warnings under routine circumstances. In fact, patrolmen of some departments almost never resort to interrogation.

In connection with major offenses, the requirement of warnings is still generally ignored. Some peace officers, especially those with special commissions from isolated and rural jurisdictions, simply are not informed of a suspect's rights and so can scarcely be expected to protect them. More often, investigators fail to give the four complete warnings prior to questioning. The overall effect of the restrictions on use of confessions has been negligible.[13] Police manage to obtain many incriminating statements despite the warnings. Many suspects may be readily convinced to speak in order to clear their own conscience, incriminate others, hopefully mislead officials as to their guilt, or gain favors for themselves. In short, the curtailment in the use of confessions has not had the dire effect on criminal justice once predicted. The daily routines of investigations continue, while the warnings tend to constitute another surmountable obstacle for police. So far as citizens are concerned, the procedural formalities mean less than substantive liberties, and these are determined more through custom than judicial interpretation.[14]

Identification

The hunt for evidence in a criminal case usually hinges upon identification of a suspect. This may occur before or after arrest and can follow any number of methods. At times, the offender will be apprehended at the scene; in other instances, witnesses to a violation supply details as to the name, description, and even address of a culprit. But often the police have no definite information, and the investigation must include a means of first locating and then identifying the criminal.

Assuming that a suspect has been taken into custody, law enforcement officials must then establish his association with the offense committed earlier. What can the apprehended party be required to do to faciltiate the identification? And what limitations are imposed upon the police in regard to the inquiry?

One obvious means of attempting to establish that a given suspect was responsible for the violation is to confront him with witnesses to the event. The observers can presumably establish the identity of the offender accurately if they are not directly influenced by the police. Traditionally the "line-up" has been employed to provide a means for prompt accusation of the guilty and release of the innocent. This normally involves a group of people, generally similar in appearance, brought together before the witnesses. Should the criminal be among those in the line-up, he can possibly be identified. The presentation may include wearing clothing or speaking words to coincide with those used during the crime.

Line-ups are somewhat restricted by legal qualification. They occur, and suspects can be required to appear in them. But courts now insist that police furnish basic rights to a defense counsel in line-ups following formal accusation. In effect, a suspect must be afforded the opportunity to have a lawyer present to insure that witnesses are not misled into selecting someone indicated by the police or prosecutor.[15]

This requirement came in response to allegations that line-ups were conducted in unfair and prejudicial ways which made proper identification during later trials an impossibility. It is believed that only an attorney can safeguard the rights of a suspect at such a critical stage. Of course, this legal protection can be waived as may those involving confession. Also, the requirement of counsel has been held not to apply when the line-up occurs prior to, rather than after, a formal accusation or indictment.[16]

The same fundamental limitations presumably apply to cases in which a witness personally confronts a suspect for the purpose of identification. This practice, now quite widely used by police, is called a "show-up." The courts have clearly recognized that emergency situations may call for taking a possible offender directly before a victim. Many departments follow a policy of taking likely suspects immediately back to the crime scene before booking. In many instances, the witnesses can then make an identification without suggestion or even questioning by officers. Show-ups may, of course, also be conducted at a police station under circumstances more similar to a group line-up.[17]

At one time, law enforcement agencies could resort to picking up masses of suspects for purposes of identification. Individuals with criminal records, appearances, or even habits which might cause them to be considered as possibly responsible for a particular offense would find themselves caught in the police dragnet. Today, such practices will not be tolerated by the courts; suspicion must be strong and founded upon probable cause before arrest, search, and forced appearance for identification is deemed justifiable.[18]

As dragnet operations became outmoded, imaginative police organizations increasingly turned to the use of technical means for associating suspects with certain violations. Identification by witnesses could, after all, be based upon photographs as well as actual appearances. Consequently, many investigators developed techniques of presenting to those having an opportunity to observe an offense a series of pictures including one or more likely suspects. In general, courts treat such indirect means of identification with more latitude than those involving the physical person, but the police must still insure that the use of such photographs is not prejudicial or unfair. Many agencies now go a step beyond the use of available pictures; representations of criminals can be created by artists working with the aid of witnesses and by kits enabling the features of a suspect to be assembled. The resulting portraits may then be distributed for use by other officers or matched with existing likenesses.

Sophisticated methods of investigation now frequently enable the police to obtain clues leading to identification without reliance on actual witnesses. Fingerprints, hairs, handwritten notes, blood, recordings of the voice, and footprints are but a few of the signs an offender may leave behind at the crime scene. Careful investigation, which is unfortunately still quite rare, may reveal various bits of evidence helping to locate a suspect. There are, of course, serious difficulties in connection with such clues. Items and marks from the scene must be carefully identified for certain future reference; a sound chain of custody has to be maintained to eliminate possible confusion as to origin; and experts are usually required to conduct laboratory tests and analyses.[19]

Nevertheless, scientific evidence is growing rapidly in both use and acceptance. In reliability and influence, it far surpasses the typical identifications by eyewitnesses. Within the last generation, this variety of proof has become basic to the system of criminal justice; its popularity and use is likely to increase in the future.

Certain problems arise over obtaining necessary personal evidence from suspects. The police might obtain clearly significant signs at the place of violation, but a suspect may object to providing samples for comparison. Suppose a handwritten note demanding money is left in a robbery. Officials would find a similar item from the possible criminal of great use. Courts generally grant considerable authority to law enforcement agencies to enable them to obtain suitable samples for purposes of comparison and expert analysis.[20]

It is well established that police may take fingerprints and photographs of those arrested. Courts recognize that such records are invaluable to those in law enforcement. Every year millions of sets of fingerprints, currently a principal means of identification, must be classified, indexed, and filed in systems now national in scope. These procedures often make possible the prompt and sure association of offender and crime.

While they are less often required to do so, police may also obtain samples of hair, blood, fingernail scrapings, and similar personal items for comparative analysis. Most jurisdictions allow such nontestimonial items to be taken once a legal arrest occurs and the investigations would reasonably be expected to benefit. Also, to aid in identification, the police may require a suspect to speak (but not admit guilt) for the assistance of witnesses to a crime. Recently, it has even become possible to establish identities through scientific analysis of voiceprints, which have characteristics as unique as the fine lines on fingers.

Investigations can also include direct invasion of the physical person. Normally, this involves proof of some condition rather than mere identification. The most common forms of these examinations are for the purpose of determining intoxication of automobile drivers. Many states now permit police, with cause, to require a suspect to give breath, blood, or urine samples for testing. As long as these invasions are conducted by properly qualified people, they are normally considered acceptable by the courts.[21] Less frequently, personal examinations are needed for narcotics, smuggled goods, or even weapons which may be taken internally be a suspect. Such invasions of the body may, of course, require the assistance of medical personnel.

The basic procedures followed by the police must be in accordance with constitutional requirements. No law enforcement agency is supposed to ever violate the rights of citizens. Of course, the rules are not always strictly followed. But, the principle remains clear. The police, like everyone else, have to follow fundamental constitutional guidelines to protect personal rights. At times, this may admittedly make the task of immediate crime control more difficult. The basic duty of all police agencies, nevertheless, remains enforcement of the law, even when those restrictions apply to themselves.

Summary

Most arrests are for lesser crimes against public peace, order, and concepts of morality. Only a small percentage of major offenses result in an apprehension, and many people taken into custody are quickly released by the police.

Searches must be based on probable cause and be limited in scope. Many problems arise over street encounters with suspicious persons, but most recent difficulties over rights of privacy concern means of electronic eavesdropping.

Confessions obtained by police are now closely scrutinized by the courts. Interrogations should be preceded by warnings of a suspect's right to remain silent and to have an attorney present.

Investigations of crimes routinely demand identification of suspects. This may be accomplished through line-ups, show-ups, photographs, fingerprints, and other types of scientific evidence; but care is required to safeguard legal rights.

Questions

1. Which offenses result in the most numerous arrests?
2. What is probable cause?
3. How can the police obtain a legal confession?
4. What is the difference between a line-up and a show-up?

NOTES

[1] Shadwick v. Tampa, 407 U.S. 345, 92 S.Ct. 2119 (1972); Coolidge v. New Hampshire, 403 U.S. 443, 91 S.Ct. 2022 (1971).

[2] Austin T. Turk, *Criminality and Legal Order* (Skokie, Ill.: Rand McNally, 1969), pp. 8–18.

[3] *Uniform Crime Reports for the United States—1972* (Washington: GPO, 1973), pp. 129–131.

[4] *Ibid.*, p. 107.

[5] *The Functions of the Police in Modern Society* (Washington: GPO, 1970), pp. 107–112.

[6] Federal Rules of Criminal Procedure, 41(c); California Penal Code, sec. 1525; Illinois Revised Statutes, chapter 38, sec. 108–3; New York Criminal Procedure Law, sec. 690.10; Texas Code of Criminal Procedure, art. 18.01.

[7] Chimel v. California, 395 U.S. 752, 89 S.Ct. 2034 (1969); Vale v. Louisiana, 399 U.S. 30, 90 S.Ct. 1969 (1970); Robinson v. United States, 414 U.S. 218, 94 S.Ct. 467 (1973).

[8] Terry v. Ohio, 392 U.S. 1, 88 S.Ct. 1868 (1968), Adams v. Williams, 407 U.S. 143, 92 S.Ct. 1921 (1972); Gustafson v. Florida, 414 U.S. 260, 94 S.Ct. 488 (1973).

[9] Wong Sun v. United States, 371 U.S. 1, 83 S.Ct. 407 (1963).

[10] 18 United States Code 2518; United States v. United States District Court, 407 U.S. 297, 92 S.Ct. 2125 (1972).

[11] Arnold S. Trebach, *The Rationing of Justice* (New Brunswick, N.J.: Rutgers University Press, 1964), pp. 32–58.

[12] Escobedo v. Illinois, 378 U.S. 478, 84 S.Ct. 1758 (1964); Miranda v. Arizona, 384 U.S. 436, 86 S.Ct. 1602 (1966).

[13] "Interrogations in New Haven: The Impact of Miranda," *Yale Law Journal* 76 (July, 1967), pp. 1519–1615; R. H. Seeburger and R. Stanton Wettick, "Miranda in Pittsburgh," *University of Pittsburgh Law Review* 29 (October, 1967), pp. 6–26.

[14] Harold E. Pepinsky, "A Theory of Police Reaction to Miranda v. Arizona," *Crime and Delinquency* 6 (October, 1970), pp. 379–392.

[15] United States v. Wade, 388 U.S. 218, 87 S.Ct. 1926 (1967).

[16] Kirby v. Illinois, 406 U.S. 682, 92 S.Ct. 1877 (1972).

[17] Stovall v. Denno, 388 U.S. 293, 87 S.Ct. 1967 (1967).
[18] Davis v. Mississippi, 394 U.S. 721, 89 S.Ct. 1394 (1969).
[19] Charles E. O'Hara, *Fundamentals of Criminal Investigation* (Springfield, Ill.: C. C. Thomas, 1970), pp. 67–82.
[20] Gilbert v. California, 388 U.S. 263, 87 S.Ct. 1951 (1967).
[21] Schmerber v. California, 384 U.S. 757, 86 S.Ct. 1826 (1966); Rochin v. California, 342 U.S. 165, 72 S.Ct. 205 (1952).

Chapter 8

Constitutional Safeguards

"No free man shall be taken, outlawed, banished, or in any way destroyed, nor will We proceed against or prosecute him, except by the lawful judgment of his peers and by the law of the land."

THE MAGNA CARTA

Due Process

The story of U.S. constitutional safeguards is, in large part, the history of mankind's continuing struggle for political and personal freedom. Over a period of centuries, people have battled for liberty against the power of tyrannical governments. In retrospect, it appears that the greatest achievements were related to individual effort and sacrifice in England and America. To a large degree, protections within the United States may be traced to origins of the common law and fundamental principles of private freedom.

Generations before the American revolution, many important concepts had developed in England. The rights of representation by counsel, trial by a jury of peers, and an independent judiciary were but a few of these vital principles. Common law heritage served as a foundation for protection against government authority and was so highly regarded as to subsequently become an integral basis for a new nation, the United States of America. In 1787, after a significant dispute between those favoring centralization and others supporting a loose confederation of cooperating former colonies, the Constitution was accepted.

But, in 1791, fear of too strong a national system led to the adoption of the first ten amendments or Bill of Rights as a curb on authority of the federal government. For nearly a century, these important restrictions had no application to the activities of the states that retained similar protections for their own citizens.

One of the most significant elements of the Bill of Rights was derived from the English Magna Carta of 1215. In 1791, the principle that government should be subject to established procedure became part of the Constitution through the part of Amendment V which reads, "No person shall be . . . deprived of life, liberty, or property, without due process of law." By these terms, the national government was required to follow previously determined rules; order demanded justice.

Shortly after the Civil War, the Constitution received a second "due process" clause. In 1868, Amendment XIV, designed to guarantee rights of former slaves, was enacted. It provided that, "No State shall . . . deprive any person of life, liberty, or property, without due process of law. . . ." Under these terms, the same general conditions which previously applied only to the single federal government became mandatory with respect to the states.

As generations passed, the U.S. Supreme Court faced many serious questions concerning the meaning and significance of these simple but important words. The due process clause of Amendment XIV gradually came to have two leading and related impacts on criminal law throughout the country. With both, continuing debate resulted.

First, due process was held to nullify any activity which truly shocks the collective conscience, offends a fundamental sense of justice, or goes beyond basic standards of civilized conduct. Federal and state authorities, alike, were forbidden to utilize measures beyond those necessary for reasonable law enforcement. As an example, the police and courts could not rely upon confessions obtained through physical torture.[1]

Second, the Fourteenth Amendment's due process clause has been used to apply *specific* basic protections of the Bill of Rights to state, as well as federal, government. While the Supreme Court has yet to determine that *all* guarantees of the original ten amendments must be directly followed throughout the nation, most portions are now so regarded. Consequently, the fundamental protections once accorded citizens against the central government now also exist when facing state or local authorities.

The principle of due process is surely one of the most basic liberties enjoyed by Americans. Yet, its application causes difficulty. Some fear that imposition of rules by a central power poses as many dangers to personal freedom as does the conduct they may prevent. Many deplore the diminution of state sovereignty and loss of local autonomy. Nevertheless, others deeply believe that basic liberties must be accorded to all, uniformly, for the ultimate safety of the nation and a free people. For them, due process demands no less. While almost everyone now agrees that the federal government properly demands basic standards, it is also widely believed that states should control and adjust formalities to meet regional and local conditions. The difficulty arises over the correct balance between the two public powers.

Very strictly defined, due process refers to the regular and established course of law. But application of the term seldom follows such a narrow meaning. In truth, due process remains a vague and constantly evolving concept. Actions termed unreasonable, capricious, arbitrary, and unfair have been held in violation. Yet, those pronouncements serve only to indicate the general scope and fundamental nature of due process. Each question must, in the final analysis, be measured by basic and widely recognized standards of fairness and justice.[2]

Within the last few years, due process concepts have indirectly brought about a revolution in our rules of criminal procedure. Reaching beyond earlier civil law applications, recent court interpretations transformed the formal requirements imposed upon police and courts. Such decisions go far beyond theory and strike the daily routines of questioning, search, counsel, and trial.

Much present confusion and considerable vocal opposition results from continuing change as well as from the imposition of higher standards for criminal justice. Our legal system, particularly in reference to the Constitution, does not entail strict adherence to precedent. Unlike the English, U.S. courts may vary from the dictates of prior decisions. This means, in practice, that policemen and judges cannot absolutely rely upon preceding cases. Due process means something quite different today from what it did a generation ago. Although major alterations occur infrequently, they impose constant stress upon essential procedures of criminal justice.

Rule of Law

It is sometimes asserted that one measure of a civilization may be found in the protections accorded criminals. In the western world, this concept receives recognition in the requirement of rule by law. Related in many respects to due process, such a principle provides numerous safeguards against assumption of unjust power by governmental officials. Some of these protections are unwritten but entrenched doctrines of common and civil law. Others have received specific recognition within the Constitution of the United States.

Paul von Feuerbach, a German legal scholar of the early nineteenth century, is credited with the formulation of an elemental maxim of personal liberty. He wrote, *"nulla poena sine lege"* (no punishment without law). Such a doctrine asserts that citizens cannot be accused, prosecuted, or corrected without clear and prior provision, normally found in statutory form.

Punishment only by law requires careful interpretation and application of criminal codes. This demands what is usually termed "strict construction." A system of justice dedicated to *nulla poena sine lege* can ill afford statutes distorted or magnified for mere convenience. It is essential that penal laws be specific and absolutely clear. Strict construction means simply that statutes must directly apply to the actual conduct and situation. Generally, words are accorded only their ordinary, logical, and appropriate definitions, to the usual benefit of a defendant. For example, should a law on operation of automobiles be applied to motorcycles, sailboats, trucks, snowmobiles, bicycles, or motorboats? Obviously the answer would depend upon individual interpretation, but strict construction should exclude some of the suggested cases. How different might the results be if the statute were amended to cover all motor vehicles?

Criminal laws are frequently struck down for vagueness. For example, "offensive" behavior could be regarded as far too broad and general for accurate interpretation. Here again, strict construction and *nulla poena sine lege* demand language which is clear and precise, although this often leads to great detail and very lengthy statutes.[3]

A second major feature of rule by law consists of protection against retroactivity. Such guarantees are found twice in Article I of the original Constitution: Section 9 applies to the federal government and Section 10 covers the states; both forbid the passage of *ex post facto* legislation. Basically, these insure that no law makes acts criminal in retrospect. The government, therefore, can only punish those things prohibited at the time of the incident or conduct. Possession of alcohol today, for example, could scarcely be made a crime tomorrow. Penal law should only be accorded prospective application.[4]

Another essential element of rule by law concerns the right to judicial hearing by anyone placed in custody. This guarantee against illegal punishment was developed in seventeenth century England and found recognition in Article I, Section 9, of the U.S. Constitution: "The privilege of the Writ of Habeas Corpus shall not be suspended, unless when in Cases of Rebellion or Invasion the public Safety may require it."

Procedures in federal and state systems permit those under restraint to demand that authorities show cause for their detention or grant release. This is accomplished by the "great writ" of *habeas corpus* (you have the body) whereby the prisoner must be brought before a magistrate and the charges examined. Such a protection does not, of course, eliminate all possible abuses of authority, but it operates as a means of preventing the ultimate danger of a police state.

Today, with statutory requirements of prompt judicial hearing, the primary purpose of *habeas corpus* is seldom required. It has become, instead, a popular means of seeking additional review of cases. The federal writ, especially, may be used by those seeking to challenge the constitutionality of actions by state authorities. Despite what sometimes appears to be excessive employment of *habeas corpus*, it remains a vital heritage of English and American justice. It truly delineates rule by law, for authority of the judiciary restricts arbitrary action by other agencies of government. As long as a magistrate may compel that prisoners be brought before the bench by *habeas corpus*, a barrier against possible police tyranny exists.

Rule of law rests upon the fundamental assumption that safeguards are needed against unjust, inequitable, and unfair treatment by the state. Without such doctrines, criminal law could become the destroyer of liberty, and the police an agency for despotism. Only by their adherence to established standards and basic doctrines of justice can such dangers be avoided.

There is, however, a totally different equally important meaning to rule of law, and it is also directly applicable to the police. The concept implies that we live in orderly and peaceful ways. Without rule of law, society would dissolve into chaos. Crime, riot, violence, and vandalism would be rampant throughout the nation. Instead, agencies of justice operate to help maintain or even improve the quality of life so that citizens need not constantly suffer or fear attack and thievery. True rule of law protects people against government abuse and ordinary criminals.

The Exclusionary Rule

A good number of criminal cases involve evidence obtained in violation of constitutional protections. The most common problem concerns action which goes beyond Amendment IV safeguards against "unreasonable searches and seizures." Two generations ago, when the due process clause still applied primarily to the national government, it was established that evidence secured through unlawful searches by federal officers would not be admissable in courts of the United States.[5] This concept, called the exclusionary rule, meant that violations of basic protections by the police would preclude subsequent use of any items seized. Of course, it might still be possible to prosecute the defendant using totally different evidence properly obtained.

Until 1961, the U.S. Supreme Court did not impose the exclusionary rule upon the states, although a majority of them adopted such a standard by either judicial interpretation or legislative act. But today, the doctrine designed originally for only federal application is controlling in all jurisdictions of the country.[6] Evidence obtained by illegal means cannot be utilized in any American court under our unique and strict exclusionary rule.

The obvious difficulty with forbidance of proof acquired through unreasonable search is that some of the guilty may escape punishment. Such instances undoubtedly occur throughout the United States. Every day, the police overstep present interpretations of proper authority and discover clear evidence of guilt, particularly in regard to vice offenses.[7]

Before assuming that an exclusionary rule only serves to subvert the purposes of criminal justice, however, one should understand that the overwhelming majority of instances where law enforcement agents go beyond their legal power could be easily avoided. Also, the vast number of improper invasions of personal privacy which produce *no* evidence of crime whatever tend to be forgotten. The exclusionary rule was created to protect ordinary citizens, not defend the guilty. Present statutes grant police considerable power to conduct searches with and without warrant; in many areas this wide authority is incorrectly understood and utilized.

By preventing admission at trial of improperly obtained evidence, another goal may, at least in theory, be accomplished. The exclusionary rule, removing the incentive for violating consitutional guarantees, reasserts the clear role of law enforcement as an arm of justice. Who can be expected to follow the rules if not those appointed to apply them? As Justice Louis D. Brandeis wrote, "If the government becomes a lawbreaker, it breeds contempt for law; it invites every man to become a law unto himself; it invites anarchy."[8] Public respect for the police and preservation of the character of democracy depend upon adherence to the highest possible standards of behavior, even though a few more offenders may escape conviction.

One basic problem with the exclusionary rule is that a single, rigid requirement now exists for all jurisdictions of the nation. This restricts local autonomy and substitutes a central judicial conscience for those of the various states. Despite the obvious scope of this broad doctrine, it would be an error to presume that the elimination of evidence seized illegally has drastically altered law enforcement. The actual effects of the exclusionary rule, viewed amid the enormity of the total crime problem, have been almost negligible.[9] Police can still violate personal rights while diligent prosecutors manage to circumvent intended restrictions.

It is possible for some officers to misinform about circumstances, through reports or testimony, and so make an actually improper search seem reasonable. Others may distort facts to more readily justify an investigation or arrest. From the standpoint of one frustrated by examples of the exclusionary rule releasing those certainly guilty, such conduct is perhaps understandable while still not legally acceptable.[10]

In practice, the exclusionary rule reaches beyond immediate circumstances. First, while it technically applies only to evidence taken by illegal search and seizure, the same general restriction extends to confessions and other proofs of guilt. It is also important to recall that the prohibition against admission applies not only to immediate discoveries but additionally to "fruit of the poisonous tree." Thus, if the police conduct an unreasonable search and uncover clues which in turn lead directly to other evidence, it would still be excluded as the product of the original intrusion.

The Constitution protects people, not just places. Exclusion of evidence taken improperly is meant to prevent invasions of reasonably expected privacy, regardless of location. That concept becomes quite significant in connection with "standing," or the right to raise issues in court.[11]

Suppose the police, acting on a hunch and without cause, break into a private home and catch a burglar carrying stolen items out a door. Could the criminal have the evidence excluded because of the unwarranted entry and search? Hardly, for the burglar has no standing to make such a claim; he was illegally in the house and had no expectation or right of privacy. Consequently, the exclusionary rule does not apply, and the evidence is admissable.

But, suppose the police discovered hidden narcotics after they had illegally entered the home. Could they use the evidence against the house owner? The answer is negative for he would have standing in court and could properly object to the use of evidence obtained through improper conduct. The officers had invaded his privacy, not that of the burglar.

The exclusionary rule's shadow extends far beyond gross violations of personal rights and privileges. What may appear to be minor procedural errors on the part of police have often eliminated quite significant evidence. Yet, the courts generally recognize the practical difficulties of modern law enforcement. Informed debate seldom arises over the need to restrict unreasonable invasions and searches by police or to permit necessary entries and investigations. Difficulties concern the proper limits of authority and its exercise in particular circumstances.

The exclusionary rule has been criticized as illogical and impractical. Yet, it is well established in modern criminal procedure. The barrier against improperly taken evidence may also be viewed in still another context. Very few other nations allow police misbehavior to become a defense. As such, the exclusionary rule indicates the value placed upon personal freedom contrasted with the enveloping power of government.

Self-Incrimination

There is probably no single aspect of Anglo-American legal heritage of greater significance than protection against self-incrimination. This vital safeguard originated in common law, developed in England prior to the "Glorious Revolution" of 1688, and subsequently became enshrined in America's written Constitution. The primary statement of the liberty resides within the Bill of Rights' Amendment V: "No person shall be compelled in any criminal case to be a witness against himself...."

While the states maintain their own protections against self-incrimination, the federal constitutional provision is now interpreted as a standard for the entire nation.[12] It would be advisable to note, however, that the general rule established only mandatory minimums. Should states desire to establish protections for the individual going beyond those required by the Constitution, they may surely do so. It is quite possible for a jurisdiction to have somewhat more expansive rules against self-incrimination than those required by federal courts.

The essence of the privilege consists of personal freedom to remain silent and refuse to divulge any information which could be useful to the prosecution. As such, the federal provision is ordinarily interpreted to cover only testimonial evidence (such as confessions). An individual state may additionally prohibit demonstrative and other forms of required self-incrimination.

Without doubt, however, the typical situation involves a statement which might indicate the speaker's guilt. The foremost example is a confession or admission made to the police. An ultimate test for the acceptance of such statements remains that of voluntariness. Basically, compulsion of any sort may be treated as a violation of the right against self-incrimination. Under this somewhat flexible rule, which legislators reaffirm, confessions or admissions obtained through force, threats, false promises, or extended questioning are regarded as compelled and involuntary.[13] Protections from required self-incrimination may, nevertheless, operate in other and broader categories. The safeguard extends well beyond the confines of police interrogation.

Under certain circumstances, the law itself may indirectly cause a type of self-incrimination. Tax forms, business files, automobile accident descriptions, and similar mandatory statements undoubtedly provide sources of frequently damaging evidence. Yet, these required reports are held to be routine and part of the regulatory power of the government. Courts, therefore, may treat such evidence as falling outside the usual scope of self-incrimination privileges. Quite often, however, required reports are subject to exclusion through special statutes.

Where mere filing of a declaration itself indicates actual guilt, constitutional protections clearly apply. For example; the central government cannot require an individual to pay taxes (under threat of federal criminal prosecution) for items or activity which the states, in turn, totally forbid. An individual would be forced to incriminate himself in one jurisdiction in order to avoid prohibited conduct in another. This situation has recently developed in the United States in regard to gambling, firearms, narcotics, and other areas which both state and federal governments attempt to regulate.[14]

As interpreted, constitutional rights relative to self-incrimination actually exist in two quite separate categories. One involves defendants, the other witnesses. Both parties have a personal privilege of refusing to give evidence which could be used against them. It is quite possible for a witness testifying in one trial, for example, to be asked questions which might lead to his eventual prosecution. Protection against self-incrimination extends to these circumstances although the state may grant immunity and thereby compel essential statements. Under these conditions, the testimony could not be subsequently used to convict the unwilling witness.

It should be obvious that protection from compulsory admissions goes beyond the confines of police questioning and courtroom appearances. Damaging statements (oral or written) could be demanded by grand juries, legislative committees, and administrative bodies. Constitutional rights, however, reach these situations almost as clearly as they do actual trials. With certain limitations, a party can remain silent as long as his testimony could reasonably tend to incriminate himself. Considerable controversy occasionally occurs with the exercise of such liberties, for the processes of justice may be frustrated as a result. The danger of encroachment upon essential personal freedom, however, discourages efforts to modify such a basic testimonial privilege.

Difficult questions involving self-incrimination sometimes arise in connection with waiver. Either the defendant or witness may forego his right to remain silent. And, once voluntarily waived, evidence given cannot be later withdrawn or restricted. The most common example concerns a defendant who elects to waive his right not to testify and swears to his own innocence. This usually permits the prosecutor to question the suspect and to introduce evidence about his veracity.[15] Otherwise, such often damaging information cannot be presented in court.

Should a defendant exercise his constitutional right against self-incrimination and remain silent before and during trial, it must never be taken as an indication of guilt. Consequently, both prosecutor and judge must not comment upon the fact or discuss the implications of such conduct before a jury. Just as the Constitution guards everyone's freedom of silence, it protects use of the right from becoming a weapon of the state. The essential element of no self-incrimination is, above all, a means of preventing the government from intimidating it's citizens. As such, the right tends to be broadly construed.

Like other constitutional protections, that against self-incrimination has evolved gradually. Popularly associated with torture or required answers under oath, the privilege of silence now stands as a paramount feature of criminal justice. There are, of course, cases when refusal to give evidence results in release of guilty parties. Critics consequently assail the privilege as illogical and unnecessary. Conversely, defenders assert that it protects against potential inquisition and oppression. And, after all, the privilege against self-incrimination originated and expanded not as an obstacle to reasonable law enforcement but as a barrier against abuse. The history of legal rights coincides directly with that of political freedom; relaxation of one soon undermines the other.

First Amendment Freedoms

Just as Americans enjoy the freedom to remain silent, they also may speak. The related liberties reside under Amendment I, which Justice Hugo Black often described as, ". . . the heart of our Bill of Rights, our Constitution, and our nation."[16] In its entirety, this fundamental bulwark of democracy provides:

> Congress shall make no law respecting an establishment of religion, or prohibiting free exercise thereof; or abridging the freedom of speech, or of the press; or the right of the people peaceably to assemble, and to petition the Government for a redress of grievances.

The First Amendment plays a significant role in criminal justice and has been construed as applying to all levels of government within the United States. It binds states and cities along with various branches of the federal system. Moreover, the provisions serve as a pivotal element in the balance of personal security and public safety. Both are essential features of a democratic society. And, the delicate yet vital role of criminal justice in protecting order *and* freedom is perhaps most easily recognized in regard to Amendment I.

Some people will occasionally abuse any liberty. Consequently, even the privileges of religion, speech, the press, assembly, and petition cannot be considered as absolute or without possible qualification. As long as conduct violates established and legitimate criminal law, it may be punished despite claims of constitutional rights. One could not, in an extreme example, commit murder and then assert a justification on religious grounds. Society grants freedom within reasonable limitations.

The prerogative of our citizens to assemble and criticize the actions of others, as well as the government, often collide with the continuing need for social order. Such confrontations are clearly demonstrated by recent civil protest, particularly from racial, student, or other groups. Here also, criminal justice must attempt to maintain a balance between the guaranteed liberty of peaceful demonstration and necessary functioning of our sensitive urban culture.

While generalization is difficult, protest cannot extend to actual violence, occupation of private or public property, obstruction of ordinary pathways and roads, or obvious disorderly conduct. Should those involved in civil demonstration overstep such boundaries, they forfeit constitutional immunity from police action and criminal prosecution.

On the other hand, penal law and government authority may not be used primarily to suppress protest through assembly and criticism. If representatives of criminal justice, for example, single out those engaged in such activity and subject them to discretionary arrest and harassment, they become agents of oppression rather than defenders of right. In practice, under the tension of actual confrontation, of course, these legal distinctions may seem blurred and confused by personal attitudes. The ultimate security of freedom, nevertheless, directly depends upon such difficult decisions.[17]

Rights of assembly and petition are naturally intertwined with those of speech. While Amendment I guarantees that government cannot directly hinder personal expression, it does not prohibit legitimate legislation designed to prevent and punish disturbance of the peace, incitement to riot, slander, and similar offenses. Criminal justice must, nevertheless, remain alert to distinguish preservation of public order from social repression.

Freedom to speak, in public or private, entails only a limited privilege. One entrusted with secret government information can, for example, be legally restricted from selling verbal reports to enemy agents. While the right of free speech must be liberally construed to protect all against the state, it does not serve as an umbrella for otherwise criminal conduct. But, as with other rights, interpretation and application pose major difficulties.

Conflict sometimes even arises between constitutional protections. One of the most graphic examples of such a collision concerns free press and fair trial. The Bill of Rights protects both, yet they can appear contradictory. It is quite possible for the press to focus such adverse publicity upon a defendant as to severely curtail the possibility of fair trial. Particularly in the case of crimes attracting widespread interest, it becomes extremely difficult to empanel an unbiased jury. Even changing the place of trial fails to avoid the problem when the offense has drawn national publicity.

In fact, no definite solution to the dilemma of free press or fair trial exists. Both are essential to democracy. When courts attempt to stifle the press, however well meaning the intentions, the door to tyranny opens. At the same time, abusive publicity can virtually determine guilt prior to adjudication. The best compromise, at present, consists of a combination of voluntary cooperation from the press and close control of those directly involved with criminal justice.[18] Discretion on the part of police, prosecutors, defense attorneys, and judges can sharply reduce instances of this impasse.

Control of speech, press, or other means of public expression involves significant problems of censorship. The applicability or proper limit to government regulation of mass communications raises serious questions. Regardless of the subject under scrutiny, censorship invariably creates power and provides opportunity for abuse.

Today, complaints are quite frequently directed against portrayals deemed pornographic or excessively violent. Is censorship a proper and reasonable solution to questionable presentations in the press, on television or the stage, and in motion pictures? The answer relates not only to constitutional and statutory interpretations, but to practical considerations of actual effect.[19]

A wide division of opinion on the results of pornography and violence exists. Critics contend that deviance and disrespect for authority are directly caused by artificial stimulation. Meanwhile, others proclaim that the public only receives what it wants and indirectly benefits from release of emotions. At present, research casts doubt on the overall effect of pornographic and extremely violent material. It appears that among well-developed personalities no harm results, but those with emotional disturbances may be incited. Possible harm depends upon the individual and his given situation.[20]

Censorship creates an ultimate threat of dictated political, moral, and social concepts notwithstanding any demonstrated harm. But under certain circumstances, the community must exercise basic authority over conduct and items for public consumption. At present the Constitution permits a tenuous balance between government restriction and the exercise of individual taste.[21]

The police are required to make decisions concerning the First Amendment every day. They must constantly balance the rights of the individual and those of the public. Courts can answer such questions by careful deliberation in quiet settings. But the policeman must face the same basic issues amidst turmoil and when emotions are highest. He has to deal with unruly crowds, antagonistic speakers, and angry citizens. Even so, his answers and actions should reflect the highest possible standards of constitutional law. Failure can lead to either anarchy or tyranny.

Summary

The requirement of due process applies to all forms of government within the United States. It provides for fundamental justice and specific guarantees found within the Bill of Rights. Rule of law, a companion of due process, rests upon principles of strict construction and no retroactive application. It involves protections against imprisonment without trial.

Evidence seized through illegal search and seizure may not be used against those whose rights are violated. This doctrine, uniquely applicable throughout all of the United States, is termed the exclusionary rule.

The privilege against compulsory self-incrimination permits a defendant or witness to avoid giving evidence against himself. As such, the right is normally regarded as personal and limited to testimonial matters, but it does reach beyond court appearances.

Amendment I protects essential freedoms of religion, speech, the press, assembly, and petition. These liberties are foundations of democracy and our Bill of Rights.

Questions

1. How has the concept of due process developed?
2. Could democracy exist without rule of law?
3. Should the exclusionary rule be abolished?
4. How far should the protection against self-incrimination extend?
5. Why do First Amendment freedoms affect criminal justice?

NOTES

[1] Brown v. Mississippi, 297 U.S. 278, 56 S.Ct. 461 (1936); White v. Texas, 310 U.S. 530, 60 S.Ct. 1032 (1940).

[2] Hugo LaFayette Black, *A Constitutional Faith* (New York: Knopf, 1969), pp. 23–42.

[3] Papachristou v. Jacksonville, 405 U.S. 156, 92 S.Ct. 839 (1972); Jerome Hall, *General Principles of Criminal Law* (Indianapolis; Bobbs-Merrill, 1960), pp. 27–69.

[4] Calder v. Bull, 3 U.S. (3 Dall.) 386 (1798); Wayne R. LaFave and Austin W. Scott, *Handbook on Criminal Law* (St. Paul: West, 1972), pp. 89–97.

[5] Weeks v. United States, 232 U.S. 383, 34 S.Ct. 341 (1914).

[6] Mapp v. Ohio, 367 U.S. 643, 81 S.Ct. 1684 (1961).

[7] Jerome H. Skolnick, *Justice Without Trial* (New York: Wiley, 1966), pp. 215–225.

[8] Olmstead v. United States, 277 U.S. 438, 485, 48 S.Ct. 564, 575 (1928).

[9] Dallin H. Oaks, "Studying the Exclusionary Rule in Search and Seizure," *University of Chicago Law Review* 37 (Spring, 1970), pp. 665–757; Hazel B. Kerper, *Introduction to the Criminal Justice System* (St. Paul: West, 1972), p. 422.

[10] Paul Chevigny, *Police Power* (New York: Vintage, 1969), pp. 180–218.

[11] Alderman v. United States, 394 U.S. 165, 89 S.Ct. 961 (1969); Jones v. United States, 362 U.S. 257, 80 S.Ct. 725 (1960).

[12] Malloy v. Hogan, 378 U.S. 1, 84 S.Ct. 961 (1964); Bram v. United States, 168 U.S. 532, 18 S.Ct. 183 (1897).

[13] 18 United States Code 3501; California Evidence Code, sec. 1204; Illinois Revised Statutes, chapter 38, sec. 109–1; New York Criminal Procedure Law, secs. 120.90, 140.20; Texas Code of Criminal Procedure, art. 38.22.

[14] Leary v. United States, 395 U.S. 6, 89 S.Ct. 1532 (1969); Marchetti v. United States, 390 U.S. 39, 88 S.Ct. 697 (1968).

[15] Harris v. New York, 401 U.S. 222, 91 S.Ct. 644 (1971).

[16] *A Constitutional Faith*, p. 63.

[17] Feiner v. New York, 340 U.S. 315, 71 S.Ct. 303 (1951); Cox v. Louisiana, 379 U.S. 559, 85 S.Ct. 476 (1965).

[18] *Standards Relating to Fair Trial and Free Press* (N.p., American Bar Association, 1968), pp. 1–14.

[19] *To Establish Justice, To Insure Domestic Tranquility* (Washington: GPO, 1969), pp. 187–207.

[20] *The Report of the Commission on Obscenity and Pornography* (Washing-

ton: GPO, 1970), pp. 23–27; *Television and Social Behavior: Television and Adolescent Aggressiveness* (Washington: GPO, 1972), pp. 383–435.

[21] Miller v. California, 413 U.S. 15, 93 S.Ct. 2607 (1973); John A. Mintz, "Comment on Obscenity," *FBI Law Enforcement Bulletin* 42 (September, 1973), pp. 21–23.

> UPON THE INTEGRITY WISDOM AND
> INDEPENDENCE OF THE JUDICIARY DEPEND
> THE SACRED RIGHTS OF FREE MEN

PART III

THE COURTS

After the police arrest someone in connection with a crime, the matter may go on to court. Such a transition is, however, neither direct nor automatic. Several steps and participants normally become involved and determine whether or not a case will ever actually come to trial. Once again, criminal justice is a peculiar patchwork of rules and customs rather than an efficient and logical process.

Soon after apprehension, a suspect usually gets an opportunity for release on bail. Under this ancient system, a guaranteed sum of money, now ordinarily provided by a professional bondsman, is accepted as insurance for the defendant's later appearance in court. If bail requirements cannot be met, the suspect normally stays in jail. This may mean incarceration for many months under deplorable conditions before trial and any determination of guilt.

Unlike police agencies, which have crime control as a primary duty, the courts are supposed to establish legal responsibility and then assign suitable penalties. Balancing the rights of the public and those of individuals, they occupy a central and critical role in American criminal justice. Our tribunals are expected to perform a multitude of social functions and still remain immune from outside influences. As a practical matter, they usually conduct routine formalities far removed from idealistic goals while standing as traditional symbols of impartial arbitration under law.

Courts do not, of course, operate with absolute independence. They are actually focal points of many aspects of justice. Despite their authority, American criminal courts rely almost entirely upon attorneys for the prosecution and defense to both present and examine evidence in what is termed adversary practice. This rather strange competitive system endures as an integral part of common law and contributes to equally peculiar dependence upon bargained justice whereby deals really determine guilt and punishment. A great many problems exist because of these odd negotiations, but at present, American justice would collapse without them.

Our judicial systems developed gradually over hundreds of years. While criminal courts throughout the United States are inefficient and archaic in many respects, they also provide fundamental safeguards to individual freedom. Rights of defendants were largely developed in seventeenth century England but are of enormous significance in twentieth century America.

Criminal cases formally commence with accusations, by information or indictment. Here, prosecutorial and grand jury discretion achieve major importance. If charges are determined to be reasonable, the matter then proceeds to a court of suitable jurisdiction. Even excluding the numberless traffic infractions, an overwhelming majority of cases involve uncontested misdemeanors.

The federal government, each state, and thousands of local areas have their own criminal courts; powers and procedures are incredibly varied. American judges, chosen politically by either appointment or election, routinely handle vast numbers of cases in almost automatic fashion. Only rarely does a defendant demand and receive trial by jury. Although the right exists in connection with every serious charge, it is ordinarily waived.

Trial itself occasionally constitutes a dramatic spectacle; more often, it resembles a soporific litany designed to meet procedural *requirements. After preliminary hearings, a contested case enters the vital phase during which evidence is formally brought forth. The finder of guilt or innocence, either judge or jury, then renders a verdict. Later, and often after some delay, courts face the difficult task of sentencing those found criminally responsible.*

During these stages of justice, cases frequently pass from one level of government to another. City police may arrest a suspect for a state offense but place him in a county jail. The case can go to a district attorney, be tried in a circuit court, and finally undergo federal review. And, punishment for the crime might also involve a variety of jurisdictions. This apparent incoherence is but another example of the confused nature of criminal justice in the United States.

Courts occupy a central position in the entire process, and many problems exist in relation to them. They are agonizingly slow, congested, and resort to impersonal mass handling. Moreover, serious questions may be properly raised over basic issues of fairness and impartiality. As just one illustration, there is an even lower proportional representation of blacks among judges than among police.

A case does not, by any means, reach a definite conclusion when the trial ends. Many criminal matters subsequently become subjects for appeal to higher courts. It may take years for a case to be transferred back and forth between different tribunals. While society suffers, the machinery of justice grinds ponderously along.

In addition to thousands of regular courts hearing cases at federal, state, and local levels, the United States has many special governmental units performing judicial functions. Our complex, technical culture has spawned countless administrative agencies with clear, immediate, and vast power to punish for violations of many types of laws.

Of more obvious and direct significance to criminal justice, however, are the juvenile courts. Today, about half of the known serious offenses involve youths. They become subject to the jurisdiction of juvenile courts. Now, yet another classification of criminal violators based upon age is emerging. Increased recognition has been accorded the unique problems of characteristics of youthful offenders who are too old for child care but too young to be treated as adults.

Finally, the military maintains separate and complete systems of criminal justice. While subject to basic constitutional restrictions, each of the armed services has police, judicial, and correctional operations for its own personnel. Trial, of course, occurs by court-martial.

Chapter 9
The Aftermath of Arrest

"Delay of justice is injustice."

LANDOR

Bail, or Jail?

After arrest and booking, a suspect usually faces a difficult question. He must either satisfy authorities that he can be released or go to jail. Of course, the apprehended person is already in custody and might have been locked in a car or cell before completion of the booking slip (a short form on which certain details of arrest are noted). The police or the courts ordinarily possess the authority to release a person suspected of a lesser offense solely upon his signature, or personal recognizance (a promise to return to face the accusation).[1] This power is routinely granted in traffic citations, where signing the ticket suffices. But personal recognizance is used very much less frequently in connection with other crimes, except when better known citizens of a community are arrested. It has recently been demonstrated that proper release on mere promises to return can be quite successful. Under careful selection, 98% of those apprehended will apparently honor their signatures and come to court when summoned; this percentage is actually higher than that obtained by more traditional means.[2]

Assuming that personal recognizance is not permitted, an arrested party normally gets an opportunity for release on bail. This is an ancient method whereby a suspect avoids custody by posting a bond, a specific sum secured by cash or property. In some jurisdictions, police resort to a judicially established bail schedule and so release a suspect when either he or someone else pays or promises to supply the required amount. For major violations, a magistrate must determine the particular bail required, and for the most serious offenses, such as murder, bond may simply be denied. The actual sum demanded varies according to the crime; it may be very little for routine public disorders or arbitrarily set high enough to preclude any likelihood of release, despite the clear requirement, in Amendment VIII of the U.S. Constitution, that "Excessive bail shall not be required...."[3]

In practice, the necessary amount is routinely met by recourse to professional bondsmen. Their offices may be found near many jails and, in some areas, they simply wait at the station for regular offenders. Profits to those supplying bail are considerable (interest rates of 15 percent are not unusual) while expenses depend upon selection of customers. Bondsmen sometimes invest great effort and large sums to locate, capture, and return suspects who jump bail and cause financial loss. In most instances, those regularly providing money for release of arrested persons are well known to police, and they sometimes work in very close cooperation with defense attorneys. At times, an efficient bondsman–lawyer team will have their clients (especially prostitutes) out on bail within minutes of apprehension, before the arresting officer has completed his written report at the station!

There are many problems associated with reliance upon the ancient system of bonding an arrested person. Originally, the purpose was to provide a guarantee for the state and permit the suspect to remain out of actual custody before trial. Today, the situation places considerable power in the hands of bondsmen and works to the clear disadvantage of a poor suspect unable to provide either his own money or the needed collateral for financial assistance. For organized criminals, the wealthy, or the influential, the requirement of funds for release poses no real obstacle. In certain circumstances, cash bail may now be simply forfeited, and the case never goes to court.

Some accused persons commit additional offenses before they can be tried for an original violation. This disturbing fact has led to limited adoption of "preventive detention" whereby, in effect, an accused party may be kept in jail without opportunity for pretrial release.[4] Such a scheme violates traditional concepts of innocence prior to proven guilt but represents a growing frustration with our presently inefficient system of justice. Whether or not such custody could be equitable, reliance on monetary bonds seems obviously outdated and might be successfully curtailed.

If an arrested party cannot be released outright or make bail, he usually remains in jail. It is no exaggeration to state that this result is, in most situations, a tragedy and a disgrace to America. Our jails can be described as antiquated detours to human despair. Persons arrested on criminal charges which often never go to trial are held under unconscionable conditions for incredible periods of time. More than half of the approximately 160,000 people now locked in jails throughout the United States have not been convicted; perhaps 20 percent of them will eventually be simply discharged or acquitted of the offense for which they were originally placed in custody.[5]

While awaiting a trial, which may never come, suspects endure appalling conditions. Most jails provide neither exercise nor education, and many are old, overcrowded, and lack facilities for either visitors or medical care. Adults and juveniles, accused of crimes ranging from disorderly conduct to murder, may be confined together with little effort at separation by age or offense. Runaways and rapists could easily share the same cell. It is yet possible in the United States to find jails operated for personal profit and those without any form of flush toilets.

Brutality and abuse by guards, though still real, do not constitute the primary danger to inmates, which comes from other prisoners. Homosexuality and extortion are rampant in American jails. In the absence of satisfactory supervision, exploitation and assault join waste and boredom. Every year hundreds of people die in American jails from suicide, murder, and failure to receive medical assistance. Guilty and innocent, they are killed because of the abject failure on the part of officials in an unredeemed scheme of organized injustice.

Problems associated with bail and jail acquire greater magnitude because of the delay between arrest and trial. It might seem that this period logically need not extend beyond a few weeks in all but the most unusual of cases. Such, though desirable, is not the situation. A typical felony charge will take at least six months to move from apprehension to a decision. Some defendants languish in jail or stay out on bail for three or four years before they ever come to trial. It is not unusual for a suspect to spend more time in confinement without conviction than he could receive as a maximum sentence for the offense charged. Simply because they cannot afford to make bond, thousands of Americans, including some totally innocent, lose weeks, months, and even years under terrible conditions which no society could properly term civilized. The consequences include lost jobs, broken homes, and serious emotional disturbances.

Adversary Practice

Criminal process depends on lawyers to provide the trappings of justice. Soon after a police arrest, prosecutors and defenders become involved, and a strange ritual known as adversary practice begins. Centuries ago, in Anglo-Saxon times, people could be represented by champions in trials of combat. From this old heritage developed the present system of attorneys for the state and the accused, fighting with rhetoric and legal rules. The court is the descendant of a field of battle and, however archaic the scheme may seem, it serves as a unique device for protecting invaluable personal liberties. While adversity appears a strange basis for justice, no totalitarian state can afford unemcumbered representation of criminal defendants. That is the heart of such a peculiar scheme, but it is vital to common law and an essential legacy of freedom.

The primary justification for adversary practice is that it allows an independent trier of law and fact (judge and jury) to benefit from hearing both sides of the case. The state prosecutor and the defense counsel have an opportunity to explain the maximum strengths of their arguments and to penetrate the weaknesses of the opposition. From the resulting controversy, the virtues and vices of each side may be determined and weighed, with a resulting variety of indirect but informed justice.[6] Another benefit of adversary practice comes from the isolation of those who must ultimately determine guilt and punishment. In the traditional civil law system, which originated in continental Europe, the judge not only serves to make such decisions but also to develop and explore evidence. In common law jurisdictions, these latter functions become the responsibility of the opposing attorneys, thus permitting the court to remain in a position of neutrality, separate and independent of the state's efforts to prosecute.

There are many problems associated with adversary practice. Individual defendants and, often, agencies of the government are interested in results rather than equity. In practice, this means that attorneys for the accused and the state have victory (in whole or part) as a goal instead of either truth or justice. When contention serves as a primary principle, humanity and foresight can reasonably be expected to suffer. Adversary practice also places such an undue emphasis on success that deceit and collusion become involved. Under such conditions, the ultimate purpose of criminal law, protection of the people, may be regarded as secondary or even ignored. If the court accepts or is deceived by such procedures, the state and public become the final victims.

The struggle between prosecuting and defending attorneys extends far beyond the confines of the actual trial. It begins as soon as the two opposing sides become involved in a case, usually shortly after arrest, and can continue over a period of many months or even years. Criminal justice involves far more than courtroom appearances might indicate.[7]

Adversary practice significantly affects rules of criminal procedure and evidence. For example, the order of trial is dependent upon opportunities for both sides to contradict and counterbalance both proof and argument. These aspects may have significant impact upon the eventual outcome. One unspectacular but important area of advocacy involves the acquisition of prior knowledge about the opponent's case. This may transpire during what is technically termed *discovery*, or pretrial disclosure of information. Such a process can materially expedite proceedings while helping to eliminate the bluffing and surprise aspects of advocacy. Discovery is quite widely utilized in civil suits but remains restricted in criminal matters. The extent to which details of evidence and argument will actually be revealed depends on statutory interpretation, local custom, and the personal relationship of opposing attorneys. Discovery can save time and effort for all concerned, but many criminal practitioners feel it militates against the best interests of those whom they represent. Courts, prosecutors, and defense counsels might benefit from general disclosure, but the process is not widely followed.

There are hundreds of thousands of licensed attorneys in the United States, but many do not practice at all and fewer still engage in criminal work. The overwhelming majority of legal activity concerns private claims, property, and technical advice. A small part of all the lawyers' time probably has a close connection with criminal justice. The reason is quite simple: Money attracts law. The financial proceeds of disputes between ordinary offenders and the state seem insignificant beside those from tax, probate, labor, patent, estate, corporate or other legal specialties.

Lack of remuneration undoubtedly contributes to the relatively low social status occupied by criminal lawyers. Another factor logically associated with attitudes toward both prosecuting and defense attorneys is, of course, the persons and problems with which they deal. All together, such conditions fail to attract large numbers of well-qualified lawyers who naturally drift toward opportunities with greater financial and social rewards. It is also unfortunately true that conditions within criminal practice scarcely promote the highest ethical standards. All attorneys are, in theory, held to certain canons of conduct by bar associations and courts. Frankly, these ethical standards are largely rhetoric except in instances of direct profiteering at the cost of clients and, strangely enough, overt efforts at advertising. Organized state bars, recognizing the popular image of lawyers, are making efforts to improve public relations. In the absence of rigid personal standards, supported with realistic canons of ethics, such measures appear designed to mislead rather than inform. Criminal practice, along with other areas of legal service, needs immediate, marked, but unlikely, forthcoming improvement.[8]

The Prosecution

Shortly after a typical criminal case is initiated by arrest, the police take the matter to the prosecutor. Across the United States there are hundreds of separate and independent agencies with the authority to handle serious offenses while many thousands of city and town officials exercise control over minor, local violations. Under our present system of justice, the prosecutor occupies a position of significance fully comparable to those of police and judges. He usually determines the charge and probable punishment.

Prosecutorial responsibility resides in various government lawyers, divided according to jurisdiction. Federal offenses go directly to attorneys working for the central government and grouped into offices matching the number of district courts. The relatively few U.S. Attorneys, each with assistants, are appointed by the President. These well-paid prosecutorial positions ordinarily serve as a means of obvious political patronage and change hands with shifts in power. The actual work of federal attorneys, however, is ordinarily performed by thousands of civil service employees. Their activities must necessarily be restricted to violations against the U.S. government, although this tends to expand rather steadily.

At the other end of the prosecutorial spectrum are those attorneys, often part-time, employed by cities and towns to present charges based upon violations of purely local ordinances. The majority of criminal cases taken to court fall under their authority. But these prosecutions are usually of routine traffic or licensing infractions.

Most serious crimes go directly to the district attorneys, some of whom are under very nominal control by a state official. These prosecutors and their thousands of employees handle the bulk of major cases. Most district attorneys (their exact titles differ by region) are elected on a county basis; four eastern states have an appointive system. The type of agency maintained under these officials varies greatly in size and organization. Most, reflecting the rural nature of their sections, are necessarily quite small. In fact, many American prosecutors work part-time, maintaining a private law practice to supplement their limited salaries. On the other hand, the district attorneys in large urban areas may employ scores of lawyers, secretaries, and investigators. Their benefits of office frequently include high rates of pay and the power of considerable political patronage.[9]

In general, attorneys who work for prosecutors have relatively low salaries and little in the form of job protection. Apart from young lawyers anxious for trial experience, the ranks tend to be filled by those who cannot find better positions. This tends to create a condition where lower ranks have rapid turnover while those of higher supervisory capacity become dependent on political support during elections. The total prosecutorial expense in the nation comprises about 5 percent of all criminal justice expenditures;[10] this fact may contribute toward a combination of limited professional opportunity and occasionally rather gross maneuvering for public attention.

The district attorney in a rural section may, personally, deal with almost every type of offense, from murder to theft. In an urban setting, by contrast, the chief prosecutor serves primarily as an administrator who makes decisions involving particular cases and appears in court only in unusual circumstances. His office will probably be quite specialized, with separate branches for felonies, bad checks, family disputes, or similar designations. It would, however, be a mistake to associate size with efficiency; to a large degree, the benefits of individual attention are lost in large organizations.

In many jurisdictions, the independent district attorneys and their investigators possess the same legal authority as policemen. Ordinarily, prosecutors rely on regular law enforcement agencies to supply charges of regular street crimes. They are, however, frequently called upon by complaints from citizens to investigate many business offenses and violations against the family. Some district attorneys also direct efforts against organized criminals, vice activities, and corruption of other officials. The exact relationship between police and prosecutors varies widely in different localities. In some communities, particularly small towns, they may work in close cooperation; in other districts, there can be competition, contradiction, or outright antagonism. At times, the police and prosecutor, because of quite different roles, operate apart and with mutual misunderstanding.

Because responsibility in larger offices must be delegated, agents of the district attorney possess far-reaching and arbitrary discretion. They have the duty to conduct preliminary investigations to determine if charges appear justified, to decide when to press prosecution either directly or through the grand jury, and to actually prepare and present the resulting case. Conversely, the district attorneys and their assistants can determine when not to proceed with an accusation. In the early stages, they exercise almost unlimited authority to release a suspect and, even after formal indictment, it is possible for them to withdraw charges by entry of *nolle prosequi* (a declaration of no further intent to prosecute).

A great deal of discretionary judgment, largely without court supervision, is involved in the operations of the district attorneys.[11] This truly immense power may, of course, be used for good or evil; it can be a vital militating element in the harsh realities of modern criminal justice or a threat to personal freedom. Examples of both aspects exist throughout the nation. Prosecutors dismiss or reduce the charge in about half of the serious cases involving adults. In many instances, these actions are meritorious, as are occasional efforts by independent prosecutors to directly expose malfeasance and crime. On the other hand, discretionary justice always opens the door to favoritism and corruption. With virtually unrestricted power to both accuse and discharge suspects, opportunities for extortion and bribery abound. In most instances, the negative facets tend to be subtle rather than overt, but the danger of improper and unethical conduct remains very high.[12]

The key to understanding the prosecutorial system is political. Elected district attorneys with extensive control over individual liberty create a dangerous formula. It sometimes surfaces in personal vendettas, crusades for publicity, or improper announcements concerning unproven guilt. Prosecutors (many of whom move on to judicial positions) should be above either imposition of personal concepts of morality or more obvious forms of political maneuvering. Unfortunately, both varieties of misconduct exist in America. Our scheme of popularly chosen prosecutors and wide discretion does maintain the invaluable benefit of ultimate community control, but it also poses serious problems of public and personal justice.

Defense Counsel

The counterparts of prosecutors are, of course, the lawyers for the defense. Only a small percentage of privately practicing attorneys take substantial numbers of criminal cases. Most work alone or in small firms; few large law partnerships encourage or even accept such financially unrewarding activity. The majority of regular defense attorneys deal with great numbers of lesser offenses, including traffic infractions. There are, in addition, a few lawyers of wide reputation who tend to monopolize the rare instances where prosperous citizens stand accused of serious violations. These well-known defenders are colorful and expert but scarcely represent the real criminal bar.

It is difficult to underestimate the role of counsel acting in behalf of an accused. With our entire system based upon concepts of adversary practice, a suspect without a lawyer automatically acquires a tremendous handicap. Although no exact comparison can be made, it appears that the rate of conviction drops by about 50 percent whenever defendants acquire counsel. How does this great discrepancy occur when the state is supposed to bear the great burden of proving guilt? It happens because a trained and experienced lawyer knows how to exploit weaknesses in the prosecution's case and marshal evidence of innocence. Without these benefits, a suspect may often be taken advantage of by police or the district attorney.[13]

A skillful defender recognizes that no advantage comes from total submission and attempts to create obstacles for the prosecution. In routine practice, this means pleading a client not guilty, delaying the trial, and threatening to undermine the state's case. Although some measures may reach the borderline of ethical standards, the defense counsel plays in a dirty game with more than monetary rewards at stake. He knows, for example, that chances of success increase markedly with passage of time and, therefore, he contributes to the slow machinations of justice. Defenders will sometimes initiate tactics designed to cause delay: exercising full rights to a jury, refusing to waive procedural formalities, and entering numerous pretrial motions. Such measures can become weapons for an accused, and no lawyer can afford to overlook them despite theoretical preachments on impractical standards for desired conduct. Finally, the experienced counsel realizes that the quest for total victory may lead to disaster; he understands that maximum benefits for a client can come through negotiation and compromise.[14] The defender must act as champion, intermediary, and counsellor simultaneously.

The vital part played by attorneys is recognized in law. Under Amendment VI of the U.S. Constitution, "In all criminal prosecutions, the accused shall . . . have the Assistance of Counsel for his defence." Today, this means that all persons threatened with confinement must be afforded a lawyer, even if the suspect does not have the means to hire one himself. In short, the right to an attorney is a fundamental right; the burden of defense rests upon the state as well as on the individual.

In truth, the responsibility of government to defend as well as prosecute is somewhat limited. Such a duty extends only to indigents (persons unable to afford bail or counsel) accused of either felony or misdemeanor offenses made punishable by confinement in prison or jail. Nevertheless, nothing requires the state to extend the means to investigate, import witnesses, and conduct scientific examinations readily available to the prosecutor.[15]

Relatively little government money is spent on defense: Perhaps 1 percent of the entire sum expended on criminal justice goes for this purpose. The scope of the problem, however, looms much larger than indicated by public cost. An estimated 35 percent of all defendants cannot afford a lawyer, while the proportion among felony suspects runs to 60 percent. Most of the people tried for serious crimes have insufficient money or property to provide themselves with an adequate defense.[16]

Counsellors for indigents are supplied in three major ways that vary in detail throughout the nation. The majority of states and localities use a system whereby attorneys receive part-time defense assignments from courts. Refusal to serve would be considered highly improper, and limited compensation may be authorized based upon duties performed. The assigned counsel system has several significant flaws. Lawyers who receive such responsibilities may demonstrate a lack of experience, interest, or concern with criminal matters. There sometimes exists a tendency either to plead a client guilty to save time or to extend the case for lengthy periods to increase fees. Most assigned counsels do neither and sincerely attempt to adequately perform their often undesired tasks despite limited enthusiasm for such causes.

The second basic method for providing indigents with attorneys is found in the office of public defenders. These regular government employees have as their full-time job the provision of legal aid to the poor. The system, now found in several hundred locations across the nation, is opposite yet similar to the prosecutor's agency. It also tends to utilize somewhat less than outstanding lawyers because of limited remuneration and opportunity. However, public defenders can likewise develop considerable skill and efficiency in repetitiously dealing with criminal cases. Unlike assigned counsel, they may rely on established agency procedures and may develop close connections with their legal adversaries in the prosecutorial arm. These can become quite significant advantages, especially within the bureaucratic organization of urban justice.[17]

The third and final scheme of affording counsel for the poor is through the voluntary defender. This arrangement exists only in a few areas, often in the form of extended legal aid (which is usually limited to civil cases). Voluntary defenders are normally organized by agencies, often privately sponsored with public support. Such a system benefits somewhat from the absence of direct government control but is usually restricted in resources, personnel, and facilities.

It is difficult to generalize about criminal defense in the United States because of the enormous variation which exists. The different systems of providing counsel for indigents and the diverse capabilities of practitioners combine to extend over a spectrum from superb to terrible. However, it cannot be denied that money is the primary determinant of a strong defense. The American system continues to operate to the considerable disadvantage of the poor, for they must face the organized and structured office of the prosecutor without truly comparable assistance of counsel. As long as a dependence on part-time defenders is necessitated, it might seem that a balance might accrue from utilization of assigned prosecutors as well. That, in essence, has been the scheme relied upon quite successfully in Great Britain for many years.

Plea-Bargaining

A tremendous number of criminal cases are actually settled outside of court. Well over half of all serious offenses reach their critical stage in the process of justice with what is known as plea-bargaining. Ordinarily, this consists of negotiations between prosecutor and defense counsel. Most cases are settled and decided before they ever come to a judge.

It might seem unlikely that a prosecutor would ever wish to enter an agreement with a suspect, but this ignores the realities of our antiquated system. In truth, the present structure would simply collapse without extensive plea-bargaining. If most defendants were to insist upon having full legal rights and privileges, the prosecutors and courts would quickly become hopelessly entangled and overburdened; a breakdown of unprecedented magnitude would rapidly develop. Consequently, negotiation occurs for purposes of superficial efficiency.

District attorneys work under a constant demand to maximize convictions and avoid acquittals; between these extremes a variety of useful alternatives exists. The greatest asset of a prosecutor's job is the guilty plea, for work can be simplified and time saved whenever a defendant admits responsibility. Perhaps surprisingly, this occurs in about 90 percent of all cases, including two of every three felony charges brought to court. To some degree, such an apparent phenomenon of conscience takes place because prosecutors dismiss the weakest cases outright and concentrate on those offering stronger evidence.[18]

The primary explanation of so many guilty pleas is the direct result of bargaining. Considerable pressure may be applied to a suspect through overcharging (increasing the degree of crime associated with a particular act), menacing relatives and friends, and threatening imposition of the heaviest possible sentences. These methods are, regrettably, quite routine.

Prosecutors negotiate for many reasons. The simple desire to expedite the case and reduce a backlog is probably most common. They also may seek to get a conviction, of any sort, when evidence is weak and might not support a contested determination of guilt. At times the prosecutor may wish to individualize a sentence, avoiding minimum penalties imposed by law or perhaps providing for disposition outside the formal scheme of justice. And, finally, he might be willing to exchange leniency for information on other crimes and offenders.

What does the prosecutor offer in exchange for pleas of guilty, testimony, or other desired performance by a suspect? He may, of course, promise to forego persecution of friends, accomplices, or relatives, but the usual consideration accrues directly to the defendant. Perhaps the most frequent benefit is that of a sentence recommendation to the judge; a guilty plea receives, in return, an agreement that the prosecutor will request less than the maximum possible punishment. The second, and frequently combined offer, is for acceptance of a reduced charge. A prosecutor will generally substitute a lesser offense for a major one in exchange for sufficient cooperation from a suspect. Finally, total dismissal of the case, regardless of apparent guilt, may be offered.[19] A diagram of dispositions for major offenses at all stages is presented in Fig. 4.

Often these lenient gestures are combined. Suppose police apprehend an offender in the course of an aggravated assault, and investigation reveals him to be wanted for a similar crime. In return for an agreement to admit guilt in one case, the prosecutor might offer to reduce the charge to simple (rather than aggravated) assault, recommend probation to the judge, and dismiss the second matter entirely. Everyone directly involved in the system benefits: The police record two clearances by arrest; the district attorney gets credit for a conviction (without need for a contested trial); the judge saves time and trouble; and the criminal receives only probation for two serious violations. The public, of course, may eventually suffer from such exchanges of leniency and expediency. But many aspects of justice indicate little consideration of the people.

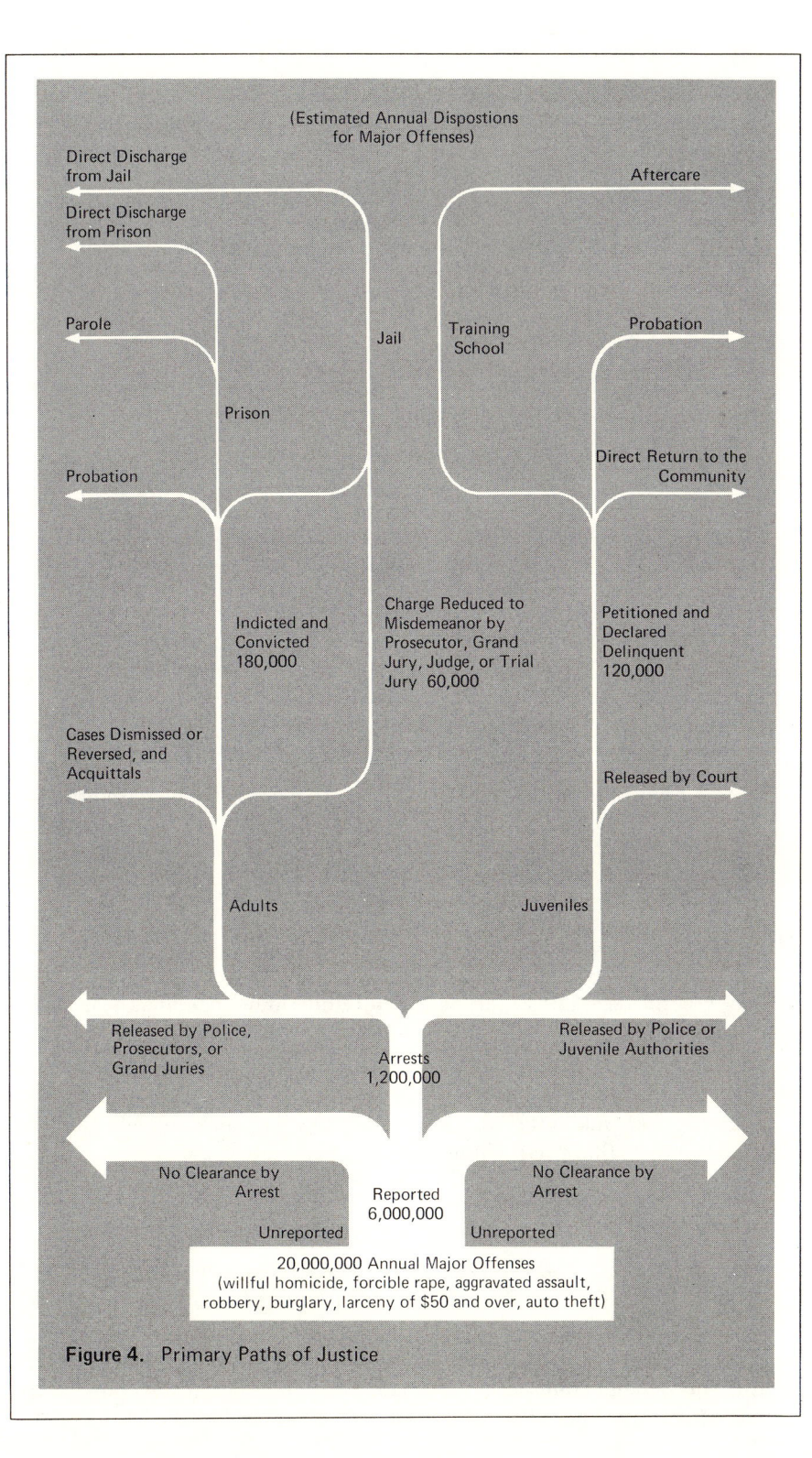

(Estimated Annual Dispostions for Major Offenses)

Direct Discharge from Jail

Direct Discharge from Prison

Aftercare

Parole

Jail

Training School

Probation

Prison

Probation

Direct Return to the Community

Indicted and Convicted 180,000

Charge Reduced to Misdemeanor by Prosecutor, Grand Jury, Judge, or Trial Jury 60,000

Petitioned and Declared Delinquent 120,000

Cases Dismissed or Reversed, and Acquittals

Released by Court

Adults

Juveniles

Released by Police, Prosecutors, or Grand Juries

Arrests 1,200,000

Released by Police or Juvenile Authorities

No Clearance by Arrest

Reported 6,000,000

No Clearance by Arrest

Unreported

Unreported

20,000,000 Annual Major Offenses
(willful homicide, forcible rape, aggravated assault, robbery, burglary, larceny of $50 and over, auto theft)

Figure 4. Primary Paths of Justice

Negotiated pleas are not binding upon the court. Judges occasionally disregard recommendations in passing sentence, but they ordinarily play a more delicate role in the process of bargained justice. A ritualistic denial of any agreement may be required although negotiations occur with overt regularity. Most judges desire expedited cases and rarely inquire too deeply into open admissions of guilt. Modern practice, however, generally requires a satisfactory basis for the plea, comprehension on the defendant's part, and appropriateness of the recommended sentence. According to the procedural rules of particular jurisdictions the court may also be called upon to approve dismissal or reduction of charges after the indictment stage, but this normally becomes a mere formality.

Although judges may choose to ignore the typical bargaining process, they sometimes must interfere to preserve a primary level of fairness. Otherwise, prosecutors might obtain admissions of guilt through outright deceit. Where promises are broken, the courts intervene and permit pleas to be withdrawn.[20] Without this safeguard, a suspect would be at the mercy of an unscrupulous district attorney. On the other hand, once a defendant makes a voluntary and knowing plea, and a prosecutor fulfills his agreement, the admission of guilt will normally be considered as conclusive.[21]

The widespread use of plea-bargaining creates many problems for American justice. Most obvious is the distinct possibility that perfectly innocent persons may be coerced into pleading guilty. Where traditional means of establishing responsibility and punishment become secondary to bureaucratic or judicial expediency, doubt arises as to the entire system's reliability. The role of the court is theoretically considered as central to determination of guilt; in practice, it has become an adjunct to administrative procedure. This is but one cause of a gulf between written and actual law in the United States. Such a condition and general use of negotiated pleas tend to undermine confidence in our scheme of justice. There must be flexibility to allow for unusual circumstances and conditions; the need for flexibility does not require the substitution of arbitrary power for the hard won protections of personal liberty and of public safety. Some authorities have recently gone as far as proposing the total elimination of negotiated pleas.[22]

Summary

Release after arrest frequently depends on bail. Those unable to post the required bond may languish in jail for lengthy periods under appalling conditions.

Adversary practice is the system of controversy between prosecutors and defense counsel. Unfortunately, criminal law repels most leading attorneys. The prosecutor possesses great power and discretion.

This condition is made critical by pronounced political considerations on the part of many district attorneys.

Defense counsel, by comparison, operates in relative independence. Because most of the people accused of serious offenses are indigent, it has become the responsibility of the government to provide attorneys. Such defenders may be assigned, publicly employed, or voluntary.

Most serious criminal charges are actually determined before trial through plea-bargaining. Negotiations between prosecutors and defenders provide flexibility, speed, and simplicity, but also pose a continuing threat to the system of justice.

Questions

1. What problems are associated with the bail system?
2. Why is adversary practice significant?
3. What are the functions of the prosecutor?
4. How are indigents afforded counsel?
5. Why does plea-bargaining exist?

NOTES

[1] 18 United States Code 3146; California Penal Code, sec. 1318; Illinois Revised Statutes, chapter 38, sec. 110–2; New York Criminal Procedure Law, sec. 500.10.2; Texas Code of Criminal Procedure, art. 17.031.

[2] Ramsey Clark, *Crime in America* (New York: Simon & Schuster, 1970), pp. 299–304; Charles E. Ares, Anne Rankin, and Herbert Sturz, "The Manhattan Bail Project," *New York University Law Review* 38 (January, 1963), pp. 71–92.

[3] Frederic Suffet, "Bail Setting: A Study of Courtroom Interaction," *Crime and Delinquency* 12 (October, 1966), pp. 318–331.

[4] District of Columbia Code, sec. 23–1322; *Compilation and Use of Criminal Court Data in Relation to Pre-Trial Release of Defendants* (Washington: GPO, 1970), pp. 7–9.

[5] *National Jail Census 1970* (Washington: GPO, 1971), pp. 1–3.

[6] Lewis Mayers, *The American Legal System* (New York: Harper & Row, 1964), pp. 99–102.

[7] Abraham S. Blumberg, "The Practice of Law as Confidence Game: Organizational Cooptation of a Profession," *Law and Society Review* 1 (June, 1967), pp. 15–39.

[8] Leonard Downie, *Justice Denied* (Baltimore: Penguin, 1972), pp. 159–176.

[9] *Standards Relating to The Prosecution Function and The Defense Function* (N.p., American Bar Association, 1970), pp. 48–76.

[10] *Expenditure and Employment Data for the Criminal Justice System, 1970–71* (Washington: GPO, 1973), p. 11.

[11] George F. Cole, "The Decision to Prosecute," *Law and Society Review* 4 (February, 1970), pp. 313–343.

[12] Alcorta v. Texas, 355 U.S. 28, 78 S.Ct. 103 (1957); Brady v. Maryland, 373 U.S. 83, 83 S.Ct. 1194 (1963).

[13] Lewis R. Katz, "Municipal Courts—Another Urban Ill," *Case Western Reserve Law Review* 20 (November, 1968), pp. 87–139.

[14] *Rehabilitative and Planning Services for the Criminal Defense* (Washington: GPO, 1970), pp. 88–91.

[15] Gideon v. Wainwright, 372 U.S. 335, 83 S.Ct. 792 (1963); Argersinger v. Hamlin, 407 U.S. 25, 92 S.Ct. 2006 (1972).

[16] *The Challenge of Crime in a Free Society* (Washington: GPO, 1967), p. 131.

[17] David Sudnow, "Normal Crimes: Sociological Features of the Penal Code in a Public Defender Office," *Social Problems* 12 (Winter, 1965), pp. 255–276.

[18] *The Challenge of Crime in a Free Society*, pp. 134–136, 262–263; Arthur Rosett, "The Negotiated Guilty Plea," *Annals of the American Academy of Political and Social Science* 374 (November, 1967), pp. 71–81.

[19] Donald J. Newman, "Pleading Guilty for Considerations: A Study of Bargain Justice," *Journal of Criminal Law, Criminology and Police Science* 46 (March–April, 1956), pp. 780–790.

[20] Santobello v. New York, 404 U.S. 257, 92 S.Ct. 495 (1971).

[21] North Carolina v. Alford, 400 U.S. 25, 91 S.Ct. 160 (1970); Dukes v. Warden, 406 U.S. 250, 92 S.Ct. 1551 (1972).

[22] *Courts* (Washington: GPO, 1973), pp. 46–49.

Chapter 10
Judicial Systems

"In court men study only their owne fortunes."
COTGRAVE

Accusation

American courts reflect the proudest heritage of the English-speaking world, but they also contain a number of serious national problems. This peculiar paradox developed largely through continued failure to adapt traditional procedures to our modern society. Decades of simple neglect and strong political resistance have combined to create a strange situation in which ancient methods of protecting individual liberty become causes of judicial inefficiency.

Before approaching the subject of criminal courts, it is wise to recall that only a fraction of all those arrested reach the stage of prosecution. Juveniles constitute a very large portion of persons arrested, and they must usually be handled by entirely separate systems of justice. Among adults, multitudes are quickly released by police or other authorities. Overall, about 20 percent of reported major violations result in apprehensions, and by no means all of those conclude in someone facing criminal charges.[1] These simple facts should dispel any notion of a direct connection between statutory violations and our courts. So few offenders reach the stage of prosecution as to raise serious questions about the old adage, "Crime does not pay." Considering the percentages of violations unreported, offenders never apprehended, and suspects released or referred elsewhere by law enforcement agencies, it should be clear that the present system serves more as a sieve than as a funnel leading to prosecution, as Fig. 4 may easily indicate.

The comparatively few who are arrested and held may eventually face formal accusation. Prosecutors and grand jurymen ordinarily perform this task in the overwhelming majority of cases. Possible homicides include an extra phase, investigation by the coroner or medical examiner. These officials determine the general cause of death—accidental, natural, or otherwise—but leave the question of personal guilt unanswered. Some jurisdictions retain the old position of elected coroners, who conduct inquests with small juries of citizens. The complexities of forensic science and a desire to remove criminal investigations from the realm of politics has, however, led to creation of the newer posts for medical examiners. Certain states and most large communities now utilize appointed doctors to perform necessary inquiries into the cause of suspicious deaths. The heavy responsibility and technical difficulties of modern autopsies appear to demand the services of trained and experienced experts rather than well-meaning but often uninformed politicians.

In many jurisdictions, felonies are taken before a grand jury. Usually composed of established citizens serving for several months, it carries the responsibility of deciding, in private, whether or not sufficient evidence exists for a suspect to be brought to trial. The grand jury may indict or *true bill*, upon substantiation of the charge presented by the prosecutor. They also can ordinarily reduce the case to a misdemeanor or decide to simply *no bill* a party and so discharge him. The role of grand juror varies by custom and personality. Most closely follow suggestions by the prosecuting attorney, but some act with greater initiative and independence.

Approximately half of the states rely upon the grand jury only in unusual circumstances. In such jurisdictions, the prosecutor may proceed on the basis of information rather than indictment for felonies and misdemeanors alike. Every state permits lesser charges to be brought directly in this manner. The vast majority of all criminal accusations are, of course, actually determined by the police and prosecutor. Grand jurors play a significant role only in regard to more serious offenses within certain parts of the country.[2]

In most of the cases reaching the trial stage, accusation remains a formality. Nearly 90 percent of all criminal charges concern rarely contested parking or traffic infractions which seldom require attention from prosecutors. Routine public offenses such as drunkenness, disorderly conduct, and petty theft comprise a large majority of the remaining accusations. These common misdemeanors, many times more numerous than felonies, are routinely processed en masse by lower courts. In such situations, arrest, charge, verdict, and sentence follow in rapid and almost automatic sequence. The formal process of accusation is important as a means of downgrading initial charges, but it may also serve to screen out weaker or undesirable cases.

Founded upon principles of common law, our judicial concepts demand that the prosecution sustain the burden of proof. Unlike some nations, English-speaking countries do not permit the state to gather evidence through what is termed the inquisitorial system. In America, the accusation must be independently supported if the defendant chooses to be silent; this is the great significance of the adage, "Every man is presumed innocent until proven guilty." In practice, it may not seem to be invariably true, but it represents the highest and most distinguished principle of common law. Derived long ago from continental usage, the presumption of innocence has become a fundamental element in American criminal justice.

Jurisdiction

Before trial may be held, the proper location and court must be determined, and this leads to questions of *jurisdiction* and *venue*. The two terms are quite distinct but closely related. Briefly, jurisdiction refers to the power of a court to try a certain case; venue deals with the actual place where trial occurs. Both must be correct, or the prosecution will be deemed improper and illegal.

Jurisdiction is established by reference to statutes. In effect, these restrict the authority of courts to certain geographic areas and a particular range of subjects or persons. Criminal jurisdiction is normally referred to as *general* (having power to hear felony charges) or *limited* (permission to try lesser violations, usually misdemeanors or crimes subject only to fine). High courts often possess no authority to decide original cases and obtain such matters only by way of appeal. It should, of course, be apparent that thousands of jurisdictions exist within the United States and may overlap to a considerable degree. Ordinarily, the statutes will specify which type of court should receive a particular case, but a choice (usually made by the prosecutor) sometimes exists between possible alternatives. When overlapping occurs, the jurisdiction is properly termed *concurrent*. When just one court has statutory power to hear a case, its authority should be called *exclusive*. Some acts violate both state and federal law while other violations may be taken before several different judges.[3] Most prosecutors and courts are perfectly willing, if not anxious, to relieve their overcrowded schedules and forego claims to cases in which others express interest.

In most instances, the primary difficulties over jurisdiction involve geography. Questions sometimes arise as to the exact place of an offense, for this can determine the proper court to hear the case. To simplify such problems, some states have county line provisions which extend jurisdiction for several hundred feet and eliminate most critical disputes over location. Occasionally, difficulties arise involving crimes committed by persons in passage through various sections, typically in a moving automobile. State laws now often provide that any jurisdiction along the path may take the case if the exact point at which the offense occurred cannot be determined.

Venue refers to selection of the actual place of trial once jurisdiction has been established. The logical and usual location is the site of the crime. In other words, venue lies where the offense occurred. Long ago, when community influence remained strong, the place where jurymen were chosen often determined the outcome of a trial. Venue still has the added meaning of the source of jurors and the location of the court which finally hears and decides the case. At times, the places of offense and trial may be separated by considerable distances. It is not unusual for defendants in major cases to request and be granted a change of venue so that trial may be shifted to another and more suitable site.

Sometimes a court encounters difficulty in obtaining jurisdiction over a suspect, particularly when he is absent from the state. In such situations, officials can resort to extradition. Briefly, this amounts to a request for the surrender of a person between cooperating jurisdictions. Statutes provide for rather rapid transfer of wanted fugitives from one city or town to another. When state borders must be crossed, extradition becomes somewhat more complex. Generally, the domestic governments and police forces work fairly closely together in permitting removal of those already in custody. On rare occasions, however, a state may feel that the wanted person may not be treated fairly if returned and therefore refuse to deliver the fugitive.

Far more involved are extraditions from other nations. Today, many countries cooperate with one another for the exchange of wanted fugitives and specify procedures in formal treaties. Defendants in major crimes, especially those involving counterfeiting or swindling, can no longer expect to find refuge in other nations. When the crime reflects political or social attitudes, however, countries sometimes reject requests for extradition. Most nations are quite reluctant to permit removal of their own citizens, although they may have committed offenses elsewhere.[4]

Sometimes a policeman will briefly go beyond his jurisdictional limits to make an arrest. Generally, this is permitted as "hot pursuit" across local or even state boundaries. The officer must then, however, take the person apprehended to a judge where the arrest occurred instead of returning him directly to the original jurisdiction. Many of our states, as opposed to nations, have entered compacts with established procedures to be followed in situations involving actual and direct pursuit of fugitives.

Should either jurisdiction or venue be held improper under statutory law, the prosecution must fail. The court lacks suitable authority, because of position or location, to hear the case. At times, such problems can be simply remedied by transferring the defendant or case elsewhere. But, if these measures conflict with established law, the only recourse becomes outright dismissal of the charges.

Courts

Comprehension of our rather involved court system requires an understanding of bisovereignty. The heart of the U.S. Constitution provides for separate federal and state systems, each retaining independence within specified areas. Consequently, we have two kinds of governmental sovereignty, with authority to organize and maintain courts. Federal and state judicial systems parallel each other in many ways, but they are separate and represent quite different authorities. Bisovereignty may seem confusing and at times inefficient, but it remains the basic element of our unique Constitution.

Federal courts with 7,000 employees try those accused of violations against laws of the United States. Most offenses involve state or local regulations, and they must be taken before different judges. Federal courts naturally devote most of their time to civil rather than criminal matters, but violations of penal laws are rising with expansion of national prohibitions. Many, but by no means all, of these offenses carry relatively heavy penalties.

The federal courts are organized in three basic tiers. Original and general jurisdiction attaches at the district level. There, juries and judges make fundamental determinations of guilt and punishment. In addition, U.S. magistrates (formerly called commissioners) may hear minor offenses, including traffic infractions, against the national government.[5] Judges of the federal courts are appointed by the President with approval of the Senate. On the district level, this means that nearly all those designated will have been active in the Chief Executive's political party and are acceptable to both senators of the locality concerned.

There are nearly 400 judges organized into about 100 courts of original federal jurisdiction. Heavily populated states are divided into more than one district which may be split, in turn, into several divisions. When necessary, judges can, of course, be temporarily moved about to meet imbalanced dockets (schedules of cases to be heard).

Above the districts are several Courts of Appeal and the single Supreme Court of the United States. The intermediate appellate level has about 100 judges grouped unevenly into ten numbered circuits plus one separately designated to hear the mass of questions coming from the District of Columbia. The Supreme Court has nine justices and ordinarily handles only appeals coming up through the federal system or directly from the highest tribunals of the states. The national system

140   THE COURTS

displays relative uniformity and simplicity throughout, though procedural differences exist.

As every state names and organizes its own courts, great variation might reasonably be anticipated. Apart from separation by limited, general, and appellate jurisdiction, there are few common features. Throughout the states, for example, the court exercising broad authority over criminal offenses may be called district, superior, oyer and terminer, supreme, common pleas, jail and delivery, quarter sessions, or otherwise. Of course, the jurisdiction of each can only be determined

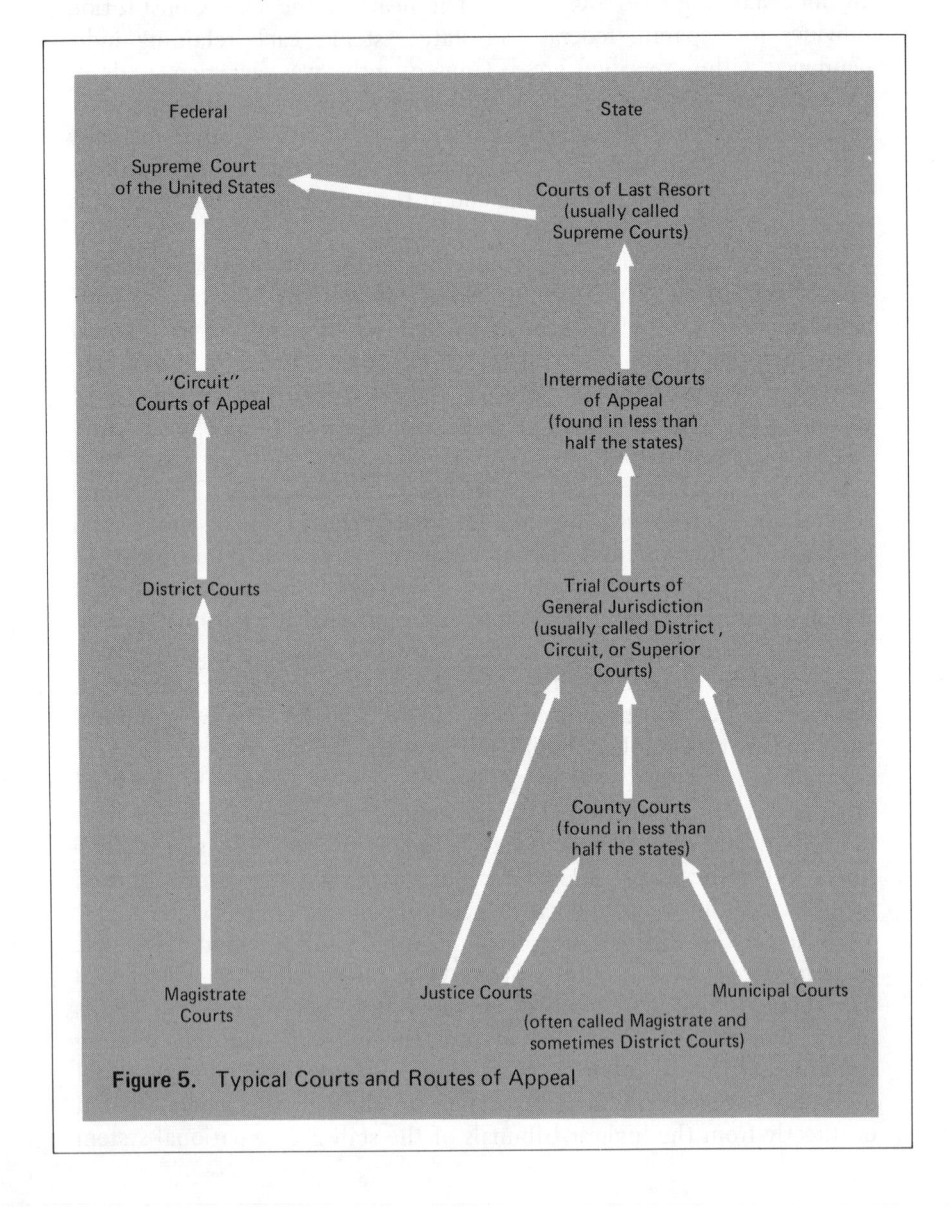

Figure 5. Typical Courts and Routes of Appeal

Federal:
- Supreme Court of the United States
- "Circuit" Courts of Appeal
- District Courts
- Magistrate Courts

State:
- Courts of Last Resort (usually called Supreme Courts)
- Intermediate Courts of Appeal (found in less than half the states)
- Trial Courts of General Jurisdiction (usually called District, Circuit, or Superior Courts)
- County Courts (found in less than half the states)
- Justice Courts (often called Magistrate and sometimes District Courts)
- Municipal Courts

through reference to the laws under which they operate. Figure 5 is a diagram of both the federal and typical state court systems showing their parallel but interrelated structures.

All together the nation has more than 3,000 state courts exercising control over criminal matters, with about 20,000 employees. The judges, most of whom handle civil cases as well, ordinarily deal with the felonies causing greatest public alarm: murder, rape, burglary, robbery, grand theft, and other serious cases. About half the states have county courts as well with a form of limited jurisdiction between the equivalent of district and purely local tribunals. Statutes and customs often assign only civil matters to particular judges. The name of a court does not invariably indicate exercise of authority.

States delegate a great deal of judicial responsibility to smaller units of government. In practice, this has led to creation of local courts with limited but significant power. The nation contains thousands of such entities with a combined work force of 90,000.[6] Bearing such typical names as municipal, traffic, police, corporation, or justice of the peace courts, they account for the vast majority of all criminal cases. Here judges determine the routine automobile violations and the multitude of such frequent misdemeanors as drunkenness, disorderly conduct, and petty theft.

Frankly, it is misleading to refer to most of the hearings in our local courts as trials. There, at least 80 percent of the defendants quickly plead guilty, very few have counsel, only a small percentage escape punishment, while most are merely fined and released. In the almost automatic sequence, guilt and sentence appear predetermined. Courts disregard constitutional and statutory rights and simply process defendants en masse. Many local judges handle 30,000 or more cases a year! As a consequence, the typical trial lasts but a few moments, and in some instances, the officiating magistrate merely glances at the arrest report, "make sheet" (police record), and the defendant before passing sentence. It is quite possible to find those accused of similar crimes to be presented for unanimous pleas of guilty.[7]

The problems of American courts are unfortunately most evident at the lower level, the only one frequently encountered by ordinary citizens. Few people could honestly report that such contacts instill respect for our system of criminal justice. Not without reason, some conclude that it appears geared for the mechanical exploitation of the unfortunate.[8] With growing alarm, a few states have recently moved toward greater standardization and minimal standards for all courts. Such efforts will, hopefully, lead to significant improvement and restoration of the element of personal concern so necessary to practical justice.

Federal, state, and local courts must devote a great deal of time to functions other than actual trials. The public view may be one of criminal judges determining guilt and deciding sentences. In truth, much effort concerns applications for warrants, preliminary appearances and pleas by suspects, pretrial motions, selection of jurors, sanity hearings, assignment and payment of counsel, writs of *habeas corpus*, and a host of similar activities. Some matters may be handled through private office routine (in chambers), but they constitute essential if less dramatic aspects of the judicial system.

A good deal of interest has been recently generated in attempts to reform the administration of our court systems. Certainly, some progress might be made through better management of existing facilities.[9] In essence, however, the operations of our courts depend far more on the quality of personnel than on schemes of organization and communication. With human liberty at stake, justice should invariably take precedence over efficiency.

Judges

Trial judges occupy a very crucial position within the process of American criminal justice. They preside over, influence, or directly make the critical determinations of guilt and punishment. Regardless of the government they serve or the jurisdiction of their court, decisions from the bench mark the ultimate difference between tragic misuse of power and balanced protection of public interest.

In general, we have a judiciary of politicians. This condition does not reflect upon overall quality but results from our system of selection. There are two basic means by which judges achieve office in the United States: appointment (ordinarily for an indefinite term) and election (usually for a period of only a few years). Criminal courts of all types and levels have vacancies filled by one or the other method.

A minority of the states utilize some form of the appointive scheme, but most allow the governor, rather than the legislature, to make the selection. Within recent years, the Missouri Plan has attained considerable popularity. This variation permits the governor to choose among candidates nominated by a bipartisan committee and requires those newly appointed to eventually seek voter approval.

Most states retain an elective system for their judges. However, a division occurs between those relying on identification by political affiliation and ballots lacking such information. Closely contested elections are, nevertheless, comparatively infrequent, and once achieved, the position tends to become secure.[10]

Strangely, the two basically different schemes of selection produce similar results. While most positions are elective, about half of American judges were initially appointed to fill vacancies. This phenomenon may contribute to the prevalence of former prosecutors, legislators, and government attorneys (rather than practicing lawyers) upon the bench.

Also, it cannot be denied that either appointment or election depends largely upon strong political support.

Many judicial positions carry with them considerable privileges of reward through patronage. Courts regularly employ commissioners, clerks, bailiffs, reporters, probation officers, stenographers, and secretaries. Such positions are usually filled by the presiding judge, and great numbers of relatives, personal friends, or those of political use consequently receive the available jobs.

While judicial salaries may not be the highest incomes of the legal profession, they are higher than the average of other criminal justice workers. Not only do judges and their employees get better compensation, they have tended to enjoy the greatest increases within the last few years. At the local level, the income situation is a bit peculiar. Most justices of the peace continue to be paid through the outmoded and much denounced fee system, whereby remuneration depends upon cases tried. In fact, there are even jurisdictions which reward their magistrates according to the number of convictions, a practice held unconstitutional by the Supreme Court half a century ago![11]

Despite growing attention and sincere effort, the quality of American criminal judges leaves something to be desired. Some never finished high school; half possess college degrees; still fewer are licensed attorneys; and only a small number could claim experience in defense or prosecution. Formal or practical education is certainly no guarantee of character and ability, but the present situation remains cause for concern. Perhaps of even greater alarm is the realization that certain criminal judges have never even visited the jails and prisons which contain their unwilling subjects.

There is, unfortunately, no simple test of potential character. Consequently, few meaningful standards exist for candidates for many judicial positions. As yet, most training programs are voluntary and cursory. Moreover, the removal of judges (usually by impeachment or forced retirement) poses serious problems. A politically entrenched magistrate enjoys almost absolute job security.

In a sense, our judges serve as policemen for lawyers. They must attempt to preserve the confidence and respect of all parties. Judges have the delicate task of avoiding both arrogance and passivity while protecting the interests of the public, defendants, and witnesses alike. A good magistrate must be knowledgeable, understanding, reliable, honest, fair, humane, and reasonable simultaneously. Furthermore, such traits are subject to constant stress and pressure. The judge represents society, but we expect him to demonstrate only our most desirable features.

Those serving in American courts do not always fulfill the highest possible requirements of office. Some judges are senile, prejudiced, vindictive, uninformed, lazy, or even corrupt. Yet, the majority certainly strive to objectively maintain the great principles of our civilization.[12] Regardless of personal flaws, incidents of penal law being imposed for political purposes are very, very rare in the United States. Not all nations possess such an invaluable heritage.

History demonstrates that judges should be independent from community pressures but still responsive to public interest. Such a balance is most difficult to obtain. Failure to do so, however, may result in recognition of mob rule or governmental tyranny.

Juries

The concept of a jury extends far back in common law. Originally, citizens were assembled only to give evidence of violations, but they eventually became responsible for pronouncing guilt. It was not until the seventeenth century that jurymen in England and America achieved true independence from judges and came to represent the power of the free community. Their unique ability to protect against abusive action by government earned due recognition in the Bill of Rights. As Amendment VI provides, "In all criminal prosecutions, the accused shall enjoy the right to a speedy and public trial, by an impartial jury of the State and district wherein the crime shall have been committed . . ." This clear language bound the federal government after 1791 but, oddly enough, has not yet been applied to state cases involving only fines or sentences of less than six months.[13]

While juries are technically available for all serious criminal charges, defendants frequently negotiate guilty pleas and waive their rights. It is only in the relatively few contested misdemeanors and felonies where heavy penalties may be imposed that claims for jury trial occur. Such insistence, often discouraged by prosecutors and magistrates alike, ordinarily means delay (perhaps while the defendant remains in jail), possibly more severe final sentences, and payment of additional fees and court costs.

Petit (trial) juries serve in no more than 10 percent of major criminal cases because most defendants simply plead guilty or elect to appear only before a judge. Nevertheless, the possibility of a demand provides a basis for considerable negotiation and bargaining between defense and prosecution. Generally, rural areas rely upon juries to a far greater extent than do cities. Perhaps the most serious effect urbanization has had on criminal justice is a destruction of community interest and involvement. The problem of public support exists in all phases but becomes most obvious at trial itself.

The typical American citizen regards jury service as a distasteful imposition. As each state sets its own standards and many judges have individual policies, those selected represent divergent aspects of society.

Generally, most of those old enough to vote who are not convicted felons may, in theory, be summoned as prospective jurors. But practice often permits exclusion of attorneys, physicians, teachers, clergymen, housewives with small children, and a host of other categories. Citizens with good reasons, and some without, can often be excused by the presiding judge.

Prospective jurors should anticipate boredom and rates of pay which may not cover their commuting expenses. Some sit about for several days and never witness a trial. The summoned panels are, in many jurisdictions, confined to spartan central jury rooms to await service on individual cases, civil or criminal. Special lists of venire-men may be drawn for unusual cases with many anticipated disqualifications.

At times, attention is drawn to the prejudice implicit in the process of choosing possible jurors. Undoubtedly, imbalance has occurred, especially on racial lines, in some areas. Today, however, the basic obstacle is not systematic exclusion of any group, but the difficulty of obtaining reasonable representation from all aspects of society. To function properly, the jury system must reflect the entire community, not just certain parts. At present, a tendency exists to primarily utilize middle-class citizens. In part, this results from the processes of original summons and subsequent selection for actual participation at a trial.

The empaneling of a petit jury becomes, especially in very serious cases, an involved and significant phase of justice. Many defense attorneys regard the process as extremely important and often determinative of the final outcome. The selection involves *voir dire* (to speak the truth) examinations during which questions may be asked of each venire-man. Answers may reveal a lack of qualification, prejudice, personal knowledge, relationship to someone involved, or other conditions which disclose a poor choice. Those obviously unsuited may be disqualified by a *challenge for cause* approved by the judge. Furthermore, statutes permit both prosecutor and defense attorney a number of *peremptory challenges* with which prospective jurymen or jurywomen can be directly excused without a stated reason. In some courts, the judges themselves expedite the process by personally conducting *voir dire*, but many prefer to merely supervise questioning by counsel. Proper selection of the jury becomes a kind of game, sometimes requiring many days, whereby the final panel should represent no bias toward either state or defendant. Naturally, both sides attempt to have a panel sympathetic to their objectives; hopefully, neutrality results.

The trial jury performs several tasks. Best known, of course, are the deliberations on fact and responsibility. In criminal cases, this usually means a final decision on whether or not the state has sustained its burden of proving guilt beyond a reasonable doubt. Also, juries often must resolve issues of sanity, as the question is now commonly raised in connection with more serious charges. In addition, they may be called upon to sentence those found guilty. Several states retain the traditional American system of having juries determine both responsibility and punishment for crime. The trend, however, is clearly against this method of sentencing.[14]

With such responsibility, it may seem peculiar that our rather intricate rules of evidence keep a good deal of information from the jury. In effect, the panel must answer important questions while deprived of details which might mislead or cause bias. Frankly, the effectiveness of a jury depends largely upon the judge. He must clarify important issues, properly apply relevant legal principles, advise upon duties, and insure that attorneys do not incorrectly influence by argument. Yet, the judge must not presume to direct or, in many jurisdictions, even influence the jury. Only then can the independent voice of the people be retained in criminal justice.

By tradition, twelve petit jurymen are expected to reach a unanimous verdict. The number of members may be reduced in certain cases.[15] Unanimity of decision, though not a constitutional requirement imposed upon the states, is quite well entrenched in America.[16] If the panel should deadlock on a decision (a "hung" jury), the judge declares a mistrial. Most magistrates attempt to avoid this outcome by insisting upon continued deliberation until the impasse appears insurmountable. When mistrials do result, the state has the option of commencing a new prosecution.

Summary

A person is formally charged with committing a crime through the process of accusation. While grand juries play a role in felony matters, the prosecution can often utilize the direct form called an *information*.

In every criminal case, jurisdiction and venue must be proper. Fugitives reaching other states or nations may face extradition by cooperating governments.

The principle of bisovereignty has produced both federal and state court systems. The latter, additionally, provide for local courts of limited jurisdiction in cities and precincts which handle the great bulk of routine cases.

Judges are selected either by appointment or election. Both methods have come to be essentially political in America. Right to trial by jury is waived most of the time, with defendants accepting decisions by a judge. Nevertheless, the principle of a verdict by representatives of the community remains fundamental in common law.

Questions

1. Does crime pay?
2. How is jurisdiction distinguished from venue?
3. What level of courts is most important?
4. Should judges be appointed or elected?
5. Does the jury system still have value?

NOTES

[1] *Uniform Crime Reports for the United States—1972* (Washington: GPO, 1973), pp. 107–109, 115.
[2] Delmar Karlen, *Anglo-American Criminal Justice* (New York: Oxford University Press, 1967), pp. 149–153.
[3] Henry J. Abraham, *The Judicial Process* (New York: Oxford University Press, 1968), pp. 158–160.
[4] Lewis Mayers, *The American Legal System* (New York: Harper & Row, 1964), pp. 81–86.
[5] 18 United States Code 3060.
[6] *Expenditure and Employment Data for the Criminal Justice System, 1970–71* (Washington: GPO, 1973), p. 36.
[7] *Crime and Justice: American Style* (Washington: GPO, 1971), pp. 169–172; Maureen Mileski, "Courtroom Encounters," *Law and Society Review* 5 (May, 1971), pp. 473–538.
[8] Leonard Downie, *Justice Denied* (Baltimore: Penguin, 1972), pp. 18–51.
[9] *Modern Court Management* (Washington: GPO, 1970), pp. 1–8.
[10] *State-Local Relations in the Criminal Justice System* (Washington: GPO, 1971), pp. 101–103.
[11] Tumey v. Ohio, 273 U.S. 510, 47 S.Ct. 437 (1927); Ward v. Monroeville, 409 U.S. 57, 93 S.Ct. 80 (1972).
[12] Stuart S Nagel, "Judicial Backgrounds and Criminal Cases," *Journal of Criminal Law, Criminology and Police Science* 53 (September, 1962), pp. 333–339; Howard James, *Crisis in the Courts* (New York: McKay, 1971), pp. 4–11.
[13] Irving Brant, *The Bill of Rights* (New York: New American Library, 1965), pp. 62–68, 176–182; Baldwin v. New York, 399 U.S. 66, 90 S.Ct. 1886 (1970); Duncan v. Louisiana, 391 U.S. 145, 88 S.Ct. 1444 (1968).
[14] "Statutory Structures for Sentencing Felons to Prison," *Columbia Law Review* 60 (December, 1960), pp. 1154–1155.
[15] Williams v. Florida, 399 U.S. 78, 90 S.Ct. 1893 (1970).
[16] Johnson v. Louisiana, 406 U.S. 356, 92 S.Ct. 1620 (1972); Apodaca v. Oregon, 406 U.S. 404, 92 S.Ct. 1628 (1972).

Chapter 11

Trial

*"With palsy'd hand, shall justice hold the scale
And o'er a judge, Court Complaisance prevail."*
                                                    JOHN WILKES

Preliminaries

Perhaps the most significant aspect of criminal trials is that they usually occur in highly abbreviated form. With less than 2 percent of serious offenses ever reaching this stage, they could also be described as relatively rare! Still, trial serves as the technically determining phase and, sometimes, even as a dramatic event within our system of justice.

The attention of the court is drawn to a criminal case long before final decision. In fact, it should begin shortly after arrest. Under the provisions of federal and state codes, an apprehended party must be taken before a magistrate, "without unnecessary delay."[1] Police may not hold a suspect for extended periods before taking him to a judge. Although the federal law has been strictly interpreted to require court appearance after arrest,[2] the states do not generally follow such rigid procedures.

Nevertheless, it is well established that an apprehension (for any offense) must be followed by an initial hearing unless the police quickly release the individual. This first appearance before a magistrate (sometimes called an *arraignment*) serves several purposes. The police should, but often do not, show probable cause for the arrest. More often, the initial hearing becomes the trial itself because the defendant in a lesser case may immediately plead guilty and receive his sentence. In serious charges, the judge usually informs the suspect of his rights, sets bail, and inquires about the need for assigned counsel. The typical initial hearing requires only a few minutes and normally takes place within 24 hours of arrest.

A felony defendant often returns to court within a few weeks for his examining trial (also called the *preliminary*, as distinguished from *initial*, hearing). In some courts, this appearance is ordinarily waived; in others, it becomes a very significant phase where over half the cases are dismissed. The examining trial should, in theory, serve as a fact-finding device utilized by prosecutor, defense counsel, and judge. But the degree of participation by the latter two figures varies greatly by jurisdiction. In effect, this phase requires the state to show cause for continuing the case. Ordinarily, witnesses appear for questioning, and other evidence may be briefly indicated. Assuming that the examining trial does not result in dismissal, the matter then proceeds to accusation by indictment or information.

The next court appearance is during formal arraignment. This normally occurs as the earliest phase of trial itself. The defendant will be called upon to enter his plea of guilty, innocent, or *nolo contendere* (not contested). The last form is most often utilized in regard to auto accidents, for it may not be relied upon to subsequently establish civil responsibility.

Nationally, two of every three felony defendants admit guilt; in some courts, the figure rises to more than 90 percent. With our present system of bargained justice, the negotiated plea becomes prominent.[3] In most instances, the judge accepts the recommendations of the prosecutor and imposes the previously agreed upon sentence. A multitude of such processed cases can be handled in one day. Otherwise, the arraignment usually concludes with a time being set for subsequent sentencing or, when the plea is not guilty, for trial to begin.

Minor errors in preliminary procedure will often not result in later reversal. Unless the defense counsel raises such issues when appropriate, they can be treated as having been waived. Because preliminary steps primarily serve the interest of an accused, his failure to request full privileges prior to trial may result in their loss.

In the vast majority of actual cases, of course, the procedures prior to trial are abbreviated, or simply absent. Only felonies ordinarily result in lengthy and formal preliminaries. A typical misdemeanor concludes when the accused appears for his initial hearing, waives rights to counsel, pleads guilty, and receives his sentence. The entire process may require only a few minutes, particularly in cases of public drunkenness or disorderly conduct. Because many charges, such as traffic infractions, are usually not even contested, a single judge may conduct dozens of hearings and "trials" every hour.

Despite the attention paid to constitutional and other rights, practical procedures evolve largely for purposes of convenience. (For a look

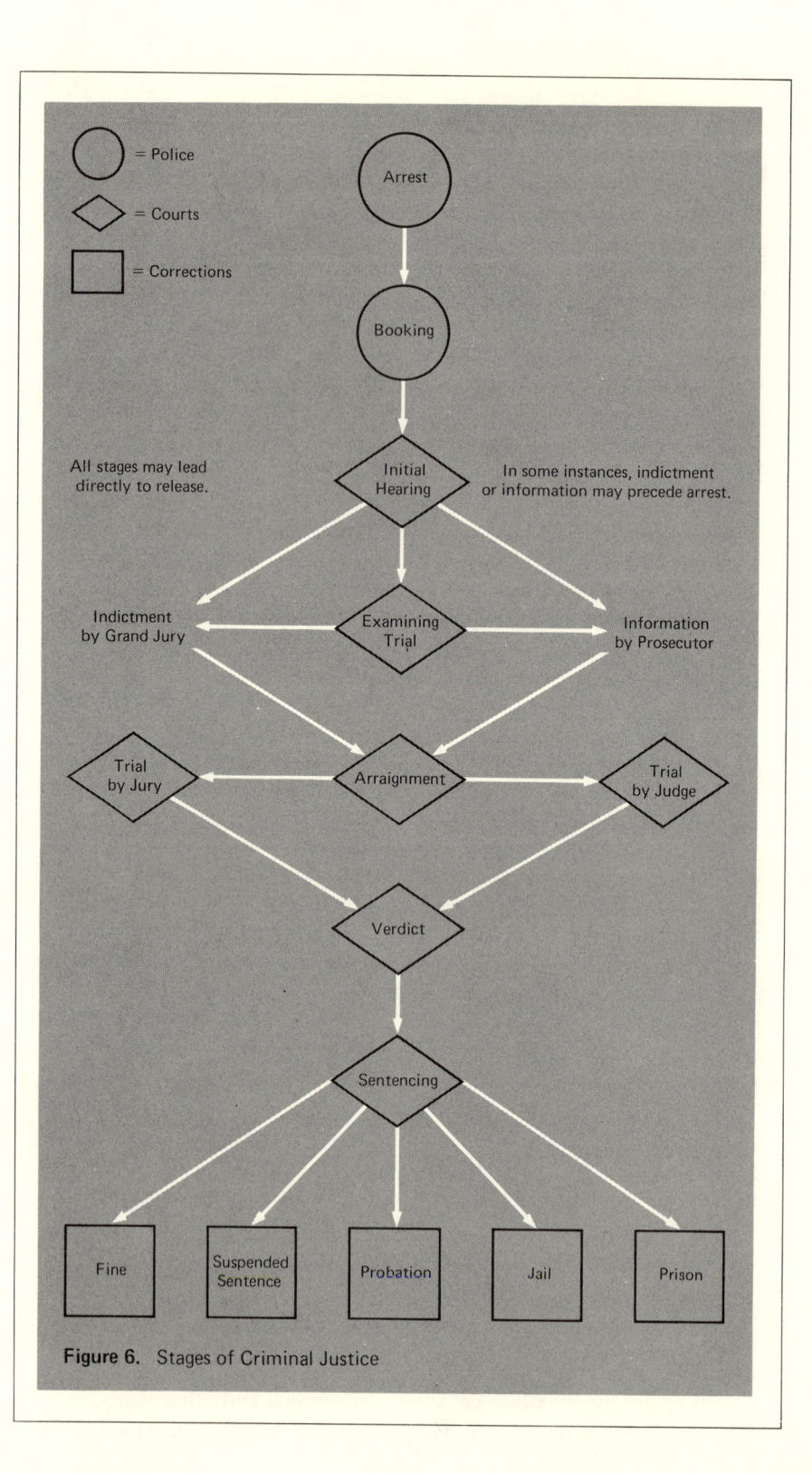

Figure 6. Stages of Criminal Justice

at the total scheme, see Fig. 6.) Custom plays a far more significant role than is generally realized, even in criminal law. So, defense attorneys, prosecutors, and judges work loosely together to insure mutual benefits and advantages. Those accused of violations may also have more to gain by cooperating than by demanding every possible safeguard. The entire system of American criminal justice depends upon bargaining and informal understandings to a far greater extent than is generally realized. Written rules often do not fully illustrate actual practices.

Procedures

With arraignment complete, the public trial contest begins in earnest. In some courts, this may, by agreement, be on the basis of the preliminary hearing transcript. More often, the trial comes closer to the traditional public contest so beloved by writers and dramatists. However, real confrontations seldom achieve comparable tension, continuity, or sustained interest.

The prosecutor begins with an opening statement generally designed to outline his case. Then, the defense counsel may discuss the intended proof of innocence. These statements are usually quite short and meant to provide a basic orientation to the major issues.

As the state carries the initial burden of proof, it must first establish the commission of a crime (*corpus delicti*) and the probable responsibility of the accused.[4] Therefore, the prosecution presents its evidence first. Upon completion of the state's case, defense counsel will routinely move for dismissal, asserting that insufficient evidence was produced to support a verdict of guilty. Should the judge agree that the state failed in its task, he will sustain the motion, and the case ends.

In most instances, however, enough proof will have been presented for the trial to continue. The defense must then undertake to raise doubts about the accused's guilt. This may consist largely of attacks upon the prosecution's evidence or independent proof of innocence and technical lack of responsibility.

Regardless of which side happens to be presenting its case, the procedures are quite similar. While many minor controversies are decided by prior agreement between prosecutor and defense counsel, most evidence actually produced at trial emanates from the testimony of witnesses. Briefly, the person will be summoned into the courtroom (he is usually not permitted to watch prior activities), sworn, and asked a series of questions. Attorneys for the side calling the witness commence the *direct examination* and attempt to elicit answers which support their argument of guilt or innocence. When finished, the opposition has an opportunity to ask their own questions in what is termed *cross-examination*.

At times, the witness may be subjected to additional periods of *redirect* and *re-cross* inquiries, limited to prior answers. Although it is fairly infrequent in adversary practice, the judge may also interrupt to clarify or seek explanations of certain points. Because of a general desire to expedite the case, testimony by a typical witness usually takes well under one hour, but unusual circumstances occasionally extend the period to several days. As a rule, questioning is fairly obvious and impersonal. The dramatics and hysterics of television and the stage rarely occur in reality.

When the defense concludes its presentation, the prosecutor may produce new evidence by means of *rebuttal*, to eliminate doubts which could have arisen. Eyewitnesses, for example, can be recalled to continue their testimony, or additional experts might be brought in to deliver fresh opinions on technical issues.

After all relevant evidence has been seen or heard, the trial proceeds to summation. By statute and tradition, the prosecutor may speak last, so the defense counsel first pleads for acquittal. At one time, in common law, the English barrister representing an accused could waive the right of presenting evidence and claim the privilege of the closing summation.

If the trial is before a jury, though two of every three are not, the judge follows summations by giving his *charge*. This takes the form of carefully worded instructions on responsibilities, major issues, and the relevant law. Some jurisdictions permit the judge to comment upon the weight of the evidence; others prohibit any such liberty. It then remains for the jury to decide the critical questions of fact. During private deliberations, the panel must fundamentally determine whether or not the state has proven guilt beyond a reasonable doubt. When the trial takes place before only the judge, the procedures, although somewhat simplified, remain basically the same.[5]

The verdict comes next, whether or not it is decided by a jury. Overall, the finding in 70 percent of contested serious cases is that of guilt. A significant portion of convictions, however, relate only to lesser offenses. For example, the indictment might have been for attempted murder, but the jury could decide that only an assault occurred. Frequently, such verdicts reduce a felony charge to a misdemeanor. Police, prosecutor, grand jury, and judge may also perform the same function at early stages.

The determination of guilt may involve several related offenses, for different violations can be combined for trial. In such instances, a defendant could stand convicted on certain charges and acquitted of others. While a jury finding of innocent is final and conclusive, a judge can refuse to accept a verdict of guilty when he feels that the state failed to produce sufficient supporting evidence. Even in those jurisdictions so permitting, the practical exercise of this authority is quite rare.

Juries are generally believed to be somewhat more lenient than judges in granting acquittal. Such tendencies, however, may frequently be explained by information available only to the bench. The judge, for example, often knows something of a defendant's prior criminal record while a jury usually does not.[6]

Nationally, perhaps 30 percent of contested felony cases result in dismissal, acquittal, or subsequent reversal. The percentage for all cases (including misdemeanors) is, naturally, far lower because of great numbers of defendants pleading guilty. While many factors contribute to acquittals, the most significant known element must be that of available counsel. When an accused has assistance from a lawyer, regardless of the seriousness of the accusation, the chances of release roughly double. The availability of counsel now exists as a constitutional right in cases which may result in confinement as a penalty.

Those discharged at trial comprise only a very small portion of persons moving out of criminal justice processes. Police and prosecutors release a greater number. The total for all phases dwindles to near insignificance when compared to offenses which go unreported or never result in arrest.

The courts are a pivotal but rarely dominant element within our system of criminal justice. Around them swirl webs of investigation, prosecution, and correction. In theory, trial serves as the critical phase at which guilt or innocence is determined. To the public, it may still represent a bitterly contested and dramatic battle between prosecutor and defender. More often, trial becomes a routine process for official pronouncement of punishment that is primarily determined by plea-bargaining. In such instances, the actual responsibilities for adjudication fall on policemen and prosecutors, rather than on judges and juries.

Our system of criminal justice has developed into a crude chain for maintaining a minimum form of social control. The courts stand as a central link between law enforcement and correctional agencies. Consequently, the handling and disposition of cases involves a multitude of interrelated practices and policies. Criminal trial concerns only those relatively few adult defendants held by police and actually prosecuted. Sentences are logically restricted by availability of appropriate supervisory and confinement operations as well as by judicial inclination.

Half of those arrested for serious offenses may require separate juvenile procedures. In addition, prosecutors and grand juries reduce many felony charges to misdemeanors. Over these decisions, the courts exercise little or no control. In reality, trial should be recognized as but one phase in the processing of criminal cases. It may be the stage at which guilt is actually determined, but the legal presumption of innocence often disappears in a sea of administrative negotiations and compromises. Trial still serves as the ultimate safeguard against the state, but its role as finder of truth has been greatly diminished by the realities of modern criminal justice.

An acquittal nearly always indicates that the case is over. Amendment V of the Constitution declares that, "No person shall . . . be subject for the same offense to be twice put in jeopardy of life or limb."[7] This section means that a government cannot re-try a person charged with an offense once he has been acquitted.

There are, however, a number of qualifications to the rule against double jeopardy. A mistrial (such as that resulting from a "hung" jury) does not foreclose the prosecution from again bringing the action, although it is customary to do so only once. Also, a single suspect can be charged on separate counts, thereby permitting a second trial despite an initial acquittal; such practice has become routine in major cases involving likely procedural error. Finally, one illegal act may easily violate the laws of two jurisdictions. Consequently, a defendant may be tried in both state and federal courts for the same conduct. Because these are regarded as separate sovereignties (unlike local governments), there is no violation of double jeopardy.

Sentencing

If a person is found guilty, he must be sentenced. This heavy responsibility falls primarily upon the judge. In many respects, this phase of the trial process is the most meaningful of all. Conviction alone may carry a degree of social stigmatism (as does arrest and prosecution), but an ultimate penalty purposefully bears specifically upon the individual.

When determining sentence, the judge must consider a host of frequently contradictory goals. Because society has failed to clearly define the purpose of punishment for the commitment of a crime, many possible objectives exist. A judge may opt for rehabilitation, in which case some form of probation might seem appropriate. Or, he could favor protection of the community and tend toward sentencing a lengthy term of imprisonment. A sentence designed to deter others from committing similar offenses might imply an extended period at hard labor. On the other hand, a strongly sympathetic community could demand only a token sentence. These are but a few of the varied possibilities confronting a judge.

While great discretion normally applies, limitations on extremes of available disposition also exist. Statutory law usually imposes maximum permissible sentences, but convictions for certain crimes carry minimum penalties as well. Ordinary burglary, for example, might be punishable by imprisonment for a period of from two to twelve years. In such a situation, minimum and maximum permissible penalties would obviously exist. Laws pertaining to habitual criminals, such as those requiring life terms for persons guilty of three consecutive felonies, also restrict discretion.

In about ten states, the jury may, within statutory limits, also determine sentences. Here, community frustration with early release sometimes produces incredibly lengthy punishments. Alarmed with crime by parolees, juries may resort to consecutive sentences and demands for the serving of hundreds of years for particularly reprehensible conduct.[8]

California and a small number of other states now provide for terms of imprisonment determined by administrative, rather than purely judicial, action. Governed by statutory maximums, a board decides upon the appropriate length of confinement. The gradual trend away from jury sentencing and toward dependence upon administrative control clearly measures the declining significance of the community and the expanding role of bureaucracy in America.

Despite such variations, the vast majority of actual decisions upon penalties must be made by trial judges. The most important device to aid in this task is the presentence report. Following most felony convictions but very rarely in cases of misdemeanors, the judge will call for an investigation of the defendant's background, usually by a probation officer. Although such reports are frequently hurried and cursory, they still contribute a wealth of valuable knowledge.[9]

The ordinary presentence investigation provides details concerning the convicted party's age, marital status, employment and educational background, and prior criminal record. Amazingly enough, judges decide the fate of thousands every year without such information. Usually the officer preparing the report will conclude with a recommendation for sentencing, with particular reference to probation. These suggestions are extremely important, for courts accept them about 90 percent of the time.[10]

Some judges, including those of Hawaii, Kansas, and California, now possess authority to commit convicted persons, prior to sentencing, for diagnosis. The state then provides experts to study an offender for short periods and make appropriate recommendations. Serious questions arise, of course, as to whether or not the results of such diagnoses or presentence investigations should be disclosed to the defense attorney and his concerned client. Some courts closely restrict the release of such information.

Most judges dislike the heavy responsibilities of sentencing and attempt to devise standards or routines for determining penalties. Without doubt, they rely heavily upon the past record and immediate crime of the person convicted. Prior felons found guilty of such serious offenses as homicide or robbery will, for example, almost always go to prison. But parties with no past histories who are convicted of theft or assault can usually obtain probation. The defendant's race has no established bearing on punishments determined by typical courts when other factors are isolated.[11]

Given the very great discretion that statutes and customs accord those responsible for sentencing, it should come as no surprise that wide disparity exists. The typical judge disposes of cases according to personal inclination within the broad limits established by law.[12] It is not unusual to find one court giving a sentence of several years of imprisonment for an offense which elsewhere might receive only a fine and short period of probation.

Some courts, particularly those in large urban areas, seem more inclined to leniency than others. Moreover, individual judges display vast differences in attitudes toward various offenses. One could reasonably regard child molesting as a morally reprehensible act deserving maximum punishment. Another might just as rationally consider such violations as the product of serious emotional disturbances best met with psychiatric care. The two views could result in very disparate sentencing practices.

Concern over variations in penalties has led to considerable concern about procedures. Most often suggested are recommended standards or guidelines, supplemented by seminars and discussions for jurists. Some authorities utilize sentencing hearings whereby the defense counsel, prosecutor, and the subject himself may have the opportunity to propose suitable penalties. Finally, a few judges now meet in councils for the purpose of mutually discussing appropriate sentences for actual cases. At best, however, such methods cannot entirely remove the disparity present in American sentencing practices.

Penalties are naturally influenced by available facilities. Confronted with outmoded prisons and overworked community authorities, some judges realize grim choices for sentencing. Until the correctional system provides adequate means, little more than equality of treatment should be expected.

Problems

Like other aspects of criminal justice, American courts are beset with problems. Among the more serious of these is the delay encountered before a case is brought to trial. At present, a typical felony matter languishes for a full six months between arrest and adjudication. In some circumstances and cities, the intermediate processes of justice can require years. Of course, the defense counsel and, less frequently, a prosecutor directly contribute to this astonishing average delay. Yet, a good portion of the blame must be directly attributed to the courts themselves.

It requires weeks and months to maneuver a case through initial hearing, examining trial, indictment, arraignment, and various other stages. The effect of such delay may be quite marked. Not only does the potential value of formal condemnation shrink, but the likelihood of successful prosecution also declines sharply. More cases are dismissed because of faded evidence than for any other reason.[13] As months go by, memories become blurred; witnesses may leave the area or even die; records can be lost; and even the significance of a charge seems to diminish. Perhaps most serious is the case of an innocent accused having to endure the unforgivable hardship of confinement while a guilty person released on bail is free to commit additional offenses.

The difficulties could be alleviated if the delays between apprehension and sentencing were reduced. It has been authoritatively urged and suggested that better court administration could establish the maximum permissible period at about three months. Frankly, even this time seems excessive. In England, for example, an ordinary indictable offense often comes to trial within thirty days. Such efficacy is virtually unknown in the United States today.[14]

In regard to trial itself, delay again poses major difficulties. While most serious criminal cases may be disposed of within a few hours, some spectacular causes take weeks or months. Repetitious and inconclusive testimony combined with contradictory evidence from "experts" may transform trials which should require days into marathon explorations of distantly related issues. Yet, few judges dare to curtail even faintly relevant presentations in serious cases.

Court congestion results in bargained pleas, disregard of personal rights, and mass processing rather than individual adjudication. The degree to which delay contributes to a lower quality of justice, though surely significant, cannot be determined. Nevertheless, many proposed solutions exist.

Among the suggestions for expediting criminal justice are tightened professional standards for attorneys (to eliminate purposeful procrastination), a reduction in total numbers of cases, limitations on the use of juries, and new scheduling techniques (often involving central administration) for court calendars.[15] Some jurisdictions have gone as far as enacting statutes establishing maximum time periods between various interim stages. Of course, it is often in the defendant's interest to waive his legal rights to speedy trial, actively seek postponement, and so further delay.

One seemingly obvious answer to the problem of court congestion is simply that of providing additional judges. Such proposals fail to recognize difficulties within the system itself. Increases in the numbers of federal judges within recent years have failed to materially reduce the time required for ultimate disposition of criminal cases. Indeed, it might be advisable to rely upon volunteer magistrates from the regular legal community rather than further expand our full-time, publicly paid bench.

On occasion, the overloading of facilities becomes especially acute. For courts, this condition achieves most dramatic scale in times of social crisis. Riots, mass civil disobedience, and serious urban disturbances may suddenly crowd hundreds or thousands of arrested persons into the already backlogged system of justice. Few cities have plans or techniques for dealing with such unfortunate occurrences while still upholding the traditional values of individual attention and trial.[16]

The tragic consequences of these crises tend to lend credence to the complaints and frustrations of dissidents. When magistrates most need to safeguard the liberties and protections of all, they sometimes resort to methods designed more for popular expedience than true justice. Courts must ultimately achieve respect by integrity and fairness rather than by power and privilege.

These qualities are perhaps never tested more severely than by purposeful disruption of criminal trials. On a number of recent occasions, the nation and the world have witnessed the travesty of overt conflict between defendant and judge, turning court into circus. Such spectacles reflect deep social undercurrents rather than personal idiosyncracies. Under such circumstances, wise judges utilize their power of contempt with great discretion, for it can easily become a symbol of ultimate failure.[17]

Beyond considerable immediate problems lies the perhaps even more serious issue of public confidence. Justice means only what people believe, and Americans are tending to doubt. A majority of citizens continue to believe that courts deal too leniently with criminal offenders. Public dissatisfaction may be related to reports of fear, corruption, and inefficiency, but present systems can scarcely be expected to instill lasting confidence. Ultimately, faith in justice can only rest upon a foundation of understanding and progressive leadership.

American criminal courts stand in a most critical position. They represent the highest ideals of our civilization, but remain in constant danger of becoming hollow shells of mediocrity. Should the courts fail in the total exercise of traditional responsibility, the entire fabric of democratic order will be in grave danger.

Appeal

After sentence has been pronounced, the next logical step is that of appeal. Some matters may be taken to higher court even before trial, but most issues await completion of final judgment. Actual routes and methods of appeal depend entirely on statute and individual case. It has, however, become well established that every criminal court disposition should be subject to at least one opportunity for review.

Most decisions, particularly those based upon negotiated pleas, are never appealed. The defendant willingly accepts his limited penalty and waives the right for higher court consideration. On the other hand, some major cases are subjected to several appeals before a multitude of judges.

A serious obstacle to efficiency among many lower tribunals is that of trial *de novo* (a new or a second time). This anachronism of repetitious proceedings arises because many municipal and justice of the peace jurisdictions prepare no transcripts. Since they are not courts of record, an appeal from them means that the entire matter must be determined anew before higher judges. With modern systems of transcription, including sound recordings, it would appear that the *de novo* trials could be largely eliminated.

Except for very limited circumstances, the prosecution may not appeal. If a defendant receives an acquittal, the case is nearly always finished, but a finding of guilty often opens the pathway to court review. Only a small majority of all decisions actually result in appeal, and perhaps 80 percent of them are upheld. For those found guilty of contested serious offenses, however, the chance of possible reversal offers only favorable opportunities. Indigents (those unable to afford counsel) have little or nothing to lose through court review.[18]

The great bulk of appeals are based on disputes over evidence and the way facts were ascertained, rather than on questions of law. Three fundamental methods of obtaining review exist within the United States: regular appeal, *certiorari*, and certification. While final results may be similar, technical procedures vary considerably. Appeal, strictly defined, refers to review of lower court decisions as a matter of right. In effect, the defendant has the right to demand the hearing. *Certiorari* is discretionary and indicates that a higher tribunal has ordered that the case be brought up for study. Requests for this method are routinely denied but may be the only means available after a prior affirmation. Certification occurs when a lower court refers a matter for review. This procedure sees rare use except when a trial judge encounters a totally new question of law.

Few jurisdictions possess appellate systems just for penal convictions. In other states, the same high courts review both civil and criminal matters. Nearly half of our states, including the more populous, now have intermediate courts of appeal between those of general trial jurisdiction and that of supreme authority. Whether two or more levels exist, the names and exact powers of the panels involved depend upon local terminology and popular usage.[19]

Complex and congested appellate procedures create serious problems of delay even after trial. A typical review by a higher court now requires more than one year, and some cases go through the process several times. Simplified processes and efficient handling could greatly reduce this waiting and duplication.

One way to reduce appellate court congestion might be through adjustment of sentences. At present, most states limit review of punishments only to insure conformity to prescribed maximums or minimums. Several jurisdictions, however, now permit reduction of sentences on appeal to avoid disparity or extreme severity. But upward revision of penalties remains almost totally unknown in America. Should criminal appeal create possibilities of increased punishment, the nation's reviewing courts might discover themselves with sharply decreased workloads.

Proposals are occasionally made to eliminate additional trials upon reversal. Under these suggestions, appellate courts would simply discharge defendants rather than referring the matter for more hearings and determinations. This might somewhat simplify present practice, but yet another means of escaping punishment would ensue.

Regardless of procedure, the present forms of criminal appeal display needless complexity and delay. Ever growing numbers of cases and concern with due process, moreover, indicate even more demands on reviewing courts. In a steadily expanding number of instances, criminal charges may raise questions of rights protected by the U.S. Constitution. Such questions make appeal to the federal courts possible after and sometimes before trial. Under such circumstances, even a relatively minor state case can be transferred for review and perhaps eventually taken to the U.S. Supreme Court.[20]

Summary

Arrest should be quickly followed by an initial hearing before a judge. Actual trial does not commence until arraignment and proceeds through presentation of evidence by both prosecution and defense. After summation, the judge or jury returns the verdict.

Wide discretion usually exists in regard to sentencing. The burden falls most heavily on individual trial judges, and considerable disparity results.

American courts are beset with serious problems of delay, congestion in time of crisis, disruption, and declining public confidence. No simple administrative reforms may be expected to remove such difficulties.

Appellate procedures and courts vary by state. It is considered basic, however, to allow at least one review by a higher court in each criminal case.

Questions

1. How can initial hearings, examining trials, and arraignments be distinguished?
2. What is the order of trial?

3. Why is sentencing difficult?
4. How might delay of trial be best remedied?
5. What means of appeal exist?

NOTES

[1] Federal Rules of Criminal Procedure, 5(a); California Penal Code, secs. 825, 849; Illinois Revised Statutes, chapter 38, sec. 309–1; New York Criminal Procedure Law, secs. 120.90, 140.20; Texas Code of Criminal Procedure, arts. 14.06, 15.17.

[2] Mallory v. United States, 354 U.S. 449, 77 S.Ct. 1356 (1957); 18 United States Code 3501.

[3] *The Challenge of Crime in a Free Society* (Washington: GPO, 1967), pp. 134–136.

[4] Jerome Hall, *General Principles of Criminal Law* (Indianapolis: Bobbs-Merrill, 1960), pp. 225–227.

[5] Delmar Karlen, *Anglo-American Criminal Justice* (New York: Oxford University Press, 1967), pp. 183–191.

[6] Harry Kalven and Hans Zeisel, *The American Jury* (Boston: Little, Brown, 1966), pp. 55–117.

[7] Benton v. Maryland, 395 U.S. 784, 89 S.Ct. 2056 (1969); Ashe v. Swenson, 397 U.S. 436, 90 S.Ct. 1189 (1970).

[8] *The Challenge of Crime in a Free Society*, p. 145.

[9] *The Presentence Investigation Report* (Washington: GPO, 165), pp. 7–21; *The Bronx Sentencing Project of the Vera Institute of Justice* (Washington: GPO, 1972), pp. 3–16.

[10] Robert M. Carter and Leslie T. Wilkins, "Some Factors in Sentencing Policy," *Journal of Criminal Law, Criminology and Police Science* 58 (December, 1967), pp. 503–514.

[11] Edward Green, "Inter- and Intra-Racial Crime Relative to Sentencing," *Journal of Criminal Law, Criminology and Police Science* 55 (September, 1964), pp. 348–358.

[12] Julian C. D'Esposito, "Sentencing Disparity: Causes and Cures," *Journal of Criminal Law, Criminology and Police Science* 60 (June, 1969), pp. 182–194.

[13] Ramsey Clark, *Crime in America* (New York: Simon & Schuster, 1970), p. 204.

[14] *Task Force Report: The Courts* (Washington: GPO, 1967), pp. 84–90; Strunk v. United States, 412 U.S. 434, 93 S.Ct. 1756 (1973); *Courts* (Washington, GPO, 1973), pp. 68–69; Moore v. Arizona, 414 U.S. 25, 94 S.Ct. 188 (1973).

[15] *Modern Court Management* (Washington: GPO, 1970), p. 8; *Reducing Court Delay* (Washington: GPO, 1973), pp. 35–65.

[16] *Justice in Time of Crisis* (Washington: GPO, 1969), pp. 97–103.

[17] *Disruption of the Judicial Process* (N.p., American College of Trial Lawyers, 1970), pp. 3–23.

[18] Douglas v. California, 372 U.S. 353, 83 S.Ct. 814 (1963); Mayer v. Chicago, 404 U.S. 189, 92 S.Ct. 410 (1971).

[19] *State-Local Relations in the Criminal Justice System* (Washington: GPO, 1971, pp. 88–90.

[20] Anthony Lewis, *Gideon's Trumpet* (New York: Vintage, 1964), pp. 3–43.

Chapter 12
Special Courts

"When the accuser is judge, force, not law, prevails."
PUBLILIUS SYRUS

Administrative Agencies

Many agencies outside the ordinary courts perform adjudicatory functions. A great deal of conduct that might easily be termed criminal is handled entirely by officials other than regular judges. Some of this activity deals with persons in special categories, while some concerns itself with limited aspects of everyday life. In both forms, the effect on the overall system of justice is quite significant.[1]

A steadily growing portion of American behavior falls under the regulation of administrative agencies. While these do not, technically, possess the authority of courts dealing with criminal conduct, the results may be similar. An urban and technical society such as that of the United States creates vast problems of public control. Rules are specialized, numberless, and frequently violated. Rather than inundate existing courts with millions of additional cases, special governmental bodies have been established to handle offenses.

The scope of administrative control is far more extensive than is generally realized. Agencies regulate business and financial activities, food and drug production, operation of motor vehicles, pollution of water and air, consumption of natural resources, construction and use of buildings, means of transportation, and assorted utilities. Under the guise of protecting public health, safety, and economic well-being, government imposes rigid rules of conduct. It also grants considerable power to established professional groups, including physicians and attorneys, to regulate activities within their special fields of interest.

This growth in administrative authority has produced a large bureaucracy devoted to social control. While these assorted boards, commissions, associations, and agencies may not possess the authority to directly imprison or even impose fines, they definitely utilize other means of state punishment. Building permits refused, prices lowered to reduce profits, corporate charters revoked, all constitute variations of administrative sanctions. In many instances, such decisions impose considerable economic suffering or personal inconvenience. And, should the situation warrant additional punishment, government agencies may bring formal criminal charges in ordinary courts.

In order to carry out their assigned responsibilities, larger administrative bodies create standards of procedure and general reference. These may approach the complexity of the regular judicial system or remain quite general and subject to flexible application. Innumerable regulatory agencies investigate, prosecute, and adjudicate while ignoring traditional rules of evidence. However, statutes ordinarily permit a party aggrieved by groundless or unfair decisions by administrators to seek court review. But time and expense discourage such procedures.[2]

Of course, it is extremely important to realize that many agencies of criminal justice, apart from the courts, actually perform what might be described as judicial functions. Police and prosecutors exercise enormous discretion in determining whom to arrest and bring to trial. While they lack legal authority to impose state punishment, their decisions often have significance fully equal to those of judges.

Similarly, the role of probation, prison, and parole agents has acquired great consequence. Modern systems of correction entrust wide discretionary power to these officers. Their decisions frequently determine the length and nature of penalties imposed by law.

While courts may be isolated in academic analysis, their essential functions actually interlock with administrative practices. Much in our system of justice lies outside the traditional trial scene. Even in court action, the usual role of neutral adjudication sometimes becomes secondary. Through injunctions or contempt citations, restriction or punishment reaches outside the ordinary scheme of criminal process. In such limited circumstances, a judge directly imposes sanctions without resort to formal trial although means of review exist in cases of arbitrary action.

Use of administrative agencies to perform functions of social control permeates all levels of government. Federal, state, and local bodies operate with broad delegated powers once thought to be the domain of legislative groups and courts. Removal of driving privileges, denial of parole, rejection of business license applications are all examples of how administrative decisions can regulate and, in effect, punish. At yet another level, interpretation of vague tax provisions or confused statutory prohibitions push government employees into the zone of legal arbitration.

Our complicated society has combined with natural bureaucratic inclination to produce a kind of rule through form. This, unfortunately, permits the abuse of discretion without practical safeguards. Where such tendencies enter the system of criminal justice (and they have become quite prevalent), danger lurks. A fundamental American principle concerns protection of the individual against the government, and this properly includes powers assumed through administrative action.

In recent years, vast discretionary authority has been broadly granted, especially in the federal system, by the legislative to the executive branch. This, in turn, results in delegation of enormous power down through bureaucratic structures. Despite theoretical possible recourse to regular courts, the practical conclusion is acquisition of capacities to punish without the normal safeguards provided by common law. Regardless of the worthy motives which may direct many functionaries, the trend should concern all Americans. History, ancient and recent, proves that power does indeed corrupt.

Juvenile Courts

Many Americans do not fall under the jurisdiction of ordinary criminal courts because of their age. Depending upon statutory provisions, each state has created special classifications for juveniles and methods for dealing with their delinquency. Despite considerable variation in definition and power, it is widely agreed that children and youthful offenders should be treated separately from adults and given individual attention.

These concepts have resulted, over the last century, in establishment of a large and disorganized set of juvenile courts with procedures quite different from those of ordinary criminal justice. A rising tide of youthful delinquency now appears to beset the nation and bring still more public attention. Every type of agency connected with our scheme of justice, from police to corrections, has special units organized to handle juveniles. Yet, this concern demonstrates little success in controlling the rate of youthful offenses.

Only about half of the approximately 2 million juveniles arrested yearly by police are referred for further action. Those apprehended may be confined in special detention centers for young people or, in smaller communities, held in jail with adults. Law enforcement officers personally handle and release nearly 50 percent of those taken into custody.[3] Welfare and other police agencies receive a small percentage of the remainder, but many result in referral to a unit assigned responsibilities in connection with additional legal action. In most communities, this task has, somewhat peculiarly, become that of court probation officers.

A very large proportion of juvenile cases referred by police or other agencies end before reaching a judge. The probation staff investigating the charges and the child's personal situation frequently handles the matter directly. Often, with encouragement from the court, they routinely dispose of more than half the cases obtained from law enforcement units. Juveniles may be sent to social welfare agencies, subjected to various forms of unofficial probation, or merely sent home with a warning for parents or guardians.

The actual percentage of youth cases resulting in formal action by a court varies by region and community. Generally, rural areas (which enjoy the lowest rates of juvenile delinquency) tend to rely less frequently upon disposal by probation officers alone. In some metropolitan areas, on the other hand, only the most serious of cases go before a judge.[4] Regardless of opinions on proper method, the number of juveniles arrested but not subjected to formal adjudication achieves great significance. With comparatively few cases reaching the courts, the role of other agencies becomes critical. Most of the time, serious crimes committed by juveniles fail to conclude with judicial action of any sort.

Only when the probation or other investigating officer decides the matter must be taken to a judge are formal proceedings which may result in a finding of delinquency initiated. Of course, traffic and certain other types of cases involving young people may be handled without petitions (formal requests for court action) in many jurisdictions. But, the present tendency is clearly toward use of special procedures for those below a certain age (frequently 18).

Juvenile courts do not try crimes. While it may seem peculiar, violations by the young ordinarily result in civil cases on the theory that care rather than punishment is the objective. This frequently unfulfilled goal is embodied in the doctrine of *parens patriae* (the state as guardian), whereby the government intervenes to correct deviant behavior when normal means fail. In truth, many juvenile judges perform a multitude of diverse functions. They normally deal with presently declining numbers of neglect and dependency cases, but they also may be assigned domestic relations, probate, or other duties.

Typical cases of juvenile delinquency involve those arrested on several prior occasions or for quite serious offenses. But difficulties at school or home also result in petitions. Some jurisdictions have special referees or hearing officials to handle juvenile traffic infractions; in others, the regular magistrates perform such functions.

The duty of courts in relation to youth crime has grown enormously in recent years. During 1940, there were about 200,000 juvenile cases (including those for automobile violations, truancy, and other forms of improper behavior). A generation later, the number reached 1.6 million annually. Although child population increased during this period, the rate of expansion failed to approach the 800 percent of indicted youth offenses.[5] While more than one in three of current cases falls into the category of traffic infractions, many others involve accusations of theft, assault, and other traditional crimes.

The theoretical function of juvenile courts is to protect and help delinquents rather than simply punish them. Limited facilities combine with sometimes repressive attitudes, however, to produce results not too dissimilar from adult cases. While the imposition of penalties may not be the announced goal, it often serves as the practical means of attempted care. The quest for a child's welfare frequently produces somewhat peculiar results. On occasion, a juvenile delinquent receives what amounts to a sentence of confinement far exceeding the maximum which might be given an adult committing an identical offense.

A hearing normally results from a petition involving youthful misconduct. In perhaps 40 percent of all cases, the judge dismisses the action, often with an admonition or other informal means of correction. Generally, juvenile procedures are far less rigid than those followed in criminal trials. Strict rules of evidence ordinarily do not apply, and opinions of probation officers, welfare workers, and parents may be given great emphasis. Hearings often appear to be more like a serious conference than a trial.[6]

Despite the widespread use of juvenile courts, legal requirements remain highly flexible and subject to local and personal application. While the juvenile's right to a jury is not mandatory under the federal Constitution, many jurisdictions extend the safeguard when requested. On the other hand, all of the basic protections of due process certainly apply. Rights to representation by counsel, confrontation by an accuser, and cross-examination of witnesses are required.[7] Here again, however, reality seldom approaches the ideal.

Many rights guaranteed juveniles are routinely waived. When defense attorneys play a role, the child from a poor family often meets his court-provided counsel just as the hearing begins.[8] Some judges routinely process thirty or more juvenile cases a day, and many rely heavily upon recommendations based on a variation of bargained justice. The results, nevertheless, range from outright discharge to confinement (at times, for years) in training schools. Despite sincere and dedicated judges, disposition often resembles that accorded adult violators.

In one essential respect, juvenile hearings differ markedly from regular criminal trials. They are normally private, and records usually remain closed to the public. Under liberal statutory provisions, juvenile proceedings *parens patriae* should protect the child's future by shielding him from damaging present or future publicity. Reports and records are ordinarily kept separate from those of adults, while general access is denied or severely limited.

Investigations involving past juvenile conduct encounter some problems. Even police may be forbidden from obtaining information from other agencies without court orders. Background investigations also meet with difficulties, but waivers secured from job applicants or recruits frequently overcome statutory obstacles. Some states, however, even deny the juvenile's own capacity to release information and destroy files after a fixed time.

Finally, it is worthwhile to note that juvenile adjudications rarely result in review by higher courts. Appeals are actually quite rare when compared with those from criminal convictions. Early involvement of parents and brief periods of confinement probably contribute to this result.

While the original objectives of juvenile procedure have never been achieved, separate agencies now represent a very important aspect of American criminal justice. About half of all serious offenses in the United States are committed by young people, and the proportion appears to be increasing. Juvenile justice consequently occupies a pivotal position from the standpoint of present and future violations.

At present, this system combines remarkable weakness and great strength. The most obvious example of this paradox concerns more flexible procedures and rules of evidence, although proof of criminal offenses must be beyond reasonable doubt.[9] Properly utilized, these allow judges to delve deeply into actual events and personal problems. On the other hand, they also permit negligence and even abuse.

Some juvenile judges rely too heavily upon reports and recommendations prepared by occasionally unqualified investigators. Others depend on unofficial disposition rather than on utilizing available community resources for assistance. A few treat juveniles with a severity caused by limited knowledge of conditions. Some fail to take essential precautions to protect society from future offenses. Combined with vague statutory definitions of delinquency itself, these problems have plagued juvenile courts for more than two generations and will probably continue in the foreseeable future. Yet, the basic difficulties of justice for the young are scarcely unique; the same conditions may generally be found among adult processes.

The concept of special procedures for juveniles developed gradually, and then spread throughout the United States during the first half of the twentieth century. A few jurisdictions have even resorted to informal juries composed of young people. But original hopes of individualized care dissolved while courts and other agencies gradually fell behind in their understanding of delinquency. Juvenile procedures, meanwhile, served as a springboard for reform across the nation. Many techniques and approaches now used for adults are adaptations of promising earlier efforts with young people.

Now, some of the legal protections once accorded only in regular criminal trials are indicated for juvenile matters as well. Rights to a prompt and fair hearing with prior notice, clear proof of charges, examination of reports or recommendations, and an opportunity for review of decisions are becoming recognized throughout America. Still, juvenile courts and their broad powers remain distinct from regular criminal tribunals.

Justice for Youthful Offenders

During recent years, much attention, within and without the courts, has been paid to youthful offenders. Although no widely accepted definition of this category of persons exists, it represents a group between juvenile delinquents and adult violators. In formal and informal ways, American jurisdictions have begun to recognize a special legal class of youthful offenders. A variety of significant procedures now exists for handling these older juveniles and younger adults.

The category of persons aged 16–20 has several interesting characteristics. It normally extends across the limits established for juvenile jurisdiction, required school attendance, voting, and military service. Also, this relatively small population group provides approximately one of every three people arrested in the United States, including about 25 percent of those placed in custody for major offenses.[10]

Youthful violators deserve special consideration for a number of reasons. They represent the ages when a shift commonly occurs from the relatively minor misdemeanors of children to the more serious and possibly violent felonies of adults. The 16–20 year old offender also poses an enormous statistical threat by way of future crime. Persons brought to court in this age bracket are far more likely to be arrested, tried, and convicted again than more mature violators.[11]

The soaring rates of youth crime, and the proportion of major offenses involved, have led most states to adopt statutory provisions permitting transfer of certain cases to regular courts. As a rule, when the young suspect has reached a minimum age (perhaps 16) and is accused of a felony, the juvenile judge may order him tried as an adult. Such measures are seeing increasing use throughout the nation, particularly when the defendant has a prior record.

A few states have attempted to deal directly with the unique problems of youthful offenders by creating courts with special procedures for adolescents falling within certain age brackets. Jurisdiction fits between those for juveniles and adults, combining the features of both systems.

Prompted essentially by innovations in youth correction, these measures provide a compromise between flexible procedures for children and more arbitrary standards for adults.[12]

Under the laws of several jurisdictions, a young adult, although tried and convicted in regular court, may now be subject to treatment as a minor. Youth Corrections Acts actually allow juvenile age limits to be raised, permitting individualization of sentence and care.

Some states have means of treating those below a set age (perhaps 19 or 21) as "wayward minors." This involves use of statutes originally designed to control incorrigible youths. Wayward minors may be subjected to various penalties, including possible confinement, but still avoid a formal label of either delinquent or criminal.

New York, Baltimore, and certain other cities devote special attention to youthful offenders within probation agencies. There, officers aid prosecutors and judges by study of cases, individual recommendations, and extended counseling designed to rehabilitate rather than punish. A variety of alternatives to ordinary court disposition may be made available.

Legislative, judicial, and administrative concern with youthful offenders does not involve any immediate desire for leniency. Rather, it reflects a growing awareness of the usual futility of applying traditional means of treatment or punishment. Declarations of delinquency or criminal guilt, followed by insufficient community supervision or extended confinement, simply do not succeed in reducing the likelihood of further violations. Thus, the system of justice is gradually beginning to rely on new means of diverting offenders from routine processing. While such measures have yet to demonstrate marked success, they represent growing dissatisfaction with traditional efforts at correction.

Meanwhile, many jurisdictions try to handle younger offenders by extralegal methods. Some courts will defer prosecution pending informal probation. If performance over a period of time is deemed satisfactory, the charge can be dropped.

Another version of informal disposition occurs after actual conviction for an offense. Judges allow a youthful violator to successfully complete a given period of probation and then return to court. It may then be possible, at times by means of a new trial, to erase the record of prior guilt.

Yet another practice, and one entirely outside the statutes, provides an option to suspected youthful offenders. Police, prosecutors, grand juries, and judges are known to frequently give young men a choice of either risking the penalties permitted under law or enlisting in the armed forces. Though officially discouraged, this procedure still concludes with many hundreds of "volunteers" for military service every year.

Courts-Martial

Millions of our citizens live under a special kind of judicial system because of their work. Many of these individuals are not even within the United States, yet they fall under a certain type of American jurisdiction. This rather peculiar situation developed because of the giant and far-flung military establishment.

Traditionally, the armed forces of a nation maintain laws and courts distinct from those for civilians. The obvious requirements of military service and a continuing demand for discipline and close regulation permit special sets of rules and procedures to exist within the framework of our constitutional government.[13] While the same fundamental protections apply, they do not connote the broad interpretations accorded ordinary citizens.

It is worth mentioning that the military may indirectly cause a person to unwillingly fall within the jurisdiction of a foreign court. Under numerous status of forces agreements (SOFA), those serving outside the United States can sometimes be tried by other nations. This creates a remarkable situation in which trial need not follow our Constitutional protections but be imposed upon a citizen who never elected to sacrifice his legal rights in any way.

Members of the armed forces of the United States are subject to what is termed the Uniform Code of Military Justice. Total numbers of persons affected by the UCMJ vary, of course, with the size of the military at any given moment. Many men became acquainted with the system during a few months or years of often undesired service. The UCMJ has undergone many changes, for military justice tends to be revised occasionally, with liberalization following each war.

Those in the armed forces can be accused of the ordinary offenses such as murder, robbery, and theft. But they also must avoid a multitude of violations which apply solely to the military. These include, for example, possible charges of absence without leave, casting away arms, cowardly conduct, dishonorable failure to pay debts, desertion, failure to obey an order, or mutiny. And, recourse to a general accusation of "conduct bringing discredit upon the armed forces" is always available.

Unlike the civilian legal system, our armed forces officially permit "nonjudicial punishment." Under Article 15 of the UCMJ,[14] minor and corrective penalties may be imposed by commanders in order to maintain discipline. But the scope of such punishment is generally limited to only one week of custody or two weeks of restriction. Far more often, assignment of extra duties, reprimand, forfeiture of pay, and reduction in grade might result. Furthermore, the present system of military justice permits an accused party to refuse nonjudicial punishment and demand regular trial. This procedure, seldom employed, would ordinarily lead to the traditional means of determining guilt and punishment within the armed forces—court-martial.

Interestingly, and perhaps surprisingly, draftees enjoy a far lower rate of violations and prosecutions within the military than do volunteers. It is the "regulars" who more frequently become involved with crime. The rate for this category is two or three times that of those arbitrarily selected for service. Requirements set for those chosen by draft may be a partial explanation.

Control of potential or actual violators demands law enforcement even within the armed forces. This need is met in several ways by different services. The Army relies upon its military police corps, the Air Force has a large security police, and the Navy still primarily utilizes shore patrol. In addition, each of the armed forces now contains a smaller unit to conduct special and criminal investigations. The distinction between the equivalent of civilian patrolmen and detectives is more clearly defined within the military system.

Each of the services' police displays unique characteristics. The Army and Air Force rely largely upon specially trained personnel, but the latter's force devotes a great amount of time to maintaining physical security of bases and planes. The Navy, on the other hand, primarily utilizes ordinary seamen briefly assigned shore patrol duties and members of the Marine Corps (sometimes with special qualifications) for police work.

Despite differences of terminology and procedure, the basic process of military arrest, accusation, and trial is comparable to that of the civilian system. In the armed forces, however, courts possess jurisdiction for disciplinary as well as penal purposes. While the primary goal of civilian justice is public security, the military looks first to the service's benefit.

The jurisdiction of courts-martial is both personal and particular. Unlike the practice of some other nations, United States civilians are not subject to military justice. This vital protection against tyranny leads to one confusing consequence. Once properly released from military duty, a person cannot be charged for an offense committed while in service.

Court-martial authority applies only to actions directly involving the armed forces.[15] Conversely, civilian judges have no direct control over offenses relating strictly to the services. It is, nevertheless, possible for an act to violate the rules of both systems simultaneously. For example, a sentry could murder a civilian. Such a situation would produce concurrent jurisdiction.

In response to claims of improper influence, the UCMJ provides for independence of courts-martial. In other words, the regular system of military command may not directly control a trial. Of course, a commander and the usual influence of rank undoubtedly have an effect, but efforts at overt influence are quite unusual.

Courts-martial probably provide hearings fairer than those civilians ordinarily receive. Mass processing and routine deprivation of due process do not occur with such frequency in the armed forces. However, punishment tends to be more severe than that found in civilian courts. Penalties for offenses in the military are controlled by specific articles and a Table of Maximum Punishments, but the services, particularly the Air Force, have adopted many progressive concepts of correction. The military system of justice has one great advantage over that for civilians: Our armed forces can often discharge their offenders and return them directly to the community.

Army, Navy, Air Force, and Marine Corps each contain judge advocates (the military equivalent of civilian prosecutors and defense attorneys). These are legally qualified persons assigned, as needed, in courts-martial. Military lawyers, of course, perform civil as well as criminal duties for the armed forces and their servicemen. Under recent revisions, the UCMJ now also provides for powerful military judges. Such specially designated officers exercise most of the general authority enjoyed by their civilian counterparts. Defendants may request that military judges determine an entire case—the equivalent of waiving rights to a jury.[16]

There are three kinds of courts-martial: summary, special, and general. Procedural rules, formation, and possible punishments distinguish one from another, regardless of service.

Summary court-martial is basically a trial before a single officer, not a military judge. Relatively minor disciplinary matters involving lower ranked enlisted personnel typically exemplify this level of military justice. Punishment cannot exceed partial forfeiture of pay or imprisonment for one month.

Special court-martial occupies an intermediate position between summary and general authorities. It may impose maximum penalties of imprisonment or partial forfeiture of pay for six months. The special court-martial consists of at least three members functioning as a kind of jury.

General court-martial attracts the greatest publicity but actually constitutes the smallest level of military justice. There are a few thousand annually, far less than the number of nonjudicial, summary, and special matters. Still, a general court-martial reflects the most dramatic and serious aspects of criminal trial in the armed forces. Its sentences can extend to dishonorable discharge or life imprisonment, although typical punishments are less severe.

The military equivalent of a jury has several distinguishing characteristics. Members of the panel (at least five for general courts-martial) are subject to the same system of challenges as in civilian criminal cases. Upon selection of a panel, the senior member becomes president (foreman). His once influential position has been curtailed through increased reliance upon the military judge, who must be present at general courts-martial.

As in civilian justice, the military has a degree of plea-bargaining. A good percentage of cases are actually settled by pretrial agreement. Here, the role of advocates can become most significant. Relations among defense and trial (prosecution) counsels, the military judge, members of the panel, and witnesses resemble those in ordinary criminal cases.

Unlike the civilian system, military sentences often receive downward adjustment. Each of the armed forces has procedures for endorsement by commanders who frequently reduce punishments. The UCMJ also requires the services to maintain courts of military review. Together with the higher civilian-staffed Court of Military Appeals, they insure that convicted parties are not deprived of their rights under the federal Constitution and the scheme of justice within the armed forces.[17]

Maintenance of discipline does not depend essentially upon threat of legal punishment. As in civilian life, order relies on general and willing acceptance of established rules. For the armed forces and our entire society, law enforcement, trial, and punishment simply serve as ultimate means for requiring desired conduct. Discipline within the military remains a basic goal of leadership; court-martial comes only as a final resort.

Summary

Through reliance on administrative agencies, many adjudicatory functions in criminal justice have reached beyond the regular courts. Government regulation may result in restrictions and indirect punishments of considerable significance.

Juvenile courts occupy a very large role in the present system of American justice. While the vast majority of children's offenses are handled by police or probation officers, only a judge may actually determine delinquency. Under the doctrine of *parens patriae*, care rather than punishment is the proper objective. The rising tide of offenses by older juveniles and young adults has also led to creation of both formal and informal processes within the courts.

Our large military establishment maintains its own system of justice. Each of the armed forces has an internal police force, attorneys, and judges. The Uniform Code of Military Justice permits nonjudicial punishment and three kinds of courts-martial: summary, special, and general.

Questions

1. To what extent should administrative agencies impose penal sanctions?
2. How do juvenile procedures differ from those involving adults?
3. What special means are available for handling cases of youthful offenders?
4. Does military discipline require trial by court-martial?

NOTES

[1] Lewis Mayers, *The American Legal System* (New York: Harper & Row, 1964), pp. 417–506; *Courts* (Washington: GPO, 1973), pp. 168–170.

[2] H. W. R. Wade, *Towards Administrative Justice* (Ann Arbor: University of Michigan Press, 1963), pp. 24–51.

[3] *Instead of Court* (Washington: GPO, 1971), pp. 56–57.

[4] *Juvenile Court Statistics 1971* (Washington: National Center for Social Statistics, 1972), p. 8.

[5] *Ibid.*, pp. 10–11; *Juvenile Court Statistics 1969* (Washington: National Center for Social Statistics, N.d.), pp. 8–10.

[6] *The Juvenile Court* (Washington: GPO, 1971), pp. 8–12.

[7] In re Gault, 387 U.S. 1, 87 S.Ct. 1428 (1967); McKeiver v. Pennsylvania, 403 U.S. 528, 91 S.Ct. 1976 (1971).

[8] Spencer Coxe, "Lawyers in Juvenile Court," *Crime and Delinquency* 13 (October, 1967), pp. 488–493; *Courts*, pp. 302–303.

[9] In re Winship, 397 U.S. 358, 90 S.Ct. 1068 (1970).

[10] *Uniform Crime Reports for the United States—1972* (Washington: GPO, 1973), p. 126.

[11] Daniel Glaser, *The Effectiveness of a Prison and Parole System* (Indianapolis: Bobbs-Merrill, 1964), pp. 36–41.

[12] *Task Force Report: Juvenile Delinquency and Youth Crime* (Washington: GPO, 1967), pp. 121–124.

[13] United States v. Tempia, 16 U.S.C.M.A. 629 (1967).

[14] 10 United States Code 815; *Manual for Courts-Martial* (Washington: GPO, 1969), pp. 26 (1–13).

[15] O'Callahan v. Parker, 395 U.S. 258, 89 S.Ct. 1683 (1969); Kinsella v. Singleton, 361 U.S. 234, 80 S.Ct. 297 (1960); United States v. Quarles, 350 U.S. 11, 76 S.Ct. 1 (1955).

[16] 10 United States Code 816.

[17] *Manual for Courts-Martial*, pp. 20 (2–5); *Annual Report of the U.S. Court of Military Appeals* (Washington: GPO, 1972), pp. 5, 18–19, 32–34, 40–41.

PART IV

CORRECTIONS

When offenders are found guilty or delinquent by the courts, they become subject to correction. The law attaches a variety of penalties, from small fines to lengthy prison terms, to different kinds of violations. These punishments, although they may entail no actual suffering, are the basis for corrections in the United States.

Society has established many agencies designed to stop future deviant behavior of juvenile delinquents or adult criminals. Ordinarily, some sort of court action is required to initiate resulting efforts at reform. Today, however, correction tends to be properly visualized as a broader scheme extending to protective services, especially for children, and means of diverting offenders away from traditional penal measures. This has come about through increasing recognition of the social and personal problems which frequently cause crime.

The concept of correction as a means of preventing offenses is only about two centuries old. An Italian nobleman named Cesare Bonesana, the Marchese di Beccaria, originated many still very important ideas about the relationship between crime and punishment. The goal of all corrections, regardless of method, has since come to be increasingly regarded as that of prevention.

Law and order is not a natural condition in complex, urban cultures. Social tranquility must be won through dedication and sincerity. Crime is prevented by people who care; not by arbitrary and hypocritical application of force. When, for example, leaders ignore or violate the law, it should be no wonder that the nation's disadvantaged also turn to crime. Justice is the beginning of prevention.

Before crime can be effectively controlled, we must understand and eliminate its causes. Such a task would ultimately demand fundamental moral, economic, and social changes of vast consequence. Agencies of criminal justice naturally do not, and never should, exercise control over such issues. Still, reform of our laws, police, and courts is an important element without which crime can never be effectively controlled. An efficient and equitable scheme of justice would undoubtedly be the logical starting point in prevention.

For practical purposes, America's efforts at stopping criminal activity revolve around correctional treatment of known offenders. Today, this commonly occurs in the community rather than in confinement. Meanwhile, all forms of correction suffer from divergent and often contradictory purposes. Some aspects reveal a traditional desire for revenge upon evildoers; others reflect a reasonable wish to incapacitate or isolate the criminal. Another purpose of punishment is obviously that of deterrence, and individual rehabilitation has become a final emphasis at present.

Correctional treatment in the United States suffers from erratic, inconsistent, and uncoordinated efforts. In practice, although not in theory, the punitive aspect still has a strong influence that undermines programs of intended rehabilitation. Americans have not yet realized that when society treats offenders as vicious animals, they will respond accordingly. But, in an apparent contradiction, we are also unwilling to keep our criminals caged.

The concept of correctional treatment actually designed to reform violators of the law has quite naturally led to the release of offenders in the community, often under supervision. After the pioneering efforts of John Augustus in Massachusetts about 1841, probation emerged *as a promising and steadily expanding method of handling offenders. Hundreds of thousands of juvenile delinquents and adult criminals are now undergoing this kind of care.*

Despite the growing use of community treatment, American corrections still strongly rely on antiquated means of confinement. Detention centers, jails, training schools, and prisons stand throughout the nation as symbols of prior failure to effectively control crime. Some of these institutions are models of progressive penology, but the majority continue to represent concepts which have failed consistently for centuries.

Since the innovations implemented by the Quakers in Pennsylvania in 1790, prison history reveals a gradual acceptance of humanitarian and rehabilitative ideals. Solitary penitence and congregate work schemes were used for awhile, and they continue to influence many institutions. During the late nineteenth and early twentieth centuries, reformatories and detention centers for juveniles came into prominence. Nevertheless, countless places of confinement in the United States remain as breeding grounds for additional crime rather than correction.

The difficulties inherent in custodial care and its general record of failure to reform have prompted various forms of early release. England had actually developed simple procedures for allowing convicts, including those deported to penal colonies, to return to the community during the early nineteenth century. But the first organized parole system appeared at Elmira, New York, in 1876 through the efforts of Zebulon R. Brockway. In the last century, release from confinement has been widely recognized as a critical and often determinative phase of criminal justice. Supervision of former inmates, whether through parole for adults or aftercare for juveniles, now constitutes a large and growing part of community treatment.

Recidivism is the final and only practical test for all corrections. When previous offenders commit new crimes, efforts at reformation have obviously failed. By almost any standard, America suffers from a disturbingly high rate of recidivism. This produces a frustrating cycle of crime whereby police, courts, and correctional agencies repeatedly handle the same offenders, frequently for quite similar violations. Recidivists create major burdens on all processes of justice. As long as those released continue returning under new charges, no solutions to the American crime scene should be expected.

Chapter 13

Prevention

"Criminal law is mainly a system of licensed revenge."
SIR JAMES STEPHEN

Before the Crime

The battle against crime can never be successfully waged in the aftermath. Our present system is devoted almost entirely to reactions rather than to attack. The police and the courts only indirectly serve to stop offenses before they occur. Consequently, we devote time, money, and effort after what should never occur has already transpired. As long as this concept predominates, American criminal justice will be inefficient and ineffective.

To substantially reduce the number and damage of violations, the causes must become the objectives. At present, the criminal justice system tries to destroy a tree by picking off leaves. Such superficial efforts will never succeed; the proper goal must become prevention instead of reaction.

Stopping crime before it occurs is an obvious but difficult and usually ignored solution. Critics demand more police and longer sentences, oblivious to the vast numbers of unreported offenses, released suspects, and discharged defendants. Such steps might accomplish something, but they cannot alter the broader problems of social control within a democracy.

Prevention of crime demands the realization of fundamental conditions found throughout our culture. It requires an understanding of justice as an involved system with a multitude of interdependent aspects, and it must overcome enormous obstacles of apathy and hypocrisy. History indicates that little improvement should be anticipated. While hope exists, the pathways to reform have been known and open for generations. Yet, vested interests of several types combine with natural tendencies to resist change. As a result, agencies and methods obsolete for centuries display remarkable endurance. Nevertheless, it would seem possible to direct new efforts at the more obvious varieties of crime prevention. From better locks and lighting to major social reforms, a spectrum of largely ignored significance lies waiting. But proper use demands knowledge of the total problem and its roots.

The few exciting and practical programs of crime prevention face the facts of widespread delinquency with its variety of types and causes. Changes in behavior require alterations of attitude; such modifications can be accomplished only through patience, care, and personal attention. Nightsticks and prison bars are no substitute for public concern and equal protection of law. People must respect the agencies of justice. If not, anarchy or tyranny result.

Efforts to prevent criminal behavior will invariably lead to concern with the reform of basic social conditions. To some degree, America's tendencies toward disorder and violence surely relate to poverty, discrimination, and ignorance. As long as conditions of the inner city remain, we can anticipate concentrations of offenses against person, property, and public. Past measures to combat prejudice, economic deprivation, and educational inequality produced ineffective and wasteful administrative programs. The future of massive social reform is clouded by past failures, but conditions of daily life undoubtedly contribute to much of American crime.[1]

On a somewhat narrower and perhaps more realistic basis, preventive efforts confront those features of family and community which relate specifically to juvenile delinquency. Home and neighborhood can contribute to the likelihood of youthful misbehavior that frequently serves as a prelude to serious adult crime. Consequently, those involved with social welfare have vital roles in practical prevention.

A multitude of techniques for those dealing directly with delinquency already exist. Trained workers, sometimes drawn from the community, can be detached for service on the streets. Agencies themselves sometimes attempt to develop and rely upon leadership within the neighborhoods themselves. Every urban section, whatever its official crime rate, contains a majority of law abiding citizens. With proper motivation, they can unquestionably become an invaluable asset for crime control. But animosity and mistrust still distinguish districts with the more serious problems.

In very few areas, readily accessible centers are now available for parents or children desiring advice and assistance. Social workers (rarely with a background in criminal justice) provide counseling services and refer clients to appropriate welfare facilities. At best, these centers aid families, schools, and police with information and consultation. Techniques of individual case and group work permit clients to progress toward solution of personal difficulties. Individuals with serious emotional problems are sent to psychiatric clinics, where available.

Unfortunately, even such rudimentary facilities exist only as isolated exceptions, and they encounter common indifference. Barriers of misunderstanding isolate much of the public, police, and welfare. Many community resources see limited utilization because of poor coordination and what sometimes appear as contradictory objectives. If crime prevention ever achieves a significant portion of its potential, the community must also become unified in purpose.

Large programs to attack the causes of crime and delinquency are limited in support and scope. Most have been experimental, directed at particular neighborhoods, and of debatable value. At present, however, interest primarily lies in the field of youth services bureaus. These would be located in community centers, receive juveniles referred from various sources, and coordinate services for young people.[2]

Ideally, preventive programs can encompass those citizens likely to become criminals and redirect their interests into more acceptable fields. But even the more progressive programs deal essentially with persons who have already demonstrated some degree of delinquency. The focus of prevention often comes too late.

Still, obvious avenues toward improvement exist. Many present and continuing forms of crime clearly reflect serious personal difficulties and have become a part of major social problems rarely reformed through punishment of any sort. How many assaults result from emotional disturbances or mental illness? To what degree are property offenses caused indirectly by drug addiction? Does not alcoholism produce public drunkenness and intoxicated drivers?

These conditions contribute a vast but still unmeasured proportion of the total crime scene. About half of all arrests can be attributed to such personal problems, and the functioning of justice holds no promise of actual correction. Efforts at crime prevention would do well to focus upon the detection, control, and reform of the millions of unfortunate sufferers who currently burden our police, courts, and systems of correction. American criminal justice has consistently demonstrated an incapability, and perhaps an unwillingness, in dealing with mental illness, drug addiction, and alcoholism. These difficult problems would best be handled by care and treatment rather than by formal law enforcement.[3]

Positive and imaginative approaches to vast social and individual illnesses rampant throughout the United States might result in enormous financial savings in addition to alleviation of incalculable personal suffering. Without doubt, present methods lead to frustration. Rather than imposition of traditional penalties, it would appear that hospitalization or other professional care and supervision might be more rewarding. Perhaps the greatest immediate potential achievements of crime prevention lie within measures to combat social rather than legal problems.

Agency Reform

Many parts of society have a potential role in crime control. Churches and charitable organizations, for example, already contribute through moral and humanitarian influences. In America, however, most duties relating to delinquency fall on the government. Because the state determines violations, it seems to naturally assume related responsibilities.

There are several government agencies that could greatly aid in preventing crime, including some rather far removed from justice. City recreation departments help occupy the abundant leisure time of potential delinquents. They also can occasionally redirect interests of juvenile gangs and detect youths with pronounced personal problems. Of course, few agencies are presently staffed and equipped to perform these services.

Schools continue to possess unfulfilled opportunities relating to crime prevention. Teachers commonly recognize which of their pupils are likely to become serious offenders, but can do nothing because of inadequate facilities for referral. Schools, particularly in ghetto districts, are striving to keep youngsters from becoming dropouts through technical training and remedial courses. But faculty members in sections with high crime rates still confront nearly impossible obstacles.

Our governments (local, state, and federal) could undoubtedly move toward remedying some of the more obvious statutory defects. Legislative initiative might, for example, remove some penal laws altogether. Statutes relating only to personal morality are surely in need of drastic revision.[4] Schemes for providing compensation to victims of crime could be created and expanded. After all, when citizens suffer personal or property violations, the government has failed in its assumed task of protection.

For the immediate future, remedial efforts will probably continue to be directed at criminal justice itself. The interrelated complex of police, courts, and corrections attracts growing attention but witnesses little concrete progress. Governments and agencies have demonstrated a primary interest in federal grants rather than in basic reorganization. Instead of efforts to involve citizens and improve conditions, the ordinary trend is toward retention of the status quo. Substantial reform of criminal justice has been an unrealized goal for generations.

Improvements in police and court service should result in greater chances of crime being solved through arrest and conviction. In turn, such changes would entail expanded public support, increased reporting of offenses, and more cooperation with authorities. The end product might well become a deterrent to criminals and reduce violations throughout the nation. Agency reforms alone will surely not eliminate all offenses, but they could contribute heavily toward a more orderly and law abiding society. At any rate, it would seem clear that major modifications of present organizations and policies will be required to produce substantial progress in the quest for a more peaceful and orderly society.

Very little police time deals directly with crime prevention. Routine patrol may act as a deterrent, but in practice, these measures sometimes only exacerbate strained community relations. Still, police reform and initiative could do much toward more successful control of crime.

The potential benefits of general force improvement are impossible to determine. If police standards could be significantly elevated, public attitudes toward crime might also change. But upgrading meets many difficulties. Present seniority systems help to relegate reforms to rhetoric while "professionalization" often only leads to alienation from ordinary citizens.

Even so, opportunities for police improvements are great. A few departments have had considerable success with "crisis intervention" in family disturbances. Similarly, policemen can be assigned to schools or social agencies to assist parents and children. Several forces maintain youth athletic leagues or other recreational programs, but the present trend is against the employment of officers in such areas.[5]

In a quite different approach, police have begun to utilize new scientific and technical devices for investigation, records, and communication. Progressive forces now include units with responsibilities for advising homeowners and businessmen desiring to prevent crime. Although costs remain high, police departments may now rely upon sophisticated silent alarm and surveillance equipment. Such methods will never replace personal attention and concern, but they indicate the variety of new possibilities for modern law enforcement.

Court reform could also materially affect public opinion of justice and crime. Perhaps the most controversial suggestions concern "preventive detention" whereby suspects could be held without trial. Improperly applied, such measures threaten the liberty of all citizens. But nothing need prevent court reforms designed to expedite cases, reduce mass processing, and balance sentencing practices. Such desperately needed improvements, together with provisions for fair representation and due process, should only serve to increase confidence and respect for our system of criminal justice.

Agency reform poses practical opportunities for direct and indirect prevention. The mere difficulty of committing offenses combined with the certainty of detection would surely discourage those with evil intent.

Increased chances of arrest and prosecution will decrease tendencies toward crime. Ultimately, conviction and correction (or legal punishment) must become likely rather than remote possibilities. The true deterrent to crime lies amid changed attitudes and personal values, but reform should begin within the agencies of justice themselves. While American history does not indicate significant or dramatic progress, recent innovative programs do indicate new hope.

The agencies of criminal justice are, perhaps by nature, quite conservative. Positive change requires some degree of individual sacrifice, and many political and administrative figures demonstrate little willingness to extend real effort or accept curtailment of personal power. Of course, there are progressive elements in criminal justice, but they almost never include the agencies most in need of reform. The best continue to improve; the worst cling to methods and practices outmoded for generations.

Effective crime prevention requires the help of citizens throughout society. They provide the reports, information, testimony, votes, and money which enable police, courts, and corrections to operate with some reasonable expectation of success. At present, many Americans quite logically place little faith and trust in their system of criminal justice. Corruption, brutality, discrimination, plea-bargaining, and general inefficiency scarcely contribute toward public confidence.

Meaningful agency reform demands a modification of outlook combined with structural reorganization. Furthermore, progress is not inherent in higher budgets, studies, and government grants. Enduring public support cannot be quickly bought, it must be slowly earned.

Purposes of Punishment

Why does the law impose punishment for crime?[6] We have become so accustomed to this relationship that confusion has resulted. Of course, certain penalties are actually imposed, in the name of justice or order, without a finding of guilt. Investigation, arrest, confinement prior to trial, and prosecution surely constitute varieties of punishment. These processes often produce neither conviction nor correction. They involve no penalty by law but result in personal and economic suffering. The system of justice can punish with threat. Yet, this can scarcely be viewed as part of correction.

Punishment, in various guises, remains a primary result of criminal law, but purposes and methods have become quite varied. The Constitution contains little guidance for corrections. While Amendment VIII does contain a prohibition against "cruel and unusual punishment" applicable to both federal and state governments, courts have just begun to expand rights of convicted persons.

Correction need not involve any given type of suffering. In fact, the clear trend of recent decades has been away from the infliction of physical pain. Punishment by the state most often takes the form of minor economic sanctions, through fines or restrictions on personal freedom. Limitations on the convicted person's liberty may exist in several versions. The most graphic, of course, would be incarceration in jail or prison. But limitations on individual freedom now frequently manifest themselves in ways more subtle than actual confinement. Probation, aftercare, and parole, which all impose restraints and requirements upon subjects, definitely constitute refined forms of state punishment although their goals, at times, may be removed from apparent suffering. With juveniles, correction has for some time theoretically excluded harsh penalties, but in practice, the result still includes obvious restrictions on personal freedom.

The purposes and varieties of state punishment are manyfold, and they reflect a multitude of origins.[7] It is popular but simplistic to equate infliction of punishment with an elemental desire for revenge. Nevertheless, such retributive designs are clearly evident in many rather primitive forms of justice. Criminal laws in less sophisticated societies often contain provisions allowing injured parties, or their relatives, to demand repayment or inflict revenge. The Bible's exposition of Hebraic justice " . . . life for life, eye for eye . . . " is but one example. Without doubt, the natural desire to take vengeance for wrongs remains a viable element in our culture. An immediate reaction to crime that is personally directed against us is a desire to have the offender pay by suffering for his act. While such wishes may rarely be fulfilled under present law, they occasionally become apparent in public outcry over particularly heinous violations. It is even possible to theorize that demands for state revenge against criminals, once accomplished through torture and death, are but a psychological expiation of our own guilt. By making others suffer, we direct internal feelings into culturally approved punishment for visible evil. At any rate, the role of revenge in present systems of correction is obvious. Lengthy periods of imprisonment under deplorable conditions occur throughout the United States. They may be easily explained in terms of retribution for criminal conduct still demanded by society.[8]

Some styles of punishment indicate a purpose of incapacitation. Removal from society, whether temporary or permanent, will at least deprive the offender of some opportunity for future violations. Originally, this role could be performed by exile, mutilation, maiming, or death. By banishing a rapist, branding a traitor, cutting off a thief's hand, or executing a murderer, society limited or eliminated the guilty party as a threat to order. State punishments are no longer as severe, but they still seek to incapacitate. Undesirable aliens face deportation from the country; those convicted of certain crimes may be sentenced to confinement for life; and vast numbers are, for a time, removed from society by virtue of jail or prison. In effect, we still attempt isolation of the offender in various formal ways. Those on probation are normally restricted in their movements and associations; officials are, in part, trying to remove them from temptation by such rules. Without actual incarceration, society nevertheless makes an effort to prevent repetition of crimes by removing the opportunity from convicted persons and vice versa.

Perhaps the most reasonable explanation for punishment is that of deterrence. Guilty persons are forced to undergo various forms of suffering to convince them and others not to participate in such acts. By demonstrating the unpleasant consequences of crime, society attempts to prevent future violations from occuring. The punishment could involve imprisonment, stigmatization, fine, whipping, probation, or death; yet the purpose remains that of deterrence. Through increasing the likelihood of detection, the speed of conviction, and the severity of sentence, we convince ourselves and others that crime simply is not worth the risk. Criminals are subjected to punishment imposed by the state to become examples of the folly involved in violations of formal regulations. In the modern world, punishment is equated with the seriousness and probability of the crime. We attach relatively small fines to routine violations, such as most driving infractions, while more alarming offenses, including murder, carry the heaviest of penalties. The state has simply adjusted the sanction to the degree necessary to deter people from committing the crime.[9]

Today, a popular explanation for punishment is based on efforts at reform. The state imposes its sanctions not to inflict suffering but to treat the offender. By attempting to rehabilitate those convicted of crimes, we try to change their destructive or dangerous tendencies and reorient them in socially approved directions. Restrictions upon the offender's freedom are, therefore, not directly intended to cause discomfort but simply to aid the treatment process. Punishment merely enables various degrees of required care; those who are found guilty of crimes indicating severe personality disorders and who pose potential danger to the community would, naturally, still require custody and perhaps long periods of confinement. Others might have an improved chance for rehabilitation through probation, counseling, education, employment, or an improved environment. In recent decades, the therapeutic approach to correction has come to occupy a very significant role. Growing numbers of known offenders find themselves involved with psychiatric examination, group therapy, early release, vocational training, and similar programs aimed at reform. Treatment, supplied by the state to proven violators, has obviously become a major focus of attention within the penal process.[10]

In practice, of course, correction involves a mixture of revenge, incapacitation, deterrence, and reform. Whatever the ideal might be, our present scheme of dealing with violators displays an often contradictory, inequitable, and confused approach. Penal sanctions may exact retribution, isolate the offender, subject him to treatment, and dissuade others from committing similar crimes. Our present schemes of correction display little coherence or logic. Often we seem to utilize legal punishment merely to briefly and erratically impose unpleasant conditions with little regard to practical results.

While it is difficult to assume that present methods of correction directly accomplish a great deal, it is similarly impossible to conclude that state punishment can be considered totally ineffective. The threat of fines, imprisonment, and social degradation undoubtedly does have some deterrent effect on most citizens. Treatment, although never proven to substantially improve overall chances of reform, surely aids in individual cases. And, however inefficient and primitive, both incapacitation and retribution occasionally fulfill community attitudes—perhaps never more dramatically than in the death penalty.

Much recent concern has been directed at questions relating to capital punishment. Several jurisdictions completely abolished the death penalty, and others sharply curtailed its applicability. As a practical matter, execution for crime virtually disappeared in America years before restrictive decisions by high courts. Hundreds waited on death row while procedural delay virtually eliminated capital punishment. History reveals that poor and black people have consistently been more likely to face execution, a factor which has undoubtedly contributed to the pattern of decline prior to actual abolition.[11]

Arguments for and against the death penalty are many. Some feel that execution is a suitable response to particularly reprehensible acts: It removes the threat of future crimes by the offender and could be more humane than life imprisonment. Those opposed argue that capital punishment has been applied to the innocent, demeans the culture, and only congests the system of justice. Despite the merit of both arguments, no clear evidence exists that the death penalty, alone, has a marked effect on known rates of crime. In truth, use of capital punishment appears related primarily to the character of civilization. In that respect, it closely resembles the entire system of corrections.

Debate over the death penalty reveals more about the deeper recesses of the human mind than about the practicalities of criminal justice. Execution has achieved such public attention as to actually detract from the realities of correction. Abolition or retention of capital punishment holds no simple solution to the routine problems of crime in America.

In 1972, the Supreme Court ruled that the death penalty, as it had been imposed in America, violated the Constitution,[12] but the dispute continues. Several states have not witnessed an execution for generations, while others have performed capital punishment hundreds of times. Despite the clear trend of history, many legislatures envision restoration through carefully worded statutes. Ultimately, the issue will perhaps be seen as one basically involving social and moral attitudes rather than political and legal questions.

The Correctional System

Upon conviction for a crime, one becomes subject to penal law. Today, however, we do not always talk in terms of legal punishment, preferring to speak of "correction." In truth, this constitutes the only significant part of criminal justice dealing specifically with prevention, for it attempts to stop additional violations by former offenders. While perhaps backward, sentences have been so used for centuries.

Regardless of other possibilities, for the immediate future, crime prevention will continue to focus upon correction of the relatively few offenders actually caught, prosecuted, and convicted. With only a small fraction of all violations reaching this stage, the significance of formal legal sanctions should not be overrated. However, many consistent major offenders eventually suffer some form of conviction and punishment. At any rate, this remains the only phase of serious effort toward correction of known violators.

History indicates two things about the treatment of convicted criminals: The methods employed measure a civilization, and they are very slow to change. By these standards, America should take little pride in present conditions and anticipate no rapid improvement. The correctional phase is the stepchild of criminal justice. It almost always comes last, in attention as well as in time.

The American system of corrections is far more inclusive than is generally recognized. One ordinarily thinks of a prison and hardened inmates behind high walls. This distorted picture represents only a small part of the present scene. Legal punishment takes many forms and often does not entail extended confinement.

About 2 million persons are presently subject to some type of formal correction in the United States. But the total number involved during a year is far higher because of frequent discharges, and, a great many individuals in the system are juveniles, although age classifications differ by state.[13]

People undergoing legal penalties for crime represent all aspects of society. But they include unusually large numbers of the poor, black, youthful, and male populations. Their offenses range from the most minor of traffic infractions to murder. However, crimes against property and those involving personal vices constitute typical violations.

Many individuals have only fleeting contact with corrections. The ordinary citizen pays an occasional fine and never deals with anyone directly responsible for other forms of punishment. Anything else seems, unlike the police and even the courts, remote from everyday life. Such impressions are common but quite misleading.

A majority of all those subjected to correction are not actually confined. At any one time, only a minority can be found within prison, jail, reformatory, training school, detention center, or similar institutions. Most convicted adults and juvenile delinquents live in the community, subject to a variety of restrictions and forms of supervision. Some serve periods of incarceration, but many never leave the environments in which they continue to reside. The most significant fact is simply that a large majority of those in the correctional process stays outside any type of institution or confinement. Conviction often does not lead directly to prison or jail.

Americans display little general interest in the correctional phase of criminal justice. Perhaps because of a tendency to equate attention with sympathy, reform in the area of punishment nearly always comes last. The police employ far more people than those utilized by correctional agencies, while those working within the courts are nearly as numerous. And, financial expenditures reveal similar discrepancies.

The entire system of corrections in the United States (federal, local, and state) receives less than half the amount of money being spent on nonmilitary space exploration. In short, remedial efforts directed toward offenders (who cost Americans untold billions every year) rank very low amid demonstrated governmental priorities. Even within criminal justice, all correctional efforts combined obtain but 21 percent of the total funds expended. The police receive about three times the amount spent on the treatment of offenders.[14] Correctional workers also average the lowest pay in comparison to other criminal justice employees (those associated with courts get the highest)—another indication of the relative value attached to punishment upon conviction. America still tends to forget those proven guilty of crimes; it has far greater interest in catching and trying them, again and again.

Within the correctional system, several basic divisions exist. First, subjects are classified as juveniles or adults. Second, they may be either held within institutions (detention or training schools for young people, prisons or jails for those over a specified age) or released for community treatment. Those convicted but never confined are on probation. Conversely, juveniles discharged from an institution are usually said to undergo aftercare, while adults receive parole. The terminology differs; the effect is much the same.

Perhaps the most obvious feature of community treatment is that of relative economy. While only a small portion of the correctional population is in confinement at a given moment, institutions require a huge share of monies expended. Comparative numbers of employees reveal even greater discrepancies. Only about 13 percent of correctional workers deal primarily with community treatment, yet they handle the vast majority of those undergoing punishment. The same general patterns apply to both adults and juveniles.

The correctional system encompasses a wide definition of punishment. Having been convicted of a crime, the offender becomes subject to sanctions and close control within the bounds established by law. According to sentence, he may be immediately placed on probation in the community or confined in some form of institution. From there, the offender commonly obtains release through parole or aftercare. While individual punishment appears to be the objective, it really represents an effort to achieve correction.

Remember, actual responsibility for crime and legal conviction are not synonymous. Most guilty people escape completely, and those sentenced to correctional programs scarcely represent all actual offenders. Our system of justice probably succeeds in catching disproportionate numbers of the inept and inexperienced. Persons able to afford skilled defense attorneys undoubtedly have a greater chance of escaping both prosecution and conviction. Consequently, the subjects of American correction include fewer white-collar criminals and more murderers than actual offense rates would indicate.[15] Police and courts rarely discriminate consciously against poor, uneducated, and black people. They still happen to be most frequently caught, tried, convicted, and legally punished.

Perhaps it is a natural tendency to assume that persons penalized, and most especially those confined, represent our criminal population. But such an assumption does *not* apply. The American system of justice, despite its admirable principles and many worthy features, deals most frequently and harshly with unfortunates. A drug addict caught stealing automobile accessories might be sent to jail while a public official taking thousands of dollars in bribes smoothly evades feeble efforts at investigation. One who commits a murder in a fit of sudden rage almost surely goes to prison, and a manufacturer of defective goods causing many deaths faces an occasional civil suit.

We comfortably regard our correctional institutions as containing the untrustworthy and dangerous members of society. In truth, a few inmates are quite innocent, and more guilty persons escape than follow the path of arrest, prosecution, and conviction. The correctional system fails to collect the offending residue of humanity. It is only the final phase of our rather ineffective justice, and nearly all of those undergoing legal punishment (in confinement or community treatment) are released within a few years.

Prevention of crime, to be a practical and partially realizable goal, involves understanding of the entire system of justice. It can only become a reality through changes throughout all of society. This most certainly will demand efficiency from police, courts, and correctional agencies. Moreover, prevention must be approached through recognition

American Corrections

	POPULATION (%)	COST (%)	EMPLOYMENT (%)
Juveniles	(28%)	(34%)	(35%)
Detention Centers†	1	6	7
Training Schools†	4	18	21
Probation*	18	8	6
Aftercare*	5	2	1
Adults	(72%)	(66%)	(65%)
Jails†	12	16	17
Prisons†	16	41	42
Probation*	36	6	4
Parole*	8	3	2
	100%	100%	100%
† Confinement Facilities	33	81	87
* Community Treatment	67	19	13
	100%	100%	100%

SOURCE: *Task Force Report: Corrections* (Washington: U.S. Government Printing Office, 1967), pp. 191–196.

of our involved and integrated scheme of criminal processes. Like so many other aspects of social problems and efforts at control, there are no simple or easy answers. Above all, serious programs require evaluation of our entire culture, including the political, economic, family, religious, and educational institutions. Criminal justice should never be separated from its dependence upon the democratic society in which we live.

Summary

Very little effort is presently directed at actual crime prevention. Most existing programs concentrate upon the problems of likely juvenile offenders.

Reform of government agencies, particularly those involved directly with justice, could help to control crime. Improvements in police and court service are obvious steps of primary importance.

Legal punishment has many purposes. It can be used for revenge, incapacitation, deterrence, or reform. Despite much recent debate over use of the death penalty, execution really disappeared from America several years ago.

The present approach to prevention lies in the system of corrections or legal punishment. This includes jails, prisons, detention centers, training schools, and other places of confinement. It also encompasses such forms of community treatment as probation, parole, and aftercare.

Questions

1. How can juvenile delinquency be best prevented?
2. Which government agencies are responsible for helping to control crime?
3. How can the purposes of punishment conflict?
4. Can correction also be prevention?

NOTES

[1] *The Challenge of Crime in a Free Society* (Washington: GPO, 1967), pp. 58–77; Ramsey Clark, *Crime in America* (New York: Simon & Schuster, 1970), pp. 56–67.

[2] *Instead of Court* (Washington: GPO, 1971), pp. 71–90; *National Study of Youth Service Bureaus* (Washington: GPO, 1973), pp. 77–126.

[3] *Diversion from the Criminal Justice System* (Washington: GPO, 1971), pp. 9–20; *Drug Use in America* (Washington: GPO, 1973), pp. 346–367.

[4] Jerome H. Skolnick, *Coercion to Virtue* (Chicago: American Bar Foundation, 1968), pp. 623–626.

[5] *Training Police as Specialists in Family Crisis Intervention* (Washington: GPO, 1970), pp. 5–7, 13–34; *Instead of Court*, pp. 55–56.

[6] Jerome Hall, *General Principles of Criminal Law* (Indianapolis: Bobbs-Merrill, 1960), pp. 296–324.

[7] Harry Elmer Barnes, *The Story of Punishment* (Montclair, N.J.: Patterson Smith, 1972), pp. 38–55.

[8] H. L. A. Hart, *Punishment and Responsibility* (New York: Oxford University Press, 1968), pp. 8–11, 230–237; Morris R. Cohen, "Moral Aspects of the Criminal Law," *Yale Law Journal* 49 (April, 1940), pp. 1009–1026.

[9] Johannes Andenaes, "The General Preventive Effects of Punishment," *University of Pennsylvania Law Review* 114 (May, 1966), pp. 949–983.

[10] Francis A. Allen, "Criminal Justice, Legal Values and the Rehabilitative Ideal," *Journal of Criminal Law, Criminology and Police Science* 50 (September–October, 1959), pp. 226–232.

[11] *National Prisoner Statistics: Capital Punishment 1930–1970* (Washington: Bureau of Prisons, 1971), pp. 8–9.

[12] Furman v. Georgia, 408 U.S. 238, 92 S.Ct. 2726 (1972).

[13] *The Challenge of Crime in a Free Society*, p. 160.

[14] *Expenditure and Employment Data for the Criminal Justice System 1970–71* (Washington: GPO, 1974), p. 11.

[15] *The Nature, Impact and Prosecution of White-Collar Crime* (Washington: GPO, 1970), pp. 54–58.

Chapter 14

Community Treatment

"To innovate is not to reform."

EDMUND BURKE

Punishment Without Confinement

The majority of people convicted of criminal offenses are not placed in actual confinement. Disregarding the tens of millions of traffic violators, most convicted individuals face no form of institutionalization. In truth, the mass of persons found guilty now receive some form of limited community treatment. Probation represents the most obvious form of such care, but many other varieties exist.

Most minor violators, for automobile infractions and ordinary misdemeanors, receive only a fine. The simple use of monetary punishment yields enormous revenues for some governments, expedites the judicial process, and is greatly preferred by most of the parties convicted. While such penalties often produce little in the way of reform, fines surely accomplish some of the other goals of state punishment. Their practical utility for crime control in an affluent society remains in doubt.

For generations, financial penalties also produced many indirect incarcerations. Those unable to pay their fines faced time in jail at a specified rate of days for dollars. Such procedures no longer satisfy constitutional interpretations, but they continue to occur in some areas of the nation.[1]

Despite the enduring reliance on ordinary fines, supervised community treatment, without confinement, has now achieved wide use.

The soaring costs of prison and jail operations have contributed to an expansion of noninstitutional sentences. Moreover, the growing concentration on principles of rehabilitation has led to innovations. Our present places of confinement are deplorable and often only induce still more criminal tendencies among offenders. Instead of bringing about reformation, American prisons and jails have become graduate schools for offenders. Consequently, the current trend is clearly toward community care.

While accurate comparisons remain beyond the range of available statistics, treatment without confinement appears to increase the chances of individual rehabilitation. Semicontrolled studies reveal a tendency toward reduction in the frequency and degree of criminal behavior through use of community, rather than institutional, correction. Not all types of offenders are, of course, susceptible to such measures. Still, probation and similar techniques appear to do no worse than the traditional, harsh and excessive means of punishment.[2]

Many imaginative programs now exist for dealing with offenders within the community. These extend through a wide range of approaches designed for particular varieties of violators. Juveniles and those suffering from personal disturbances are especially likely subjects for treatment without confinement, but the trend is toward still wider application.

Young persons may, in extreme cases, be removed from their homes and placed in the care of foster parents. Today, the emphasis lies upon the attempted retention of a family atmosphere. This has led to development of new techniques whereby brothers and sisters can be kept together with children of somewhat different ages. A number of state agencies now maintain programs under which groups of young people receive responsible care combined with personal opportunities for guidance. While traditional foster homes appear to be losing popularity, they remain well entrenched in the American scene.[3]

People suffering from mental illness, drug addiction, or alcoholism are also involved with diverse forms of community treatment. Courts have begun to rely on referral of individuals to appropriate clinics, counseling centers, doctors, and groups working for rehabilitation. Many of those with emotional disorders can be helped through psychiatric care without costly hospitalization. Alcoholics Anonymous can aid individuals with sincere desires to stop drinking. And, supportive therapy could probably redirect many drug addicts away from crime.[4] Modern rehabilitation programs usually recognize that no cure of socially connected problems should be expected unless the victim is successfully reoriented within the community. Such a task is far more difficult to accomplish when an offender is confined in an institution.

While these measures stress treatment rather than punishment, they cannot be divorced from criminal justice. In many instances, courts or other agencies induce offenders to seek rehabilitation. Threats of legal penalties rarely begin such rehabilitative schemes with favorable settings, but they often constitute the only link between violators and reasonable chances for reform. At the very least, programs can be publicized, expanded, and coordinated with systems of justice so that those wanting assistance can be afforded a chance.

In recent years much attention has been directed toward group interaction, often in the community setting. Briefly, the method of therapy depends upon peer influence. By bringing together a number of individuals with similar difficulties, self-analysis and improvement can be induced through open, directed discussion or argumentation. Groups may even live within a household, intensifying the effects of interaction.[5]

Residential treatment centers, in various guises, combine some features of institutionalization and community care. Sometimes called halfway houses, they feature controlled rehabilitation in relatively normal environments. Benefitting from opportunities for dealing with practical problems, residential treatment has shown considerable promise for particular types of criminals. The halfway house permits reliance on ordinary means of education and employment and may involve the offender's own family. Again, it substitutes more humane conditions than those of our prisons and jails while moving treatment into a more realistic and practical setting. Counselors can work with continuing, actual problems on a daily basis.

Community treatment, despite recent expansion and experimentation, has yet to approach its potential. Supervision or care of those awaiting trial, for example, remains almost unknown. Existing programs are primarily limited to probation for particular types of offenders, particularly juveniles. Meanwhile, bureaucratic superstructures bury innovative schemes for community treatment and the dreams of imaginative social workers.[6]

Economy and a desire to reduce crime through reform of proven offenders would appear to dictate still greater use of community care. Yet, society and government move slowly in the direction of promising innovation. Correction continues under the domination of methods proven unsatisfactory a century ago despite much progressive effort. (See Fig. 7 for a total picture of corrections today.)

Ideally, community treatment serves as the normal means of attempting correction. Offenders, juvenile or adult, should be channeled into individual programs through probation, aftercare, or parole. Diverse forms of treatment available through a multitude of agencies can then provide care, assistance, and supervision. Where such facilities and attitudes exist, jails, prisons, and training schools become secondary measures applicable only to unusual and difficult cases. The savings to the public in terms of both operating costs and eventual reduction of crime should easily cover any additional immediate expenses.

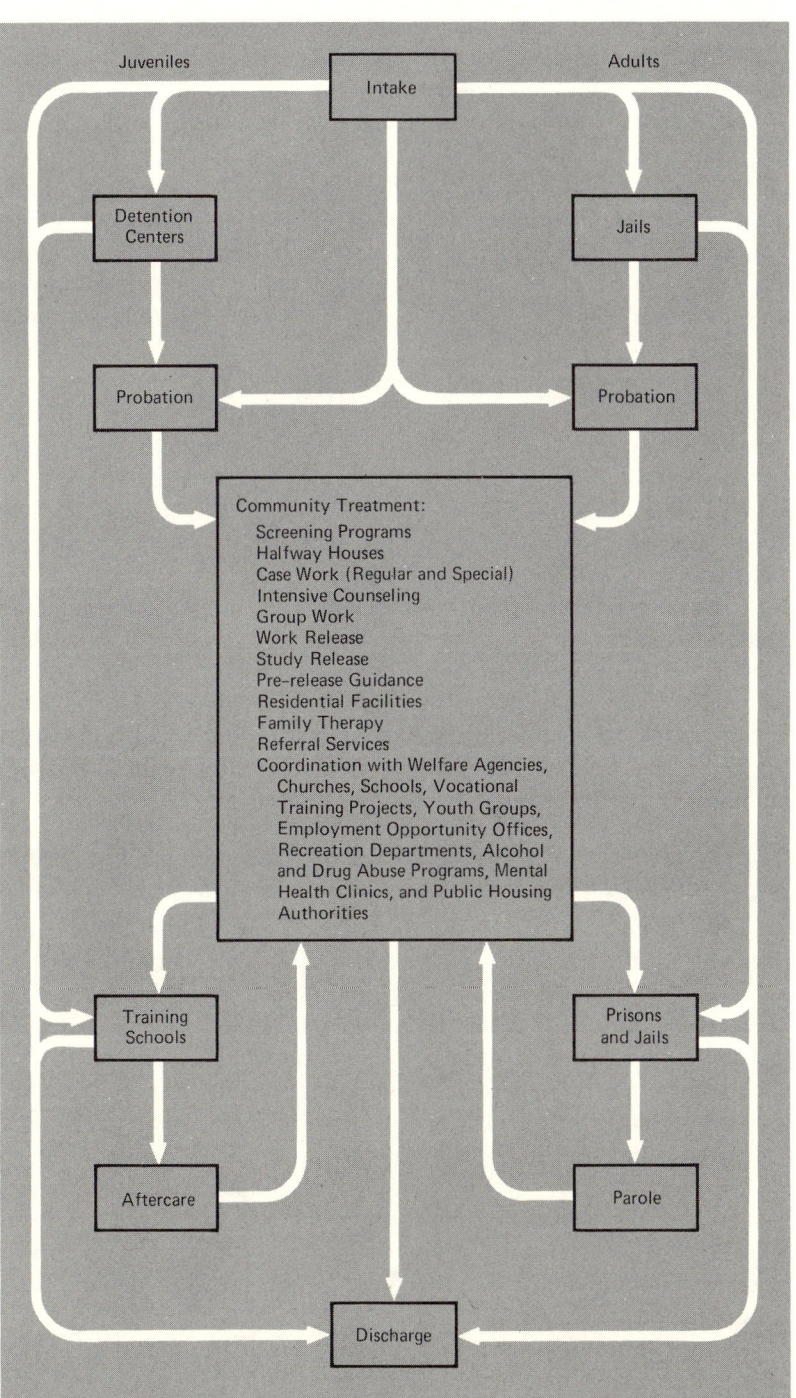

Figure 7. Major Correctional Activities

There is increasing awareness that corrections, and especially diverse forms of community treatment, should begin with intake when a person first becomes involved with agencies of justice. Instead of waiting weeks or months until possible determinations of guilt or delinquency, efforts can start almost immediately after arrest or referral. Proper handling at intake could divert millions of subjects away from the usually harmful effects of jail, prison, and training school. Many offenders, in truly innovative programs, might more easily achieve reform if they were screened, counseled, and guided without first going to court.

New forms of community treatment aimed at improving personal values suffer from coercive atmospheres, prior labeling, and retaliatory measures. Conversely, ordinary social relationships, prompt involvement, and individual consideration are conducive to character reformation. With new projects aimed at intervention upon intake, community treatment appears ready to emerge as the central rather than a peripheral activity in modern American corrections.

Despite inherent difficulties, there exists a growing recognition that reformation must eventually involve the social environment. A coordinated effort involving welfare agencies, schools, churches, and the offender's family probably has the most realistic chance of success. The great obstacle, of course, may be the very conditions which contributed to the original violation. To a degree, treatment must adapt to the community and prepare offenders to deal with its problems.

Agency Supervision

Probation, for adults and juveniles, looms as the largest single segment in the correctional scene. From the standpoint of subject population, it contains many times the number found in confinement. Technically, probation should be considered as the legal status of those persons found guilty of a crime but permitted to remain within the community under supervision. A variation on this scheme is the *suspended sentence*. Such penalties ordinarily differ from probation in that the judge announces a regular punishment, but then permits the convicted party to stay in the community without direct supervision, assuming good behavior. Under either scheme, additional arrests or violations of predetermined rules can result in the criminal's return to court for imposition of traditional penalties (usually confinement in an appropriate institution).

America was a pioneer in probation, and it has gained great popularity throughout the country. Originating in Massachusetts well over a century ago, the concept of supervised community release achieved early popularity for humanitarian reasons. Unconscionable conditions then (and still) found within prisons led to the realization of the sufferings and actual dangers of incarceration. Later, the practical considerations of expense and individual reform contributed toward expanded use.

With special emphasis on supervision of children, probation took on organized form throughout New England shortly before the beginning of the twentieth century. From there, it spread slowly but steadily across the nation. By 1925, all states maintained some variety of juvenile probation, but more than thirty additional years passed before there was similar recognition of adult services.

Today, supervised community release is utilized in more than half of all sentences for major crimes. The growth of probation has been dramatic and sustained for more than a generation and shows no indication of abatement. Authorities now tend to believe that supervised community release *should* be granted unless: confinement is necessary for public safety, treatment in custody would be more effective, or the violation's seriousness does not permit such apparently minimal punishment.[7]

Probation officers possess widely divided responsibilities. In a sense, of course, they are agents of criminal justice charged with enforcement of particular laws, but they also function as social workers, with responsibilities to their delinquent and often resentful clients. The combination of repressive, diagnostic, and rehabilitative duties can pose difficulties of divided or even contradictory goals. Yet, there appears to be no immediate solution to the dilemma.

America displays a wide variety of administrative schemes for all phases of correction, perhaps never more clearly than that for probation. The centralized federal system differs by jurisdiction and type of violator supervised. Those working in juvenile probation generally fall under the local control of separate courts while officers dealing with adults usually are directly employed by centralized state agencies.[8] Of course, many organizational patterns and combinations of function exist.

All together, about 15,000 probation officers now work within the United States. The majority of case workers probably have bachelor's degrees, while their supervisors should be graduates of professional schools of social work. However, actual educational backgrounds often do not relate directly to reformation, public welfare, or criminal justice. For some, the job has little connection with either prior training or personal interest.

Probation officers are generally overworked. Many have caseloads (the number of persons to be individually supervised) several times larger than suggested or reasonable maximums. In addition, they may be required to devote much, or even most, of their time to presentence investigations and reports for courts. To reduce probation workers' duties within boundaries of practical reason would require more than doubling present numbers. Even if funds were available for such an expansion, qualified applicants might be difficult or impossible to locate.

The immediate situation can scarcely be described as conducive to individual attention and reformation. Those on probation need frequently only appear for short, prearranged monthly visits. Except for isolated experiments, close supervision and differential treatment remain distant goals despite the indicated value of such care.[9]

The effectiveness of probation now apparently depends more on the choice of subject than on the form of treatment. Intensive counseling may indeed have negative results with certain kinds of offenders. There is no evidence that correctional innovations can actually reform those unsuited to rehabilitation.[10] However, that does not diminish the practical utility of probational schemes, given present conditions and selected violators.

While judges technically decide who is fit for community correction, the presentence recommendation serves as a determining factor. Often, the court merely approves a routine administrative determination. Judges follow recommendations for probation about 95 percent of the time, and when the presentence report suggests confinement, that is the sentence in 80 percent of cases. In practice, the decision whether or not to attempt correction by the ordinarily requested community supervision hinges upon rather basic criteria. The significant and normally determining factors are: prior criminal record, confinement status, number of arrests, type of offense, and employment history.[11] Special considerations may, of course, affect any case, but an unemployed jailed person with a record of several earlier arrests and convictions, found guilty of a crime of violence, will nearly always go to prison. On the other hand, the bailed and working party with no prior involvement with police, found guilty of a property offense, can almost invariably obtain release.

Naturally, not all courts follow the same criteria for granting probation. While the national average of such felony sentences now exceeds 50 percent, some courts and states use community treatment in almost every possible case while others very infrequently rely upon such resources.[12]

Probation is a form of punishment, although its purpose remains that of treatment, and despite burdensome caseloads, the supervising officers must attempt rehabilitation of each individual offender. This involves at least three fundamental efforts: restoring ties to the normal community, reducing the extent and significance of criminal contacts, and promoting success in ordinary activities. Naturally, every case involves special factors and obstacles, for the individual violator displays unique problems and characteristics. The probation officer must attempt the delicate task of eliminating weaknesses and developing strengths within an often quite resistant personality. Frustration frequently results.[13]

Community treatment holds no simple answer to the problems of crime. Probation is revoked in roughly 25 percent of cases, with presentence recommendations proving slightly more accurate than judicial determinations. And, naturally, many of those who successfully complete their period of supervised treatment later reappear, charged with additional offenses. Still, the rate of apparent reform through probation appears generally higher than those for other major types of correction. This may, of course, merely prove the failure of confinement rather than the success of community supervision.[14]

Efforts to evaluate the success or failure of probation must begin with a realization of the numerous and quite restrictive rules which ordinarily apply. The person under supervision must do far more than simply avoid another arrest or criminal charge. While jurisdictions and officers vary in their requirements, many prohibitions exist. For example, those on probation or other forms of community supervision must ordinarily request permission to temporarily leave the community, change their place of residence or employment, or apply for any type of license (hunting, driving, marriage). They are frequently forbidden use of drugs, weapons, or alcohol, and association with persons of bad repute, including prostitutes. In addition, the probation officer usually demands prompt replies or regular reports and may unexpectedly visit the home, school, and place of work.

These conditions obviously limit activities of those under supervision, and major or repeated minor violations can result in confinement. In many instances, such rules of behavior conflict directly with community life-styles, especially in the urban ghetto. As a consequence, a considerable range of attitudes exists among agencies and supervisors.

At one extreme, probation can suffer from excessive leniency. Supervision founded upon sympathy or sentimentality yields little more than increased opportunity for additional delinquency. On the other hand, probation may be conducted primarily as a police function. Where the officer watches for misbehavior and acts repressively for community protection, suspicion and distrust soon dominate. At best, supervision should involve a carefully designed strategy for individual reformation. Such treatment demands diagnosis and solution of individual problems, with a balance between personal understanding and public safety.[15]

Despite its essentially bureaucratic nature and often dull routine, probation service includes a number of progressive features. Transfer of subjects is possible between different communities and agencies. Today, interstate compacts even permit movement and continued supervision in distant cities. These programs provide valuable assistance by facilitating removal from problem neighborhoods and demoralizing associations.

Some agencies now also rely upon volunteer help in community treatment. Private citizens, acting as friends or employers, assume responsibility for people on probation. While such aid may not meet the standards of professional service, it occasionally provides desperately needed personal interest and relieves the congestion and pressed finances of most correctional efforts.[16]

Juvenile Probation

Despite long and widespread popularity, many counties in the United States still have no organized system of juvenile probation. While the law permits such care, no facilities or personnel may exist for supervision. This does not preclude the possibility of appointing temporary supervisors or assigning special duties, but absence of regular services surely reduces practical application.

On the other hand, urban areas ordinarily contain large staffs of juvenile probation officers with entrenched bureaucratic structures matching those of other government agencies. Here, duties may be quite specialized and almost inundated by oceans of formal reports and records. Courts naturally tend to use such existing services.

Juvenile probation costs considerably more than similar supervision for adults. This does not result from any special expenses entailed, but comes about through lower caseloads. Still, the typical juvenile probation officer supervises more than seventy released individuals, roughly twice the suggested figure. This burden prevents the specialized and individual care recommended, but it permits more differentiation of treatment than that routinely available for adults.

Probation for youthful offenders lasts an average of about one year. This naturally means that supervision must frequently be terminated before achievement and demonstration of actual reform. Meanwhile, those working with delinquents must further reduce their limited opportunity for care to perform a variety of related duties.[17]

Ordinarily, juvenile probation officers devote much effort toward preliminary processes. The typical agency receives cases from the police and diverse welfare organizations in great numbers. Probation officers must undertake primary investigations to determine if additional action, including a petition to the court, appears warranted. This often entails a review of previous reports, interviews, and inquiries into available community resources. In addition, the probation officer will often be called upon to personally make critical decisions as to whether or not a youth should be released or held in detention to await further disposition.

Formal diagnoses and recommendations to the court engage still more time. Here, the careful officer will investigate not only the individual juvenile's attitudes but also conditions of the home and neighborhood. Such tasks really involve prediction of human behavior, based on a multitude of changing factors. But, the final conclusions will frequently determine the outcome of cases and the course of lives.[18]

Supervised treatment remains the essential mission of the probation agency despite other responsibilities. The officers must devise plans for care, often without resort to formal court action. At least three essentail functions are involved. First, surveillance of the subject's major activities must be maintained. This may range from careful checks of the youth's friends and relationships within the family to brief questions about continuance in school and additional contacts with the police. In practice, performance nearly always falls between the two extremes.

The second primary aspect of supervision involves provision of services for the child's benefit. Here, the probation officer seeks out various community agencies and brings them into contact with his charge. Then, he tries to coordinate a program of treatment to effect individual reformation. Deep mistrust of government and social welfare may only complicate this difficult but often vital task.

Finally, probation workers personally counsel and advise juveniles, family members, and others connected with each case. It is today widely realized that practical efforts at rehabilitation involve far more than the youth immediately concerned. Changes in attitude come about only through acceptance and adaptation of conditions, but in many instances, this can only be accomplished with support and assistance from others. Probation officers face the trying responsibility of involving parents, school-teachers, and possible employers to create an atmosphere more conducive to rehabilitation.

Even beyond these responsibilities, agencies are commonly called upon to fulfill other duties. Some large, urban probation offices maintain mental health clinics to facilitate diagnosis and treatment of children referred for care. Also, some jurisdictions delegate administration of juvenile detention centers, foster homes, and additional treatment facilities. In a few communities probation officers occupy a major role in municipal planning and programs for crime prevention.

Added duties can overburden existing facilities for individual case supervision. They may, furthermore, appear disconnected or even unsuited to those essentially responsible to a court for treatment of young offenders. But, in many communities, such diverse functions have been acquired largely through default. Frequently, no one else seems willing and able to do the tasks at hand. At least juvenile probation remains in contact with the overall problems of society and, perhaps reluctantly, obtains still more responsibilities.

More than 100,000 young people enter the system of criminal justice every month; each year 200,000 of them are put on juvenile probation. Obviously the future of many lives and perhaps the security of our entire nation rests with successful treatment and correction. Today's youthful offender is tomorrow's hardened felon. While misguided sympathy serves no goal, undue harshness is just as unproductive; personal reformation requires a firm but sensitive hand. For overworked juvenile probation officers, the task is difficult but essential. Their efforts will very probably determine the future of crime control in America.

Adult Probation

Probation for adults falls into two fairly distinct categories: supervision of released felons and supervision of misdemeanants. These are combined in some jurisdictions and share the common problems of all types of community treatment. Probation for convicted felons, however, looms larger in terms of subjects, costs, and employment than that for misdemeanants.

Supervision of adults found guilty of crimes has several distinguishing characteristics. Unlike juvenile probation, that accorded felons must ordinarily meet quite specific requirements. For example, the statutes of most states directly control decisions to grant release without confinement. Persons proven guilty of murder or rape are often simply not legally eligible for probation, regardless of possible opportunities for rehabilitation. Legal restrictions on probation for misdemeanants less frequently preclude community care. Perhaps the most common statutory prohibitions refer to previous convictions or offenses against public morality, but provisions vary widely.[19]

Regular criminal judges (unlike their counterparts for juvenile dispositions) frequently impose rather detailed conditions and terms of release. Among the requirements sometimes attached are those for restitution (financial repayment to the victim) or a short prior period of confinement. While brief incarceration may seem warranted in many instances, the ordinary effect is detrimental. Shocking conditions within American jails cause even temporary detention to more often undermine reform efforts than to serve as a worthwhile deterrent. In addition, removal from the community can result in job loss, interruption of education, and further weakening of family ties. Supervisors generally agree that, in a typical situation, such tastes of confinement serve more as hindrance than help.

Average caseloads in adult probation currently surpass 100 in the United States; some officers must attempt to handle more than 200 individuals scattered throughout the community. This means that personal treatment remains an even more impossible goal than that for juveniles. Only a few of the nation's probation workers supervise small enough numbers to permit more than cursory counseling and verification of compliance with formal conditions.[20]

Despite the great preponderance of lesser violations, most adults placed directly under community treatment have been convicted of felonies rather than misdemeanors. Those found guilty of serious offenses constitute a clear majority of nonjuveniles presently on probation. Quite naturally, they consume most of the available supervisory time and expense.

Adult probation, unlike service for juveniles, generally operates as a state rather than local function. In fact, duties are commonly combined with centralized parole schemes. In many jurisdictions much work concerns presentence investigations and recommendations on suitability for probation, rather than direct supervision.

Perhaps the most surprising thing about all forms of community treatment is the relative economy involved. It now costs about $15 a day to maintain one adult offender in confinement, and this does not include allowances for the often resulting family support provided by the state. Probationary supervision, conversely, runs approximately $1.50 daily per subject. With hundreds of thousands presently undergoing correction, the actual and potential savings achieve very significant proportions. Since the average adult probation lasts about two years, thousands of dollars could be conserved on each subject. In fact, economy and reason would indicate reducing the numbers now in confinement by 80 percent and increasing probation services 400 percent. But such conjectures go far beyond the range of realistic expectation.

While probation for adult felons faces major limitations, the situation appears far worse in regard to misdemeanants. Several states and most counties contain absolutely no organized means of releasing under supervision those convicted of lesser crimes. In fact, misdemeanant probation (which sometimes includes juveniles as well as adults) exists almost entirely in the larger urban centers, usually combined with centralized agency supervision of felons.

Supervision of lesser offenders has quite unique characteristics. Use of misdemeanor probation varies enormously by region, state, and individual court. In some jurisdictions, the scheme is followed with some regularity, while in others it remains totally unknown.

Although probationary periods for misdemeanants average approximately one year in length, they very rarely even exist. For each lesser offender accorded community supervision, at least four simply go to jail.[21] And, the choice rarely depends upon any sort of presentence investigation or agency recommendation. Unlike felony and juvenile offenses, misdemeanors usually conclude with almost automatic established penalties. Only the most industrious of lower court judges take the time required to closely match criminal and punishment. Even when supervision is available and ordered, it often occurs in the form of *summary probation*, without prior study and determination of suitable treatment possibilities.

Individualization of penalties, while rare for misdemeanors, may still occur. Although the simple fine remains an ordinary punishment, this often accompanies a suspension of sentence whereby the guilty party returns to the community but without formal supervision. Should he violate the condition imposed, the judge can impose the prior penalty. In some courts, another variation involves the practice of giving *deferred convictions.* These imply a willingness to clear the record of any finding of guilt upon completion of certain requirements, perhaps including good behavior for a specific period.

During recent years, probation has been placed under growing judicial scrutiny. Not long ago the supervising officer held a position of enormous authority over his charges. A determination that rules had been violated or that probation was unsuccessful would almost invariably mean extended confinement for the convicted person. Today, however, conditions no longer permit such discretion. Judges must be considerably more careful about revoking probation. Hearings upon these matters may take on the trappings of a regular criminal trial. At present, actions on revocation of community supervision and deferred sentencing entail full constitutional rights of due process. Probation, once granted, has become more than a discretionary privilege despite its original imposition as punishment for crime.[22]

The ordinarily quite destructive effects of correctional confinement prompt authorities to revoke an order for community treatment only under pressing circumstances. Minor violations of probation rules, for example, may only lead to a review of conditions, followed by a conference and warning. With present emphasis upon aid rather than repression, supervisors are sometimes restricted from making direct arrests of their charges and are required to file applications for appropriate warrants for renewal of custody.

When serious new violations occur, the only alternative may be a hearing to revoke probation. Authorities generally believe that such efforts should include basic elements of due process. The hearing normally demands prior written notice, possible assignment of a defense attorney, proof of improper conduct, and provision for a record which may serve as the basis for appeal.

America has obviously developed gradations of punishment and control. A finding of guilt may no longer be considered as removing the convicted party from basic legal protections. These attitudes reflect growing concern with defense of individual liberties, but they also pose serious administrative difficulties in criminal justice. Unfortunately, social reform and personal freedom do not always coincide.

Summary

Most of those convicted for crimes stay within the community without confinement. Several varieties of treatment, especially for juveniles and adults with personal problems, now exist.

Probation, or community release with supervision, occupies a very large role in American corrections. While frequently revoked, it still provides a greater chance for reform than any other major form of sentence.

Juvenile probation entails a host of duties, with supervision of youthful offenders holding the principal position. Officers must counsel, assist, and also correct their numerous young charges.

Supervision of adults involves both felons and misdemeanants, but some states have services only for the former category. Very large sums could be saved through increased reliance upon all forms of probation.

Questions

1. What is residential treatment?
2. When should probation be used?
3. What are the functions of juvenile probation?
4. How does probation for felons differ from that for misdemeanants?

NOTES

[1] Tate v. Short, 401 U.S. 395, 91 S.Ct. 668 (1971).

[2] *Task Force Report: Juvenile Delinquency and Youth Crime* (Washington: GPO, 1967), pp. 107–113, 124–129, 422–424; Dean V. Babst and John W. Mannering, "Probation versus Imprisonment," *Journal of Research in Crime and Delinquency* 2 (July, 1965), pp. 61–69.

[3] *Community Based Correctional Programs* (Washington: GPO, 1971), pp. 22–26.

[4] Edwin M. Schur, *Crimes Without Victims* (Englewood Cliffs, N.J.: Prentice-Hall, 1965), pp. 145–152.

[5] Fritz Redl and David Wineman, *The Aggressive Child* (Glencoe, Ill.: Free Press, 1957), pp. 29–57; LaMar T. Empey and Jerome Rabow, "The Provo Experiment in Delinquency Rehabilitation," *American Sociological Review* 26 (October, 1961), pp. 679–695.

[6] *Rehabilitative Planning Services for the Criminal Defense* (Washington: GPO, 1970), pp. 40–69, 172–174.

[7] *Standards Relating to Probation* (N.p., American Bar Association, 1970), pp. 30–31.

[8] *Task Force Report: Corrections* (Washington: GPO, 1967), pp. 35–37, 200–201.

[9] *A Quiet Revolution: Probation Subsidy* (Washington: GPO, 1971), pp. 17–32, 48–83.

[10] James Robinson and Gerald Smith, "The Effectiveness of Correctional Programs," *Crime and Delinquency* 17 (January, 1971), pp. 67–80; Leslie T. Wilkins, *Evaluation of Penal Measures* (New York: Random House, 1969), pp. 74–89.

[11] Robert M. Carter and Leslie T. Wilkins, "Some Factors in Sentencing Policy," *Journal of Criminal Law, Criminology and Police Science* 58 (December, 1967), pp. 503–514; David Fogel, "The Fate of the Rehabilitative Ideal in California Youth Authority Dispositions," *Crime and Delinquency* 15 (October, 1969), pp. 479–498.

[12] *Task Force Report: Corrections*, pp. 27–28.

[13] David Dressler, *Practice and Theory of Probation and Parole* (New York: Columbia University Press, 1969), pp. 159–180.

[14] Sol Rubin, "Illusions of Treatment in Sentences and Civil Commitments," *Crime and Delinquency* 16 (January, 1970), pp. 79–92.

[15] *A Study of Practice Theory in Probation/Parole* (Washington: Youth Development and Delinquency Prevention Administration, 1971), pp. 39–65.

[16] *Guidelines and Standards for the Use of Volunteers in Correctional Programs* (Washington: Law Enforcement Assistance Administration, 1972), pp. 1–34.

[17] *Task Force Report: Corrections*, pp. 133–141.

[18] Robert M. Terry, "The Screening of Juvenile Offenders," *Journal of Criminal Law, Criminology and Police Science* 58 (June, 1967), pp. 173–181.

[19] 18 United States Code 4202; California Penal Code, sec. 1203; Illinois Revised Statutes, chapter 38, sec. 1005–6–1; New York Penal Law, sec. 65.00; Texas Code of Criminal Procedure, art. 42.12.

[20] *Task Force Report: Corrections*, pp. 34–35, 173–174.

[21] *Ibid.*, pp. 157–161.

[22] Mempa v. Rhay, 389 U.S. 128, 88 S.Ct. 254 (1967); Gagnon v. Scarpelli, 411 U.S. 778, 93 S.Ct. 1756 (1973).

Chapter 15

Imprisonment

"While we have prisons it matters little which of us occupy the cells."

GEORGE BERNARD SHAW

Confinement

Correction revolves around imprisonment. While the majority of sentenced persons remain in the community, confinement remains a critical factor. Failure of probation means incarceration, and those released on parole have already been imprisoned. In addition to those serving sentences, thousands are held pending trial or other court action. Though the image of close confinement still represents correction to many Americans, reality displays many variations. Because of the character of offenders and efforts at rehabilitation, the image of high-walled structures filled with hardened men serving long sentences has become rather misleading. Yet, the concepts and attitudes of another time continue to influence present conditions.

Today, nearly 500,000 people (young and old) are confined in several quite different types of institutions throughout the United States. Juveniles stay in detention centers and training schools; adults endure prisons and jails. But, absolute lines regarding places and varieties of incarceration cannot be easily established. Names of institutional types and categories of inmates shift by jurisdiction and locality. Conditions also differ according to statute, custom, and practice.

Some of the approximately 5,000 places of imprisonment are exemplary, modern institutions staffed by dedicated and efficient employees. At the other extreme, some stand as monuments of human depravity and official ineptitude. Despite marked but isolated improvement, the majority of confinement facilities constitute a national disgrace, symbolic of antiquated systems of justice.

Neglect now poses the greatest threat in all forms of correction, but nowhere more clearly than in confinement. Unquestioned progress has reduced the prevalence of actual mistreatment. While brutality and overt corruption on the part of workers may never be totally eliminated, they now exist only in unusual circumstances. Most inmates receive enough to eat and some degree of medical care, although deficiencies continue even in these areas. More common current problems include inadequate supervision and lack of attempted rehabiltiation. Boredom, danger from assaults by other prisoners, and existence in an atmosphere inducing still stronger criminal intentions are the major defects. Inmates simply wait for release, and society than suffers its punishment.

More than 100,000 people are employed, usually full-time, in confinement operations. Most sincerely try to accomplish their difficult and exasperating jobs, but many do not possess the temperament, education, training, or experience for such work. Correctional employees receive some of the lowest average salaries among those involved in criminal justice, and those handling imprisoned men and women get the least of all. Either as cause or effect, jobs relating to confinement generally carry less status and general appeal. Here, working conditions are worse than those usually encountered in other criminal justice positions. Tasks tend to be dull, repetitious, sometimes dangerous, and removed from population centers. Consequently, it becomes extremely difficult to recruit qualified and psychologically well-suited individuals. Confinement facilities often must accept almost anyone meeting very basic standards and sincerely wanting a job. Larger institutions sometimes provide rudimentary forms of inservice training, but smaller facilities usually have no means for improving the standards of service. Most confinement workers are well-meaning people who gradually accept their authoritarian and often unrewarding roles with equanimity.

Imprisonment naturally breeds resentment and violence. After all, inmates are contained by the ultimate (though sometimes quite removed) threat of force. It is not difficult to understand why such repression occasionally produces rebellion. Prisons and jail riots have been part of the American scene for generations. They may erupt from several causes, but they always seem to fail.

Most places of incarceration are quiet and well ordered, but a spark of resistance will sometimes ignite a social conflagration. Because control remains the key purpose of nearly all confinement operations, violence normally elicits prompt attention and suppression. Our prisons prevent most riots from ever really beginning. But, massive discontent does sometimes explode, with seizure of hostages and destruction of property.[1]

These occasional riots may call for the use of force from beyond the institutional organization. At times, local and state police are summoned and the National Guard might even appear. Only in such situations does public attention focus, however briefly, on American imprisonment. Some proclaim the absolute necessity of maintaining order; others vociferously demand alleviation of the prisoner's plight. Both sides typically ignore the mutual, shared, and long-lasting problems of guard *and* inmate. After a temporary increase of public interest things usually return to normal—until the next riot.[2]

Still, gradual changes do occur, even in our schemes of imprisonment. New concern with legal and social rights for inmates has appeared. Even more significant are those slow trends toward reform of criminal justice in general. The greatest change of recent generations concerns treatment instead of simple incarceration of those confined. This has led to a blurring of the distinction between imprisonment and other forms of care. Correction now includes halfway houses and residential facilities, which lie rather far from traditional concepts of tight security. Mental hospitals, drug rehabilitation centers, and similar institutions also demonstrate new awareness of treatment opportunities. These facilities, standing on the outskirts of criminal justice, display certain characteristics of penal institutions, but they permit experimentation and demonstrate expanding concepts of care.[3]

At least three general trends can be discerned amid the complexities of American confinement systems. First, the need for adequate classification of new inmates now receives considerable recognition. Otherwise, widely divergent kinds of criminals would be grouped together without adequate discrimination by age, offense, or likelihood of reform. Second, rehabilitation has taken precedence over punishment. Education, counseling, and vocational training now occupy positions of real importance in many institutions. Finally, correctional administration is being gradually centralized, usually under state agencies. This often leads to a diminution of political control and establishment of basic standards. These modifications, of course, were proposed generations ago; they unfortunately remain distant goals in parts of the United States.

Any appraisal of confinement requires understanding of misconceptions concerning immediate crime control. The natural assumption is that incarceration automatically reduces the number of violations, simply because offenders cannot get out to commit them. But this overlooks the realities of modern American justice. Most crimes result in no one being imprisoned, and those persons placed in custody obtain release after fairly short periods. The overwhelming majority of present and prospective offenders are not behind bars; they live among us even now. If all persons in confinement were released today, the overall effect on rates of crime tomorrow would be moderate. Others may be deterred and the individual prisoner conceivably reformed, but his brief incarceration contributes relatively little to *direct* prevention. Confinement for extended periods occurs rather infrequently and, while perhaps most often imposed upon incorrigible or dangerous offenders, could scarcely serve as a primary means of crime control.

Prison conditions have been attracting steadily growing attention from the courts. Today, confinement by no means deprives an inmate of fundamental rights, but these must constantly be balanced with the necessities of internal order and security. It is now clear, however, that arbitrary censorship of mail, excessive disciplinary punishment, physical brutality, and racial discrimination violate constitutional restrictions.[4]

Juvenile Detention

Juvenile detention is essentially jail for children. Facilities of this type do not, in theory, serve as places of punishment or reform but merely hold young people awaiting court action. In practice, they often become convenient places for temporary deposit and disciplining. Official functions remain those of support and custody for juveniles, but they perform a host of duties in different communities.

Detention houses and centers are almost entirely located in larger urban areas. Only a few hundred of them operate, but they serve areas containing about half the total population of the nation. Where no detention facilities exist, and this includes several entire states, juveniles are usually placed directly in jail. While normally demanded by statute, local authorities often do not segregate children from adults. It is not yet uncommon to find runaways placed in a cell with sex offenders, drug addicts, and violent offenders. Given the shocking conditions and lack of supervision found in many jails, the importance of separate juvenile detention becomes obvious. Of course, many local officials make efforts to hold young people apart from adults, but inadequate facilities complicate the problem. About 25 percent of all confined juveniles awaiting court action are housed within institutions essentially for adults. Most jurisdictions still do not maintain separate places for detention of young people. No area in corrections probably cries more desperately for prompt reform.[5]

A few states, mostly in New England, have established regional detention centers for juveniles, with centralized support and regulation. As a consequence of delay and disregard on the part of communities, this presently represents a promising trend. But most existing places for juvenile detention remain under purely local control, administered by the courts through probation departments.

While hundreds of thousands of juveniles undergo detention annually, only about 15,000 are in custody at a given time. The average confinement lasts several days; a few children, however, remain for many weeks. As a rule, the police place the juvenile in detention, and probation officers arrange for his or her release. Some young people stay in custody for a few hours (at times being discharged before formal reports can be completed and filed); others languish in confinement over very long periods. Parental attitude, social position, and official policy play major roles in determining actual lengths of incarceration.

Detention centers usually serve as convenient catch-alls in which to place the young. Policemen and employees of other agencies deposit troublesome youths in them. Judges allow juvenile detention to serve as informal and unofficial punishment. Social workers even resort to them for custody of neglected, abandoned, or abused children. This leads to problems of classification and segregation matching those found in adult institutions.[6]

While most detention centers provide minimal medical and dental facilities, this marks the ordinary extent of available services. No significant means for recreation, education, counseling, or therapy usually exist. The emphasis clearly rests upon custody rather than treatment. Separate detention facilities do ordinarily maintain sizeable staffs for supervision, but there is little inservice training for custodians. A few detention workers still have 72-hour alternating shifts (three days on, three days off). But, standards and conditions of service have generally improved in recent years.

While they do not always receive adequate attention, juveniles held in temporary custody benefit from the highest proportional number of employees found in any general type of confinement. Furthermore, those communities with detention centers often make a sincere effort to obtain qualified personnel.

Little uniformity in use of confinement for juveniles exists. Some jurisdictions routinely place nearly all young people arrested into detention. Others very rarely hold those taken into custody. Proportionate numbers of juveniles detained extends from close to 100 percent to under 5 percent. Decisions frequently hinge upon existence of facilities, departmental policies, and personal inclinations.

Nearly half of the juveniles incarcerated are never formally charged with an offense. They may be held for a few days and released, having not yet seen a judge or probation officer. In many such cases, the detention center has been utilized to inflict a form of punishment through temporary deprivation of freedom, without an adjudication of guilt.

The majority of boys and girls detained will eventually be discharged into the community without any sort of supervision or care. Less than 10 percent of them will later be confined in an ordinary correctional institution after adjudication of delinquency. The obvious conclusion is that too many juveniles presently go into detention. Appropriate policies depend upon community conditions and facilities, but present practices of temporarily confining thousands of American young people, sometimes innocent and very rarely dangerous, obviously demand modification.[7]

Some areas have developed imaginative programs whereby juvenile detention is controlled by agency policy and rapid court review. When combined with state assumption of responsibility for planning, support, consultation, and inspection, these centers can provide efficient custodial care without undue expense.

Training Schools

Juveniles declared delinquent may be sent to a correctional institution, usually called a training school. These are really specialized prisons for the young, with emphasis on reform rather than mere confinement. All together, about 350 institutions for the confinement and correction of juvenile delinquents exist within the United States. About 250 are training schools (frequently termed reformatories, youth centers, or otherwise). In addition, about 100 ranches, forestry camps, and reception facilities operate across the country.

In many respects, training schools present the most favorable part of the American confinement system. Here, at least, the goal is *supposed* to be reform of offenders instead of mere control or punishment. Consequently, teachers and treatment personnel constitute a considerable proportion of employees. On the other hand, the mass of group or cottage supervisors (who often function as guards) receive the lowest average salaries in the entire correctional scheme. These important positions remain difficult to staff with capable men and women.

Approximately 50,000 juveniles are currently in correctional confinement, with training schools containing far more than do camps or diagnostic facilities. Boys comprise 77 percent of the total; a greater percentage of girls face confinement than do women. Most delinquents, of course, never go to correctional institutions; they more often receive community treatment.[8]

Training schools began in the Northeast before the Civil War. But more than a century passed before every state contained at least one such facility. Now the trend is toward establishment of specialized smaller institutions. Several states have ten or more diversified training schools; others maintain only a single correctional institution for juveniles. In design, they range from traditional reformatory structures resembling factories or concentration camps to modern residential communities without walls or fences.

The vast majority of children under rehabilitative confinement are held in state (and three federal) institutions, usually administered by departments of correction or welfare. A smaller number stay in locally operated camps and schools, primarily in California. Additionally, some authorities still place children in privately run facilities which often operate under public subsidy.

One generalization applicable to most juvenile facilities concerns expense. Training schools, essentially because of their large staffs which contain many professionals, cost a great deal of money. Maintenance of a juvenile in correction costs roughly twice that for an adult. America spends about $300 million annually on its training schools. Average expenditure per inmate varies fantastically by state. Some jurisdictions spend more than five times the amount required by others, ordinarily with marked differences in degree of care.

Training schools process about 100,000 admissions and discharges every year. The typical juvenile inmate remains in confinement for only a few months (state averages range from 4 to 24). In addition to these relatively brief imprisonments, authorities frequently transfer children between institutions, contributing to high rates of statistical turnover. Approximately 60 percent of admissions to training schools are first commitments; about the same proportion of releases involve aftercare.[9]

Viewing inmates of all institutions simultaneously, juveniles represent a broad spectrum of delinquent behavior. Murderers, rapists, burglars, and robbers may be found, but most of those confined have committed such lesser offenses as petty theft, vandalism, and disorderly conduct. In addition, good numbers were guilty of no actual crime; they merely ran away from home, disobeyed parents, loitered about, broke curfew, or performed other acts constituting legal delinquency.

Most American training schools properly stress education for their youthful inmates. This frequently includes both regular academic and practical vocational courses. But education in these institutions poses many unusual problems. Students come with vast differences in background, aptitude, and motivation. A class may include juveniles of quite different ages and degrees of social adjustment. Also, the rapid rate of admission and discharge means a continual turnover of students. Administrators consequently strive to maintain small classes and promote personal attention by teachers. Considering obvious obstacles, educational efforts within our training schools merit general commendation.

Custodial aspects of juvenile correctional institutions also encounter grave difficulties. Security and a positive environment for reform seldom go together.[10] Supervisors and guards frequently resort to corporal punishment in training schools, although this receives continual criticism. But control in these facilities is no simple task; escapes and inmate assaults occur with regularity.

Reformation and custody suffer from overcrowding. Many training schools contain far more children than they can successfully control. While total numbers of inmates have remained relatively constant in recent years (because of increased use of probation and aftercare), overcrowded conditions continue in many institutions. Most experts also believe that care is facilitated by smaller schools limited to confinement of about 150 boys or girls. Nearly half of our training schools now exceed this recommended maximum.

Jails

Jails are the worst means of confinement in America; they also constitute probably the most disgraceful feature of corrections in all criminal justice. This condition results from combinations of antiquated and overcrowded facilities, inadequate budgets, reactionary concepts, corruption, and general disinterest. While progressive attitudes now influence most detention centers, training schools, and even prisons, jails have continued with operations unchanged for generations. At present, they may, collectively, do more harm than good.

A simple description of a jail might be that of a place of confinement for misdemeanants. But only a tiny fraction of such institutions fall solely within such a restricted category. Jails really serve to hold the human residue of criminal justice. Throughout the country, these cages (for nearly all fit that description) perform a host of logically separable functions.

Jails do contain those sentenced to relatively short terms for misdemeanors. But 70 percent of facilities also accept juveniles for detention, and 90 percent hold adults not yet proven guilty. They contain a wide assortment of people with legal difficulties. Parents failing to provide child support, witnesses, runaways, child molesters, bank robbers, drunkards, illegal immigrants, murderers, and embezzlers can be found within these facilities, often with only the slightest effort at segregation and supervision.

Over 4,000 jails, primarily operated by counties and some cities, exist within the United States. In addition, countless local agencies maintain small lockups for prisoners. These usually consist of a few cells temporarily confining suspects and parties awaiting transfer elsewhere. Prisoners seldom remain in such facilities longer than 48 hours; in most instances, a transfer or release occurs the same or following day.

Approximately 160,000 persons are now confined in jail. Of these, about 70,000 have actually been sentenced to terms ranging from days to years. Half of all those confined simply await trial (usually upon failure to meet bail requirements). The remaining 10,000 are in custody for additional court action or transfer to other institutions. A typical jail contains felons, misdemeanants, contrary children, and possibly innocent people. The "drunk tank" remains a common feature, and communal cells without plumbing or electric lighting may still be found.[11]

Only a few jurisdictions maintain separate buildings for such obvious categories as women and juveniles, each of which comprise about 5 percent of the total number of present inmates. Modern structures do exist, but most jails are antiquated strongholds, hiding shameful conditions. Overcrowding, filth, and obsession with security continue in many localities.

While thirty states restrict maximum jail sentences to twelve months, those serving terms are often mixed with persons in pretrial detention or with those being held for other authorities. Progressive jurisdictions concentrate on reducing inmate populations. Many of those now confined should be released on personal recognizance, judicial hearing, and prompt trial. Conscientious management has, in a few places, changed jails from museums of social failure into useful community assets. The task demands ability, patience, and public support.

With about 30,000 employees, jails have more prisoners per worker than any other means of confinement. Only about 2 percent of the staff provides any form of treatment, and custody remains the only function in many localities. Many jails have only one guard on duty for scores of prisoners; such inadequate supervision can lead directly to homosexual assaults, financial exploitation, kangaroo courts, suicides, and murders. Of course, officials and administrators deny and ordinarily escape any responsibility for these deplorable and inexcusable conditions.

American jails rarely provide any sort of positive care for inmates; half do not even have medical facilities. Counseling, educational programs, organized recreation, and partial release are most unusual. Some jurisdictions actually obtain benefit from retention of the ancient workhouse concept whereby misdemeanants serve out sentences by laboring on public projects. Today, most inmates simply wait out their time in boredom and despair. They are largely a forgotten people, caged in conditions far worse than those accorded in other forms of correctional confinement, including prison.

Most jails are administered by county or city governments. A few states (Connecticut, Delaware, Rhode Island) have pioneered by assuming full responsibilities for such facilities, but most have no control whatsoever of local confinement operations. The federal government utilizes community jails to temporarily house its prisoners, and this entails approval of food, security, and other features. Few American jails can meet the basic requirements set by the Department of Justice.[12]

While generalization is difficult, administration of local confinement facilities leaves much to be desired. Corruption and personal profiteering still exist; inadequacy and lack of concern dominate. The reluctance of local officials to develop and encourage innovative programs, change attitudes, and maintain fundamental standards of humanity creates problems for the entire country. Jails should be thrown open to public inspection and, if necessary, placed under centralized control. Significant progress in criminal justice can never be achieved with the continuation of present deplorable conditions.

Local confinement and correctional institutions include an assortment of jails, camps, and farms. Nearly all share problems of boredom, insufficient classification of inmates, poor physical facilities, and low standards for employees. Two of every three jails have no rehabilitation programs of any type. It should come as no surprise to discover that prisoners flow out and back in with appalling regularity. Some inmates have served more than 100 short sentences, typically for drunkenness or disorderly conduct.

America's jail population is not evenly distributed throughout the nation. California and the South contain highly disproportionate numbers: About 90,000, or more than half the total number of inmates, can be found within these sections. New England states, by contrast, incarcerate relatively few persons in jail.[13]

Significant improvement in local confinement will require major alterations of policies and practices. Jails could be removed from political control and subjected to strict standards, including provision of reform opportunities. Separate facilities for the insane (still frequently housed with other prisoners) are essential. Finally, it would seem advisable to expand the use of misdemeanant probation and transfer those serving longer sentences directly to prison, rather than retain them in our ineffective jails. A growing awareness by administrators holds promise of improvement, but change will undoubtedly be gradual and slow.[14]

Prisons

The United States pioneered in prison reform during the early nineteenth century but now largely follows outmoded concepts. Penal institutions, run by state and federal governments, contain sentenced adult felons (and misdemeanants in certain cases). Approximately 400 prisons exist in America though they may actually be called penitentiaries, industrial schools, road camps, or otherwise. Larger systems have specialized units for reception and diagnosis, medical or psychiatric care, and for particular categories of inmates, including women, young adults, and first offenders.

Prison populations grew rapidly prior to 1900, then stabilized, and have tended to decline during the most recent decade. Increased use of probation and parole helped shrink inmate numbers in a period of soaring crime rates. But about 200,000 (3 percent female) are in prison today (including 20,000 in federal institutions).[15] Of these, perhaps 20 percent pose some actual danger to society although most have served time before. The average convict was sentenced for a crime against property or public rather than for an act of violence. Despite popular misconceptions, prisoners do not usually spend decades or a lifetime awaiting freedom. The typical stay is now less than two years, and forms of authorized absence, transfer, and formal release actually produce nearly a quarter of a million departures annually.

With prominent exceptions, prisoners are pathetic rather than deviant or dangerous. The majority never attended high school, come from poor homes, belong to social minorities, and may encounter not one personal visitor during their entire time behind bars. Most have no close family or job skill; in some systems, 25 percent of the inmates are believed to be mentally retarded. So, they enter and leave lonely, embittered, and tragic figures—both offenders against and victims of society.[16]

Administration of prisons is now almost entirely vested in centralized state agencies. Not long ago, appointment of wardens and employment of guards were politically managed. But today most workers come within the scope of civil service, and directors often rise through professional ranks. The scope of prison administration depends entirely on state size and attitude. Larger systems (California, New York, Texas) maintain twelve or more separate institutions while the smaller (Wyoming, New Hampshire, North Dakota) have only one facility. These extend in size and concept from small work camps with fewer than 40 convicts to giant fortresses containing more than 4,000. Experts now urge establishment of new community-related institutions, each holding no more than a few hundred inmates. But, dozens of century old isolated penitentiaries continue in operation.

Among the many thousands of persons employed by our prisons, 60 percent are concerned with custodial duties. Thirty percent perform various maintenance or service functions, leaving no more than 10 percent to engage in treatment. Few institutions have adequate numbers of psychologists, counsellors, or teachers. Meanwhile, standards for regular custodial officers remain fairly low, and some prisons still utilize armed inmates as guards.

Control remains the first task in adult correctional confinement. Prisons are routinely classified by degree of security (minimum, medium, maximum), with careful assignment of inmates. Consequently, successful escapes from American facilities occur quite infrequently.

Some systems place great emphasis on work, often significantly reducing the cost of upkeep. Prison industry and agriculture may provide a side benefit of vocational training for inmates, but labor often goes toward products with little or no outside competition. Items for government use dominate correctional industry.[17]

Rehabilitation now constitutes a function of considerable significance in many institutions. Treatment teams strive toward reform in "open communities"—prisons without walls. Such techniques as counseling by former inmates, partial release, practical job preparation, and guided group therapy hold promise for improved adjustment. Yet, progress is quite slow. Only about 2 percent of inmates undergo essentially rehabilitative treatment. The rest encounter more traditional approaches stressing custody or work, but the majority of prisons do provide limited opportunities for academic education, vocational training, recreation, and professional counseling. Some institutions even allow inmates to attend regular college classes, seek individual outside employment, and participate in assorted community activities. These progressive and usually quite successful programs are, however, still exceptions.

American prisons typically display an atmosphere of repression and depression. Inmates are handled en masse, subjected to exploitation, debased, and isolated from family and friends. Guards cannot satisfactorily supervise huge dormitories and must conduct repetitious counts and searches. Rules are necessarily arbitrary, and discipline rigid. Yet, inmate subcultures remain strong, sometimes demanding covert concessions from custodians.

Our prisons serve as graduate schools for crime. Convicts conduct their own form of education in thievery, deception, and violence. Inmates usually become more experienced and deviant as a result of confinement; some even become addicted to narcotics while in prison. Of course, these conditions are more prevalent in closed and traditional institutions than in those receptive to principles of reform, but they exist to some extent in all facilities.

American penal methods are considered quite barbaric throughout much of the world, particularly in matters relating to sex and the family. Incarceration in the United States promotes abnormality and isolation. Some prisons in other lands actively encourage conjugal visits (whereby wives can stay with their husbands), allow children to remain near their convicted mothers, and provide attention and assistance for pregnant women behind bars.[18]

Despite their enduring problems, America's adult correctional institutions have progressed considerably over the last several decades. Imaginative programs and receptive administrators can, when permitted, accomplish much even within traditional prisons. Here, public and political attitudes sometimes pose the greatest obstacles.

American prisons form a peculiar, isolated, miniature society, by nature abnormal and authoritarian. These institutions develop terms of reference and personal relationships quite different from those of an ordinary community. Inmates lose far more than the obvious freedom to leave. They must conform their individual habits, associate almost entirely with other convicts, face deprivation of countless common conveniences, and enter a world of potential violence, homosexuality, thievery, and deception.

Prisons normally maintain two obvious groups: the staff and the inmates. Perhaps surprisingly, the keepers cannot maintain absolute authority by threat of force or additional punishment upon their charges. Guards routinely compromise and transmit messages, overlook minor infractions, or deal informally with prisoners. In exchange, they receive a degree of cooperation, secret reports, and assistance in performing a multitude of duties.[19]

As staff members tend to assume attitudes of superiority and righteousness, inmates develop feelings of inferiority and resentment. Each group views its opposite with natural suspicion and distrust. The result, of course, hinders all efforts toward actual rehabilitation.

Correctional institutions have their own social classes and values. Convicts occupy varying positions of power or prestige, ranging from those with political influence or close connections with organized crime down to the mentally retarded or abnormal sex offenders. Also, many prisoners (male and female) occupy particular homosexual roles, with newcomers frequently subjected to exploitation or assault.[20] Finally, inmates perform special functions or demonstrate significant personal interests. For example, some distribute contraband goods, give legal advice, dedicate themselves to religion, resist the exercise of authority, tyrannize the weak, or become informers. The majority, however, merely want as rapid a release as possible.

Prison inmates are the final residue of American criminal justice. Consequently, they collectively represent only those who committed offenses, did not avoid prosecution, were found guilty, and then received heavy sentences. They stand at the bottom of the sieve which collects our disadvantaged social deviants. It should be no surprise that, of all prison inmates in America, nearly half are black and an even higher proportion were raised in poverty.

Summary

American confinement facilities fall into four major categories: detention centers, training schools, jails, and prisons. Each type displays common problems and unique characteristics.

Juvenile detention centers provide temporary custody and shelter for the young. Their operations are primarily restricted to larger urban areas. Training schools and camps confine juveniles declared delinquent; they ordinarily stress education during rather short terms of custody.

Jails are the catchalls of confinement, and they generally display the worst features of the American correctional system. Poor management, lack of supervision, and inadequate service produce deplorable conditions. Prisons hold adults in correctional confinement. They are primarily operated by state agencies and vary greatly in size, security, and approach.

Questions

1. Who should be blamed for prison riots?
2. How widely is juvenile detention used?
3. What purpose do training schools serve?
4. How can jails be improved?
5. Should prisons be abolished?

NOTES

[1] *Prevention of Violence in Correctional Institutions* (Washington: GPO, 1973), pp. 1–32.

[2] Frank R. Prassel, "Rebellion in Miniature: A Sociological Analysis of the Prison Riot," *Proceedings of the Southwestern Sociological Association*, 20 (1970), pp. 369–373.

[3] *A Nationwide Survey of Mental Health and Correctional Institutions for Adult Mentally Disordered Offenders* (Washington: GPO, 1972), pp. 43–56; *The St. Louis Detoxification and Diagnostic Evaluation Center* (Washington: GPO, 1970), pp. 9–59; *Alternative Approaches to Opiate Addiction Control* (Washington: GPO, 1972), pp. 55–59.

[4] *A Program for Prison Reform* (Cambridge: Roscoe Pound-American Trial Lawyers Foundation, 1972), pp. 47–62.

[5] *Task Force Report: Corrections* (Washington: GPO, 1967), pp. 121–122.

[6] *Task Force Report: Juvenile Delinquency and Youth Crime* (Washington: GPO, 1967), pp. 13, 36–37.

[7] *Corrections* (Washington: GPO, 1973), pp. 269–272.

[8] *Statistics on Public Institutions for Delinquent Children 1970* (Washington: National Center for Social Statistics, 1971), pp. 4–5.

[9] *Ibid.*, pp. 11–12, 15, 17.

[10] Mayer N. Zald and David Street, "Custody and Treatment in Juvenile Institutions," *Crime and Delinquency* 10 (July, 1964), pp. 249–262.

[11] *National Jail Census 1970* (Washington: GPO, 1971), pp. 1–6.

[12] *Task Force Report: Corrections*, pp. 23–25, 75–80, 162–168.

[13] *National Jail Census 1970*, pp. 1–2.

[14] *Manual on Jail Administration* (Washington: National Sheriffs' Association, 1970), pp. 190–215.

[15] *National Prisoner Statistics: Prisoners in State and Federal Institutions for Adult Felons* (Washington: Bureau of Prisons, 1972), pp. 1–9.

[16] *The Challenge of Crime in a Free Society* (Washington: GPO, 1967), pp. 45, 160; Ramsey Clark, *Crime in America* (New York: Simon & Schuster, 1970), pp. 130, 219, 233.

[17] *The Role of Correctional Industries* (Washington: GPO, 1972), pp. 4–6.

[18] Paul W. Tappan, *Crime, Justice and Correction* (New York: McGraw-Hill, 1960), pp. 679–680; Columbus B. Hopper, "The Conjugal Visit at Mississippi State Penitentiary," *Journal of Criminal Law, Criminology and Police Science* 53 (September, 1962), pp. 340–343.

[19] Gresham M. Sykes, *The Society of Captives* (New York: Atheneum, 1970), pp. 13–39.

[20] *Homosexuality in Prison* (Washington: GPO, 1972), pp. 12–21, 28–35; David Ward and Gene Kassebaum, *Women's Prison* (Chicago, Aldine, 1965), pp. 80–101.

Chapter 16

Release and Recidivism

"The way of transgressors is hard."

PROVERBS 13:15

Discharge from Confinement

Nearly all of those incarcerated will be released, usually within a period of months, and return to the community in which they previously lived. At least 95 percent of convicts in prison eventually obtain a discharge; jails, detention centers, and training schools naturally let free almost every inmate. But release from confinement is more than an automatic phase of justice; it poses serious problems of adjustment and sometimes involves continued supervision or assistance.

Only a small fraction of those imprisoned serve their full sentences. Most convicted felons and many misdemeanants obtain some form of early release. If all sentences were fully served, our inmate populations would probably triple. Instead, total numbers are held in check through parole and other versions of early release.

Those convicted of crimes against the person or serious violations affecting public morality remain imprisoned for the longest period. Persons found guilty of homicide, rape, robbery, sex, and narcotic offenses usually face the longest periods of actual confinement. Those sentenced to "life" rarely remain in custody much longer than ten years. Administrators are especially anxious to bid farewell to troublemakers, regardless of their original offense.

Under "good time" provisions, prisoners almost automatically shorten their terms of incarceration by satisfactory behavior. Some institutions grant additional reductions based upon work, giving blood, participation in research projects, or other voluntary acts by inmates. Furthermore, these measures often apply to compound the effect of parole. This means that prisoners can obtain the benefits of several sentence reductions cumulatively. Good time release and parole are separate means of getting out of prison and can, ordinarily, be utilized in combination.

Some prisoners are discharged through direct executive intervention. At one time, pardons issued by governors served as frequent means of release. This discretionary exemption from punishment, derived from royal powers, can include removal of the original finding of guilt. Pardons may be either full or partial, absolute or conditional. In addition, America has seen occasional instances of "amnesties" or general exemptions, applicable to entire categories of offenders, that purposely overlook prior violations.

Pardons were once routinely obtained through bribery or political influence. Excessive and improper use of this traditionally executive function caused many states to restrict the power by statute and assign authority to administrative boards.[1]

Two closely related grants are those of commutation (executive clemency, whereby a sentence may be reduced or shortened) and reprieve (temporary withholding or delay of punishment). The latter is applied primarily in cases of the death penalty, and the former sometimes fits unusual cases deserving special sympathy and consideration.

Growing numbers of prisoners now serve terms which are, in effect, determined by administrative rather than judicial means. Aside from ordinary release through parole, our correctional system has edged slowly but steadily toward use of *indeterminate* sentences. Under provisions of the federal and several state systems, judges may merely establish maximum periods of incarceration, leaving time of release to be determined by a board or commission. If a burglar became liable upon conviction for confinement of up to fifteen years, and the judge imposed a term of ten, correctional authorities could discharge the inmate after only a few months. Indeterminate sentences, in theory, permit those trained and experienced in personal reform to match individual release times with apparent rehabilitation. But they also can lower prisoner morale and rely far too heavily on nonexistent expertise.[2]

Indefinite sentences lack any judicially set maximum. A person confined for any penal offense could be discharged by administrative action only when he was believed reformed—a condition that might never occur. American criminal justice does not include this practice in pure form, although incarceration of the mentally ill may appear quite similar. Often, however, the terms *indeterminate* and *indefinite* are loosely interchanged in statutes and commentaries.

Any release from confinement is widely recognized as a critical phase in correction. Planning for discharge and readjustment should, but almost never does, commence with sentencing. Many progressive institutions now include programs to assist in this difficult process. Some enable carefully selected inmates to receive partial release, usually designed to permit them to work or study within the community and return (voluntarily) to confinement at night. This scheme seems especially advantageous to local jails that provide few facilities for care or treatment while simultaneously destroying the continuity of previously undertaken jobs and classes. At present, however, it is used primarily and quite successfully in positively oriented prisons.[3]

Even our traditional penal institutions occasionally permit temporary home release. Inmates are allowed (sometimes without guard) to leave their prison in times of family crisis, as rewards, or in other exceptional circumstances. Permission for these absences nearly always depends upon the discretion of the institution's own administrators.

Controlled release is now utilized to promote readjustment to the community. Realizing the harm inherent in captivity, some authorities recommend *reception center discharge*, whereby sentenced persons thought likely to be adversely affected by confinement are promptly paroled. Also, a few facilities now rely upon temporary release for diagnostic purposes. Actions of inmates who are permitted to briefly visit their home and community can certainly provide clues for further supervision and assistance.

With growing understanding of the frustrations and temptations awaiting discharged persons, several institutions have installed pre-release classes and guidance centers. Convicts nearing the completion of confinement are instructed in common social skills such as safe driving, budgeting, insurance, union memberships, social security, standards of dress, employment opportunities, religious activities, manners, borrowing money, veterans' benefits, and otherwise prepared for life outside the walls. In some instances, these programs phase into halfway houses that are actually located within the community. Here, offenders wear civilian clothing, freely receive visitors, and are gradually reintroduced to ordinary society. Ambitious pre-release efforts provide close supervision and counseling while individuals seek jobs and places to live.[4]

Guidance classes and halfway houses are far removed from traditional concepts of punishment, but they merely face the fact of correction realistically. Inmates do not stay imprisoned; they return, one way or another, to society. Pre-release care and assistance attempt to provide a realistic bridge toward rehabilitation. Inmates deemed uncooperative or unsuited for release may also be returned directly to prison.

Discharged persons suffer many handicaps. Convicted felons usually lose a variety of civil rights, such as voting and holding public office. Of more practical concern, job opportunities are few while chances for return to criminal behavior beckon. Former friends and relatives show distrust and even fear. Police and other officers of justice remain suspicious and watchful. For most released offenders, the road of lasting reform is long, difficult, and lonely.[5]

Aftercare

Discharge from confinement may involve a variety of controls and formal regulations. Those released from custody by the police or the courts are simply freed and returned directly to the community. But persons coming from correctional confinement frequently must undergo extended periods of supervision. Adults are usually paroled from prison. Juveniles released from training schools receive aftercare. Both groups supposedly benefit from assistance and guidance provided by officers of justice. Community supervision is very rarely available for offenders emerging from jail, and it enjoys no direct application following temporary detention of young people.

Aftercare actually means juvenile parole. The concept of placing conditionally discharged youths under continued supervision and care originated rather peculiarly with indentured children from workhouses. Youthful offenders would simply be contracted out to labor for often quite mercenary employers. Today, rehabilitation is believed to be facilitated by individualized support and treatment. Aftercare places discharged juveniles under the supervision of professional government workers, with the goal of promoting readjustment to the community and reform of personal attitudes.

The decision to release juveniles from training schools usually rests with institutional authorities. Most jurisdictions empower agency administrators to determine appropriate times for discharge. Some experts, however, believe that such determinations are more appropriately made by independent bodies, along the lines of adult parole boards; several states have adopted this method. At the other extreme, a few jurisdictions still require the committing judge to make the ultimate decision on release of juveniles. In such instances, a proposed discharge may originate at the training school but must gain approval of the magistrate concerned.

Most statutes now accord wide flexibility in determining times of release for those in youth correction. Authorities ordinarily possess considerable discretion in evaluating reform and estimating chances for successful return to the community. Some states impose specific minimum terms, especially in cases of serious crimes of violence.

Supervised release for juveniles has grown to great significance in America. About 60,000 young people (20 percent girls) are currently undergoing aftercare. Several states have yet to establish centralized programs for discharged youths, but major cities usually have some form of service available. Administration of aftercare is ordinarily performed by departments of public welfare or correction. These agencies commonly operate at the state level and also manage the training schools. In some areas, aftercare remains a local operation, regulated by the courts through their probation officers.[6]

Conditionally released juveniles seldom stand entirely apart in the system of correction. Aftercare counselors frequently are charged with probationary or other welfare duties. Furthermore, they routinely conduct the pre-release investigations of children in confinement. In some regions, they handle adults on parole as well as juveniles.

Supervisors assigned essentially to aftercare average caseloads of approximately 65—a condition scarcely conducive to individualized treatment and guidance. With little support or counseling possible, workers tend naturally to concentrate on unusual cases. Often, aftercare consists largely of the completion and study of written reports (sometimes prepared by the juvenile himself). Supervisors may have, or make, time to see their youthful charges only during emergencies. Consequently aftercare seldom achieves its potential worth to the individual and community.[7]

Problems in the supervision of released young offenders are frequently complicated by distance. Some states maintain only a few aftercare counselors, usually located at the training school or in larger cities. Juveniles may be several hours travel away from a "supervisor" who has insufficient time for visits. Interested agencies or courts can, of course, assign aftercare responsibilities to local officers or private citizens, but this part-time or voluntary service may suffer from lack of interest, ability, or experience.

Despite admitted handicaps and failures, community supervision following periods in training schools has many valuable attributes. One obvious benefit is that of economy: Confinement of a juvenile costs ten times as much as aftercare. Furthermore, reform is often much more likely within the family and community rather than within an institutional setting. In many cases, continued incarceration of juveniles only contributes to further criminal behavior after release.

Aftercare provides an opportunity to observe and assist the discharged youth. Support and therapy, hopefully involving others in the community, can materially increase chances for lasting reformation. Aftercare typically lasts slightly more than one year, a period which often marks society's last opportunity to prevent youthful delinquency from developing into serious crime. Yet, it constitutes a largely undeveloped field of correction in many areas. In fact, many communities provide less supervision and guidance for released juveniles than for adults.

Parole

The idea of supervised release from prison for convicts goes back quite far in history. England forced inmates into indentured labor and transportation to colonial regions (including America). Others were released from prison under *tickets of leave* which permitted a return to home and the search for acceptable employment. Then, about a century ago, an innovative penologist, Zebulon R. Brockway, organized a formal system of parole in New York. Supervised release was developed as a regular part of the correctional system.

Adult parole has grown from isolated experiments to become a basic feature of American criminal justice. The percentage of persons conditionally released increased sharply after World War II and now includes two of every three departures from prison. Overall, a majority of those persons discharged are placed upon parole. All together, approximately 100,000 adults presently live within the community under various forms of guidance and supervision. The total is, however, remaining relatively stable because of increasing probation and less reliance upon confinement. Because fewer persons go to prison, decreasing numbers eventually depart.[8]

Use of parole varies greatly by jurisdiction. Some states (New Hampshire, Washington, Kansas) rely upon supervision in well over 90 percent of prison releases; others (South Carolina, Wyoming, Oklahoma) resort to this version of correction for less than 20 percent of cases. The South traditionally avoids parole while New England favors its use, but regional comparisons no longer reveal sharp discrepancies.

Community supervision does not correlate closely with time served. Jurisdictions giving heavier prison sentences or requiring longer periods of incarceration show no strong inclination to either greater or less use of parole. In short, early and conditional departure from prison does not indicate marked leniency or severity. The extent of reliance upon parole scarcely measures the efficiency of a particular correctional system; too many other variables are present to permit such simplification.[9]

One aspect of supervised release seems apparent; it rarely applies to misdemeanants. While often permitted by law, parole services very infrequently apply to persons discharged from American jails. This form of correction is almost entirely limited to felons, the kind of offenders perhaps most in need of, but least susceptible to, rehabilitation. Instead of relating to chances of reform or lack of danger to the community, parole application appears more closely tied to tradition. At any rate, those convicted of serious violations carrying longer sentences enjoy a far greater likelihood for early discharge than do people found guilty of lesser and repetitive crimes. The reformative goal of supervised release remains essentially limited to persons discharged from prison, rather than from jail.

Likelihood of parole for adult felons depends upon many factors. Some 80 percent of American jurisdictions have statutory requirements for eligibility. Many specify a particular portion of mandatory confinement, sometimes set at one third of the maximum sentence imposed. Those given "life" are usually legally eligible for parole within a few years.[10]

Not long ago the prospect of immediate employment was almost essential to early discharge from prison. Today likelihood of parole usually depends upon recommendations from administrators, with particular reference to inmate adjustment and rehabilitation. The nature of the original offense, prior history, personality, and efforts to continue education or participate in positive prison programs often attain significance.

Once the prerogative of governors, responsibility for granting parole now rests upon state commissions or boards. Jurisdictions naturally differ in procedural detail, but general similarities apply. The typical parole board has about five members appointed by the governor for either four or six year terms. In more populated states, these can be full-time and well-paid positions; elsewhere they may require temporary service with limited remuneration.

While essentially responsible for conducting hearings on applications for parole, board members often have a variety of additional duties. In some states they grant "good time," pardons, and commutations. Furthermore, the board frequently appoints officers and administers the state's parole service. Some authorities believe that decisions on discharge could be more efficiently handled by the confinement institution, as it is routinely practiced in training schools, or that hearing procedures might benefit from standardization and written policies. Meanwhile, parole continues to be based upon combinations of intuition and prediction.[11]

Board approval does not lead to immediate release. A considerable period of time may elapse before actual discharge and assignment to a supervisor. America has only about 2,000 parole officers, but the number is somewhat misleading. A great many states combine responsibilities for community supervision of those just convicted and of persons being discharged from confinement. Only in more populous areas are parole and probation services clearly separated. Consequently, those responsible for conditionally released felons usually have a multitude of duties. In addition to probation tasks, many agencies assign preparole duties to officers. This requires study and recommendation on applications for early release. A few jurisdictions now have special examiners to perform such tasks.

Caseloads are almost as heavy for parole as for probation supervisors, and duties appear similar. Of course, problems of readjustment to community life following conviction for more serious crimes complicate work with those coming out of prison. Years of incarceration naturally affect attitudes and desires. In an attempt to provide more individualized treatment, some agencies now resort to specialized caseloads, permitting supervisors to concentrate on certain types of offenders or personal problems (such as narcotics addiction or alcoholism).

Ideally, parole should consist of separate but interrelated phases. The first, naturally, involves selection of appropriate subjects followed by study of the individual case and pre-release planning. Next, supervision and assistance within the community occur, buttressed by essential policies on revocation and recommitment. In practice, these tend to be treated as quite distinct and independent stages.

Parole typically lasts somewhat more than two years, but individual state averages range from one to seven. The Midwest traditionally has the shortest periods of supervision. The strictness of agencies and officers varies extensively. But parole supervisors tend to be generally less flexible than their counterparts in probation.[12] Those handling adults conditionally released from prison commonly possess the authority to order renewed confinement. With considerable responsibility for law enforcement as well as assistance, parole officers often work rather closely with the police. A good deal of useful information may be exchanged between cooperating agencies. Nevertheless, observers believe that parole agencies should avoid law enforcement functions whenever possible.

Adult parole is revoked approximately 30 percent of the time,[13] a rate slightly higher than that for probation. About 20,000 released individuals face recommitment to prison every year. Procedures generally requiring board approval do not involve the full technicalities of trials but must insure due process and a fair hearing.[14] Most revocations do not involve commission of another felony or serious crime. The conditions imposed for release indirectly bring many back to prison.

Parole violations that lead toward revocation include: drinking or drunkenness, changing residence or job without authorization, associating with undesirable or disapproved individuals, marrying or driving without permission, and failing to keep appointments or complete required reports. Additionally, a released convict may be warned or recommitted for ignoring the advice of supervisors, having generally uncooperative attitudes, keeping late hours, neglecting family, and taking improper trips. Finally, revocation of parole almost automatically follows disappearance from the community or arrest and conviction for another offense. Still, most of those released under community supervision do fulfill required conditions satisfactorily.

Tens of thousands of people depart from prison every year through forms of release other than parole. Many get out early by compiling "good time," often while serving as a trustee. Their release is conditional upon satisfactory behavior but normally involves no formal supervision. And, of course, many inmates do serve an entire sentence and so qualify for direct discharge.

Regardless of the form used, release from prison poses as many problems for society as does continued incarceration. Confinement provides no real solution to the overall crime problem, but returning uncorrected offenders to the community also holds no answers. At present, many American prisons are only making conditions worse by producing ever more hardened and devious offenders. And, until suitable alternatives are made available, the situation is unlikely to change.

The Cycle of Crime

Crime is a repetitive phenomenon. Those who commit one offense tend to do so again. When a person previously convicted and subjected to correction commits another crime, the term *recidivism* applies. In a sense, the prevalence of recidivism measures the success or failure of reform efforts and, more broadly construed, the entire system of justice.

The extent of recidivism depends almost entirely upon the frame of reference used. Studies have revealed great discrepancies, largely because of incomplete data, selected sampling, or outright bias. But most experts agree that recidivism poses a major problem in America. Our correctional system very often falls short in its goal of permanent reformation.

Prisons truly succeed about 25 percent of the time; training schools probably do slightly better. In short, most of those discharged from confinement will commit new offenses. The typical person taken into custody has been arrested several times before. A clear majority of serious known crimes are performed by those having police and prison records.[15] If our scheme of justice operated more successfully, the rate of violations would fall drastically. Instead, the police, courts, and correctional agencies encounter the same offenders time and again.

While accurate and comprehensive analyses of recidivism in the United States do not exist, several tendencies are generally recognized. Quite logically, those acquitted or dismissed (without conviction) apparently seem most likely to commit another offense. Among the guilty, recidivism tends to increase with the severity of punishment. Probation accomplishes reform more often than does confinement, and those paroled are rearrested less frequently than persons released unconditionally (at the conclusion of a full sentence). Of course, these results reflect effective selections as well as treatment. Naturally, the criminals thought least likely to reform face long periods of incarceration.

Recidivism does not correlate with seriousness of offense. Those convicted on charges of auto theft or burglary demonstrate a relatively high statistical likelihood of returning to crime. Rapists and embezzlers enjoy comparatively low rates of recidivism. It should be obvious that present categories of crime bear little relation to chances of rearrest.

In general, those most likely to originally commit offenses also have high rates of recidivism. The young, males, and blacks are most frequently subject to another arrest, trial, conviction, and confinement. Renewed violation usually occurs quickly. Recidivism tends to take place quite soon after discharge. About 40 percent of those released from the criminal justice system will be back in custody within two years. After that period, rates decline rather sharply.[16]

Understanding of recidivism is quite limited and encounters several serious obstacles. First, studies are based primarily on those who are released from confinement and *arrested* again. Based only on repeatedly *convicted* offenders, the situation appears not as disturbing. Second, available figures might be misleading because alert police and correctional officers naturally watch people with prior records more closely. On the other hand, it is quite possible that former convicts have become more skillful in escaping arrest. Finally, even modern police records and means of identification permit frequent omissions or errors. Consequently, a person arrested again (especially for a minor offense) will often not be recognized as having been previously convicted or confined. In cases of offenses committed in distant states or other countries, officials may never know of prior records.

Attempts to treat recidivism in strict statistical terms meet many problems.[17] How, for example, should revocations of probation or parole for violations of minor rules be regarded? Has a murderer who commits only lesser offenses against the public peace been reformed? And, what of rearrests that seem unreasonable or lacking probable cause? Some authorities feel that individual performance after release is properly described as successful, marginal, or unsuccessful, with questionable cases assigned the middle classification.

Some nations report recidivism rates far lower than those of the United States. Why do American correctional efforts fail so often? The failure is due, in part, to retention of outmoded policies and techniques quite unsuited to a complex, technical society. Our means of treatment are overburdened and often poorly administered. Correctional institutions reveal conditions ranging from antiquated to barbaric. Convicted people are discharged from the system with little preparation and, usually, an absence of meaningful support. Those completing full sentences, probation, or parole almost never receive any additional study or assistance. Authorities simply close the appropriate files until the next arrest or trial.

Meanwhile, released convicts encounter enduring public suspicion and discrimination. They usually go back to the very community conditions that contributed to their original offense, with jobs and positive relationships even more difficult to acquire. In addition, the previously confined may have knowledge, habits, or acquaintances that create opportunities for additional criminality. In typical situations, crisis and temptation combine to form the reality of recidivism.[18]

Our methods of prediction are far more accurate than our methods of rehabilitation. Statistically, we know who is likely to commit an additional offense, but we seem unable to effect major changes in performance. Experimentation has demonstrated the value of individual treatment, but this has not led to acceptance and use on a wide scale. America could undoubtedly reduce recidivism by total reform of the correctional system, but necessary steps have been rejected for generations.

Still, promise of improvement exists. Ex-convicts have organized groups to maintain contact and provide continuing assistance for released inmates. These programs have demonstrated the potential value of programs designed to capitalize on sincerely motivated subjects.

Despite high rates of recidivism, many people convicted do *not* return to crime. Instead of concentrating entirely upon failure, it must be recalled that correction often succeeds. Because most of us display some criminal tendencies, we can scarcely expect to impose unrealistic standards of behavior on known offenders. No conceivable system of justice and form of correction could possibly eliminate *all* recidivism.

In many instances, the practical goal might be reasonable adjustment rather than total rehabilitation. Criminals are people with serious and probably chronic personal problems. Some have lasting emotional disturbances, addictions, and dependencies. Others were raised in and will return to an atmosphere scarcely conducive to model behavior. Under such circumstances, only partial reform can be marked improvement. This by no means serves as an excuse for crimes against person or property, but it may indicate the necessity of establishing more practical objectives and adopting imaginative and flexible methods of treatment.

Finally, the damage caused through current recidivism presents a significant dilemma to society. Even our limited understanding of criminal activity indicates its repetitive nature. Consequently, it is obvious that certain categories of violators will continue to pose a danger to the community. This may reflect the ineptitude of present correctional efforts; such a realization provides no additional measure of public security.

Some offenders should probably never be released unless society is prepared to tolerate seemingly endless cycles of crime, prosecution, conviction, and unsuccessful correction. Certainly, we cannot afford the potential threat to personal liberty and the immediate economic cost of confining large numbers of offenders. However, a graded system of continuing community supervision might curb the number of repeated offenses. Combined with practical approaches to social and personal problems, such schemes would hopefully curtail rates of recidivism and help in the general control of crime.

While no simple solution exists, several routes of correctional improvement seem indicated. Expanded use of community treatment with lower caseloads for supervisors and provision of services for misdemeanants will combat recidivism. Shorter terms of treatment, institutional group work, and prompt release following rehabilitation also appear to hold promise.[19]

Meanwhile, the general failure of our correctional system places constant stress upon all phases of justice. Improvements in the police or the courts will have little effect upon rates of crime as long as pronounced recidivism endures. Arrest, prosecution, and conviction would merely recycle the same offenders at higher speed. In short, significant progress toward solving the crime problem must directly involve corrections. Recidivism places heavy burdens upon the entire system of justice, and society suffers the consequences.

When offenders continue to commit violations (despite the efforts of law enforcement agents, judges, and correctional officers), we all pay. The end results of recidivism include ever-rising crime rates, public fear, higher taxes, additional insurance costs, and immeasurable losses in property and personal suffering.

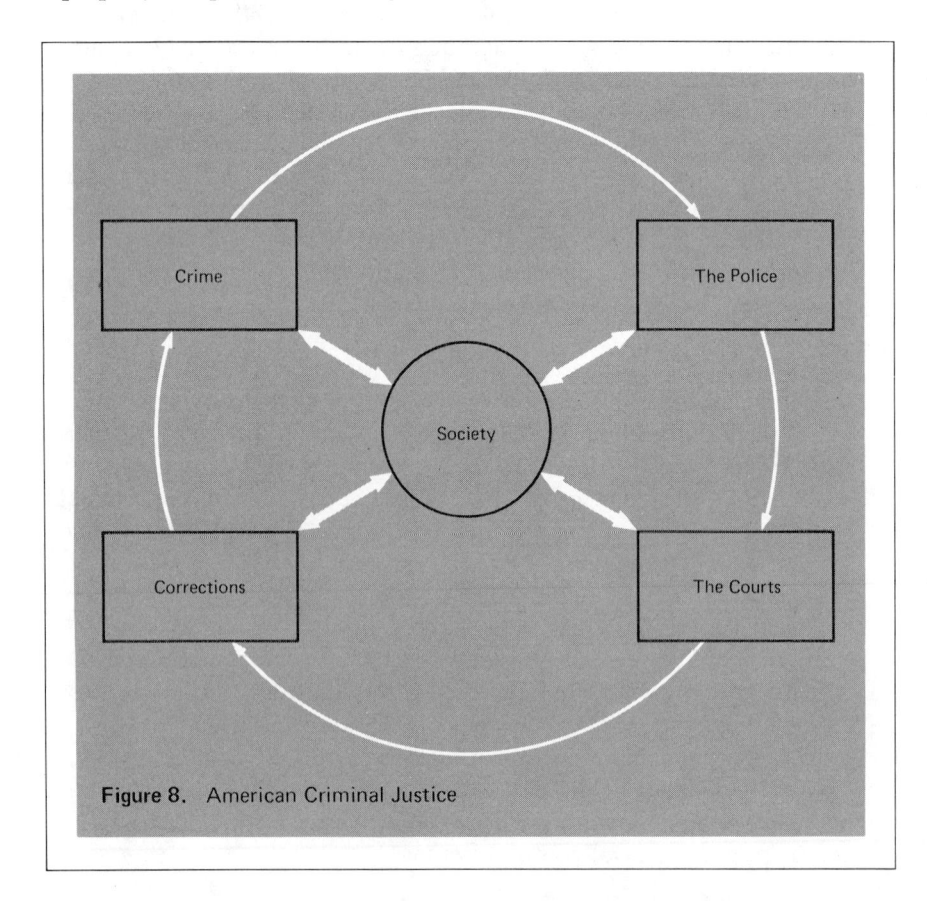

Figure 8. American Criminal Justice

Summary

Almost all of those confined will soon be returned to the community. Release, which usually occurs long before service of a full prison sentence, poses many difficulties.

Supervision for conditionally discharged juveniles is technically termed *aftercare*, and that for adults *parole*. In both fields, rehabilitation through support and treatment is the goal. A majority of prison inmates are now released through parole, but aftercare remains a somewhat less developed aspect.

Our correctional system very frequently fails to accomplish lasting reform; a great deal of American crime occurs through recidivism. Meanwhile, the system of justice continues to process the same offenders endlessly. Although no easy answers can be anticipated, new programs for reduction of recidivism now exist. Their success or failure may ultimately determine the future of crime control in America as well as the kind of society in which we will live.

Questions

1. Should the indefinite sentence be used?
2. Why has juvenile aftercare become popular?
3. What are the primary purposes of parole?
4. Why does recidivism exist?

NOTES

[1] Hazel B. Kerper, *Introduction to the Criminal Justice System* (St. Paul: West, 1972), pp. 378–380.

[2] *Struggle for Justice* (New York: Hill & Wang, 1971), pp. 67–82, 91–96.

[3] Daniel Glaser, *The Effectiveness of a Prison and Parole System* (Indianapolis: Bobbs-Merrill, 1964), pp. 402–422; *Ordering Time to Serve Prisoners* (Washington: GPO, 1973), pp. 2–10.

[4] *Graduated Release* (Washington: GPO, 1971), pp. 3–22.

[5] *Reintegration of the Offender into the Community* (Washington: GPO, 1973), pp. 42–52.

[6] *State-Local Relations in the Criminal Justice System* (Washington: GPO, 1971), p. 241; *Corrections* (Washington: GPO, 1973), p. 408.

[7] *Task Force Report: Corrections* (Washington: GPO, 1967), pp. 150–154.

[8] *National Prisoner Statistics: Prisoners in State and Federal Institutions for Adult Felons* (Washington: Bureau of Prisons, 1972), pp. 8–9.

[9] *Task Force Report: Corrections*, pp. 60–62, 186–187.

[10] 18 United States Code 3651; California Penal Code, secs. 3040–3065; Illinois Revised Statutes, chapter 38, sec. 1000–3–3; New York Correction Law, sec. 212; Texas Code of Criminal Procedure, art. 42.12.

[11] Karl Menninger, *The Crime of Punishment* (New York: Viking, 1969), pp. 81–83.

[12] Elmer H. Johnson, "The Parole Supervisor in the Role of Stranger," *Journal of Criminal Law, Criminology and Police Science* 50 (May–June, 1959), pp. 38–43.

[13] *National Parole Reports* (Davis, Calif.: National Council on Crime and Delinquency, 1973), pp. 1–17.

[14] Morrissey v. Brewer, 408 U.S. 471, 92 S.Ct. 2593 (1972).

[15] Ramsey Clark, *Crime in America* (New York: Simon & Schuster, 1970), p. 215.

[16] *Uniform Crime Reports for the United States—1970* (Washington: GPO, 1971), pp. 37–42; *Uniform Crime Reports for the United States—1972* (Washington: GPO, 1973), pp. 35–39.

[17] Leslie T. Wilkins, *Evaluation of Penal Measures* (New York: Random House, 1969), pp. 41–59.

[18] Daniel Glaser, *The Effectiveness of a Prison and Parole System* (Indianapolis: Bobbs-Merrill, 1964), pp. 311–401, 465–496.

[19] *State-Local Relations in the Criminal Justice System*, pp. 53–63.

Conclusion

An understanding of American criminal justice must begin with a general knowledge of actual conditions and meaningful relationships. Unreasoned praise is as useless as blind denunciation. *Introduction to American Criminal Justice* should provide a realistic survey rather than either a glorification or denigration.

Our scheme of dealing with offenders deserves a measure of considered criticism. At present, it does not adequately prevent, detect, prosecute, or correct criminal behavior. While no single element carries the blame, generations of neglect and misuse have resulted in public suspicion and disregard. The processes of justice stand condemned, as both reactionary and radical, for being too lenient and too harsh. Each of these several allegations is founded upon a degree of truth. There are, in fact, so many variations that generalization is very difficult.

On the other hand, few countries provide the legal protections accorded defendants in America. The United States does not have the highest crime rates in the world; our police, courts, and correctional programs remain superior to those of many other societies. Moreover, we continue to operate within a fundamentally democratic though constantly threatened framework of government. Criminal justice in this nation is progressing and continues to earn a proper degree of praise.

Introduction to American Criminal Justice has scarcely touched upon many specific areas and fields of interest. The theories of delinquency, principles of police administration, rules of criminal procedure, and techniques of rehabilitation exemplify topics for further exploration. Above all, the interrelated and interdependent nature of all such aspects should be apparent. Piecemeal analyses and efforts toward reform will produce little beyond inadequacy and frustration; conceptual integration must accompany effective renovation.

Can American criminal justice be substantially improved? The answer, of course, is yes. We can curtail but never eliminate crime by first taking action against the social conditions which contribute to violations. Then, America might reform its currently very inefficient agencies of justice. Police departments, courts, and correctional agencies need total reorganization. Higher standards for personnel, rigid adherence to requirements of integrity, elimination of provincial and political influences, and adoption of modern procedures can be accomplished in a relatively short period of time. In addition many of these steps will actually produce substantial savings to the public through eventually reduced taxes, lower insurance costs, and fewer personal losses.

Methods of improving criminal justice have been known for decades. Largely repetitious recommendations, suggestions, and guidelines abound. We already have the knowledge; the obstacle is lack of will. Many people appear to understand the answers, but very few are putting them to use. The public does not display an unwillingness to get better service from their agencies of justice. But, citizens seldom benefit from the sincere and informed political leadership that they deserve and should demand.

Many administrators in all phases of criminal justice operate largely by tradition and custom instead of by logic and imagination. They attempt to perform outdated functions by means that once may have worked. To some, change is regarded as a threat rather than an opportunity. Others may be willing to attempt reform but encounter strong resistance from those with vested interests. Improvement is seldom easy; inertia usually wins. Reform sometimes occurs by accident and not design.

Criminal justice is only one aspect of our troubled and complex civilization. It now consists largely of well-meaning men and women seeking to perform impossible tasks in impractical ways. Still, the only real answers lie in the interest, support, sacrifice, and dedication of concerned individuals and groups. The public, legislators, police, lawyers, judges, and correctional workers all share in the responsibility of improving criminal justice. Objective study, controlled experimentation, and willing acceptance of the results can transform yesterday's failures into tomorrow's successes.

Recent decades have witnessed very definite progress. Twenty years ago, for example, the college-educated patrolman was almost unknown. Today, a growing number of local and state police departments require applicants to hold degrees and encourage all officers to continue with advanced training.

The chances of significant progress have certainly never been better. Opportunities for worthwhile employment in criminal justice are great, especially among progressive police and correctional agencies. Few other fields enjoy comparable challenges and potential rewards. Despite the difficulties endemic to our whole society, a multitude of excellent jobs exist. Many agencies display degrees of imagination and innovation unknown in prior generations.

And, after all, criminal justice thrives on problems. Ultimately, they are the only reason for its existence.

Glossary

Adversary Practice. The opposing action of attorneys to further the development of truth and justice.
Aftercare. Supervised conditional release (parole) of juveniles who have been previously found delinquent and sent to training schools.
Amnesty. A general pardon applicable to entire categories of offenders, usually for earlier political offenses against the state.
Arraignment. The final preliminary process before actual trial at which the defendant pleads to an indictment or information.
Arrest. The placement of a person in custody under legal authority or the apprehension and detention of a person with cause.
Bail Bond. A guarantee or obligation (usually in terms of money) that secures the release of a defendant pending trial (as distinguished from personal recognizance).
Canon Law. The body of ecclesiastical or church law; special decrees and orders governing the clergy.
Certiorari (sŭr′shĭ-ō-ra-rē). A means of review by a high appellate court involving a writ that brings a case on for further inquiry.
Civil Law. The legal system developed on the European continent (as distinguished from common law) or the rules and matters dealing with private claims (as distinguished from criminal law).
Closed Institution. A traditional confinement facility, stressing security (as distinguished from open community).
Common Law. The legal system and concepts based upon case precedent that were developed in England (as distinguished from civil law).
Conjugal Visit. Occasional or continued resumption of the marital relationship by prison inmates under conditions of privacy.

Corpus Delicti (kŏr′pŭs dē-lĭk′tī). The "body of the crime"—evidence sufficient to establish the commission of an offense (not guilt).

Crime. Acts that are directly punishable by the state; divided into offenses against the person, property, and public.

Criminal Law. The legal system and rules applicable to violations punishable by the state (as distinguished from civil law).

Criminalistics. The specialized field using scientific and laboratory means to investigate offenses.

Crisis Intervention. Application of therapeutic techniques in time of serious personal disturbances; practiced by social workers or police to avert harmful reactions of emotionally involved people.

Dangerous Drugs. Stimulants, depressants, and hallucinogens subject to government regulation (as distinguished from narcotics).

Due Process. The constitutional requirement that government follow established rules and not offend fundamental standards of justice.

Electronic Eavesdropping. Use of technical listening devices to secretly invade privacy; now closely regulated by statute.

Entrapment. The inducement by law enforcement officers of the commission of a crime; requires an implantation of intent and constitutes a valid defense.

Ex Post Facto (ĕks pōst făk′tō). After the fact; retroactive prohibitions making illegal or punishing a previous act.

Exclusionary Rule. The doctrine forbidding the use of evidence obtained through illegal search and seizure.

Felony. A serious crime, usually punishable by death or imprisonment in a penitentiary (as distinguished from misdemeanor).

Habeas Corpus (hā′bē-ăs kor′pŭs). The "great writ" that compels authorities to produce the body of a prisoner and show just cause for his restraint.

Halfway House. A correctional facility that combines the features of confinement and community release; used for those on either probation or parole.

Indefinite Sentence. Correctional confinement with no fixed maximum length, release being entirely discretionary with administrative authorities; often used synonymously with indeterminate sentence.

Indeterminate Sentence. Correctional confinement with a judicially fixed maximum, actual time for release being determined through administrative action; often used synonymously with indefinite sentence.

Indictment. An accusation of a serious offense that is determined by a grand jury (as distinguished from an information).

Information. An accusation brought directly against a suspect, normally by a prosecutor, and not involving action by a grand jury (as distinguished from an indictment).

Inner City. The central districts of urban areas that are marked by high rates of crime, low income, unemployment, and concentrations of minority group members.

Jurisdiction. The authority of a court to decide a case; also used in reference to the capacity or power to legally act.

Juvenile Delinquency. Offenses or misbehavior by minors that can result in court action for the control and benefit of the child.

Larceny. Stealing another's property; often used synonymously with "theft" to include the crimes of false pretenses and embezzlement.

Law. Enforceable standards of social behavior; involves substantive and procedural aspects.

Misdemeanor. A lesser crime, usually punishable by fine or jail sentence (as distinguished from felony).

Narcotics. Technically, sleep-producing or pain-relieving substances; generally used to mean forbidden or closely regulated drugs, including opiates, cocaine, and sometimes marijuana (as distinguished from dangerous drugs).

Nolle Prosequi (nŏl'ē prŏs'ē-kwĭ). In criminal law, the formal declaration of the prosecutor that he will not take a case to trial.

Nolo Contendere (nō'lo kon-ten'de-rē). A plea, other than guilty or innocent, which indicates that a defendant will not contest a criminal charge but may dispute a related civil suit.

Nonjudicial Punishment. A means of imposing disciplinary correction within a military unit without resort to trial by court-martial.

Nulla Poena Sine Lege (nŭl'a pē'na sī'ne leg'e). No punishment without law; the legal doctrine which requires strict construction and non-retroactivity of statutes.

Open Community. Prisons without walls that are used to permit rehabilitation in relatively normal and therapeutic social settings (as distinguished from closed or traditional institutions).

Organized Crime. Offenses by well-established groups that are in control of gambling, narcotics, loan-sharking, or other illicit transactions.

Pardon. An act of executive or administrative grace providing an exemption from punishment and, usually, removing the original finding of guilt.

Parens Patriae (pă'rĕnz pă'trē-ī). The doctrine which allows the state to intervene for the purpose of protecting a child's welfare; a basis for juvenile justice.

Parole. Supervised conditional release of convicted people following correctional confinement, usually granted by administrative action.

Personal Recognizance. Acknowledgment of a debt or duty; a recorded agreement to obtain release pending trial (as distinguished from bail bond).

Plea-Bargaining. Negotiations between the prosecution and defense to reach an agreement so that admissions of guilt may be more readily obtained, cases expedited, and sentences limited.

Police Ratio. The number of law enforcement officers per 1000 inhabitants of a given community or area; formerly expressed in terms of the number of citizens per policeman.

Polygraph. A "multiwriting" device which ordinarily records respiration, blood pressure, and galvanic skin response; used as a "lie detector."

Precedent. A previously adjudged case or earlier decision that furnishes an example or authority in later legal controversies.

Presentence Investigation. The study and recommendation of punishment, usually made by a probation officer to a court.

Preventive Detention. Retention in custody pending trial by denial of bail; theoretically designed to prevent additional offenses prior to conviction.

Probable Cause. Facts and circumstances which would lead a reasonable man to believe that a crime has been committed; it must go beyond mere suspicion but need not extend to certainty of guilt.

Probation. Supervised conditional release of convicted people without prior correctional confinement (as distinguished from suspended sentence which ordinarily involves no supervision in the community).

Recidivism. Habitual criminal conduct as measured by repeated arrests, convictions, or correctional confinements; the return of a person to custody following an effort at reform.

Sociopath. One who lacks a conscience or fails to meet the usual cultural standards for acceptable behavior; also described as a "psychopathic personality."

Special Police. A general term applied to officers other than those in full-time public employment; used to include members of private, honorary, reserve, and auxiliary forces.

Standing. The right to either bring a suit or exercise the privilege of excluding evidence through timely objection.

Suspended Sentence. Conditional release without supervision following conviction (as distinguished from probation which ordinarily involves supervision).

Trial *De Novo* (dē nō′vō). A retrial in higher court as if the previous determination had never occurred; used when the lower tribunal was not of record.

Voir Dire (vwor dēr). Examination of prospective jurors (or witnesses) to determine their eligibility "to speak the truth."

Warrant. An oral or written judicial order that is commonly used to permit arrest or search and is based on probable cause.

White Collar Crime. Offenses committed by ordinarily respectable people in the course of routine employment.

Suggested Readings

The suggested items that follow do not constitute a complete listing of useful materials. Rather, together with the notes to each chapter, they indicate essential publications for additional inquiry and study. While arbitrarily grouped by general topic (crime, the police, the courts, and corrections), many of the references apply to several aspects of criminal justice.

During recent years, countless related publications, including several detailed bibliographies, have appeared. The following selected readings, with statutes omitted, encompass only singularly significant and valuable items, regardless of age. Some were written centuries ago by gifted observers; others are statistical analyses updated yearly and released on a continuing basis.

In the past, those concerned with particular aspects of criminal justice have tended to rely upon certain types of materials. Criminologists often use government documents; specialists in police science frequently turn to technical books; cases sometimes dominate literature relating to courts; and penologists commonly resort to articles in leading periodicals. All of these kinds of sources are included in the suggested readings.

While only items of great importance appear, they will themselves provide references to thousands of additional entries. The short accompanying comments are intended only to indicate primary applications, not broader significances. Identifying classification numbers, assigned by the Superintendent of Documents, follow the U.S. Government Printing Office publications. Individually and collectively, the selected readings contain a wealth of information awaiting the diligent reader and concerned citizen. Most of them are available in all adequate college and university libraries throughout the nation.

Innumerable collections of readings covering various aspects of criminal justice now exist. However, two notable collections have appeared in recent years. Readers desiring useful secondary sources might well consult: Radzinowicz, Leon and Wolfgang, Marvin E. eds. *Crime and Justice*, 3 vols. New York: Basic Books, 1971; and Kaplan, John ed. *Criminal Justice: Introductory Cases and Materials*. Mineola, New York: Foundation, 1973. Both of the above contain many valuable selections. They do not, however, provide the scope and depth of the following original and primary sources.

Part I: Crime

Abrahamsen, David. *The Psychology of Crime*. New York: Wiley, 1964.
   Well-organized introduction to the psychological roots of deviance and criminal behavior.

Capote, Truman. *In Cold Blood*. New York: New American Library, 1965.
   Superb account, in popular novel form, of a true and shocking mass murder, its causes, and aftermath.

Becker, Howard S. *Outsiders: Studies in the Sociology of Deviance*. Glencoe, Ill.: Free Press, 1963. Marijuana use, social control, deviant careers, moral crusades, rules, and the practicalities of enforcement.

Bentham, Jeremy. *A Fragment on Government and an Introduction to the Principles of Morals and Legislation*. Oxford: Blackwell, 1948. First published in 1789, a most influential study on the purpose of penal law.

The Challenge of Crime in a Free Society. Washington: GPO, 1967. Pr 36.8: L41/C86. The basic report of the President's Commission on Law Enforcement and Administration of Justice.

Cressey, Donald R. *Theft of the Nation*. New York: Harper & Row, 1969.
   Organized crime and its impact on society, the economy, and government.

Drug Use in America: Problem in Perspective. Washington: GPO, 1973.
   Y 3.M 33/2: 1/973. A thorough and detailed preliminary examination of the narcotics dilemma in the United States.

Hart, H. L. A. *The Concept of Law*. London: Oxford University Press, 1961. The role of sovereignty, continuity, and limitation in law.

Hoebel, E. Adamson. *The Law of Primitive Man*. Cambridge: Harvard University Press, 1954. Anthropological survey of law and procedure in primitive cultures.

Holmes, Oliver Wendell, "The Path of the Law." *Harvard Law Review* 10 (1897): 457–478. Legal realism outlined by a famous teacher, scholar, and judge.

Kantorowicz, Hermann. *The Definition of Law*. London: Cambridge University Press, 1958. A brief but brilliant analysis of the significance and limits of law.

Mannheim, Hermann. *Comparative Criminology*. Boston: Houghton Mifflin, 1965. A leading, scholarly discussion of the many theories on the causes of crime.

Not the Law's Business? Washington: GPO, 1972. HE 20.2420/2: L44. A survey of homosexuality, abortion, prostitution, narcotics, and gambling in America.

Powell v. Texas, 392 U.S. 514, 88 S.Ct. 2145 (1968). The Supreme Court decision that alcoholism need not constitute a defense to charges of public drunkenness.

Report of the National Advisory Commission on Civil Disorders. Washington: GPO, 1968. Pr 36.8 C49/R29. The causes and immediate results of unrest and riots in the inner city.

Robinson v. California, 370 U.S. 660, 82 S.Ct. 1417 (1962). Addiction, as opposed to sale or possession of drugs, held not to be punishable as a crime.

Schafer, Stephen. *The Victim and His Criminal*. New York: Random House, 1968. The history, relationships, restitution, and functional responsibilities of victims.

Schur, Edwin M. *Law and Society*. New York: Random House, 1968. Sociological analysis of jurisprudence, law, order, and change.

Sutherland, Edwin H. *White Collar Crime*. New York: Holt, Rinehart & Winston, 1961. The extent of violations by corporations and persons in business.

Task Force Report: Crime and Its Impact. Washington: GPO, 1967. Pr 36.8: L41/C86/3. Detailed report on the scope and results of crime in America.

Task Force Report: Juvenile Delinquency and Youth Crime. Washington: GPO, 1967. Pr 36.8: L41/J98. Excellent collection of papers on diverse aspects of delinquency.

Thrasher, Frederic M. *The Gang*. Chicago: University of Chicago Press, 1927. Dated but excellent study of delinquent behavior by youth groups.

Uniform Crime Reports for the United States. Washington: GPO, published annually. J 1.14/7: Statistical summaries of reported index offenses, arrests, and police employment.

Wolfgang, Marvin E. *Patterns in Criminal Homicide*. New York: Wiley, 1966. Statistical and sociological study of 600 homicides in Philadelphia.

Wormser, Rene A. *The Story of the Law.* New York: Simon & Schuster, 1962. Fine account of the historical development of legal systems from Moses to the United Nations.

Part II: The Police

Black, Hugo LaFayette. *A Constitutional Faith.* New York: Knopf, 1969. Distinguished commentaries by a famous jurist on due process, Amendment I, and the role of courts.

Brant, Irving. *The Bill of Rights: Its Origin and Meaning.* New York: New American Library, 1967. A fine study of personal liberties and protections against the state.

Brown v. Mississippi, 297 U.S. 278, 56 S.Ct. 461 (1936). Due process applied to the states, preventing the use of confessions obtained by torture.

Chevigny, Paul. *Police Power.* New York: Vintage, 1969. Liberal examination of police abuses in New York City.

Chimel v. California, 395 U.S. 752, 89 S.Ct. 2034 (1969). Searches incident to arrest are restricted to areas under immediate personal control.

Expenditure and Employment Data for the Criminal Justice System. Washington: GPO, published annually. J 1.37:. Detailed statistics on federal, state, and local agencies.

The Functions of the Police in Modern Society. Washington: GPO, 1970. HE 20.2420/2: P75. Review of the basic characteristics, practices, forces, and possible models.

Miranda v. Arizona, 384 U.S. 335, 86 S.Ct. 792 (1966). Warnings on the rights of silence and counsel required of police prior to interrogation of suspects.

Morris, Norval and Hawkins, Gordon. *The Honest Politician's Guide to Crime Control.* Chicago: University of Chicago Press, 1969. Realistic discussion of the practical problems of modern American law enforcement.

Mapp v. Ohio, 367 U.S. 643, 81 S.Ct. 1684 (1961). The federal exclusionary rule preventing use of illegally obtained evidence is applied to the states.

Niederhoffer, Arthur. *Behind the Shield.* Garden City, New York: Anchor, 1969. Police cynicism, personality, and attitudes in urban society.

Piliavin, Irving and Briar, Scott, "Police Encounters with Juveniles," *American Journal of Sociology* 70 (September 1964): 206–214. Discretion and prejudice in connection with investigations and dispositions.

Prassel, Frank Richard. *The Western Peace Officer: A Legacy of Law and Order.* Norman: University of Oklahoma Press, 1972. Origin and development of American law enforcement agencies.

Reiss, Albert J. *The Police and the Public.* New Haven: Yale University Press, 1971. An outstanding study of relationships between the community and police officers.

Schmerber v. California, 384 U.S. 757, 86 S.Ct. 1826 (1966). Blood tests may be required by police, under appropriate conditions, to determine intoxication.

Skolnick, Jerome H. *Justice Without Trial*. New York: Wiley, 1966. Police operations, investigations, use of informers, and relations with other agencies of justice.

Smith, Bruce. *Police Systems in the United States*. New York: Harper & Row, 1960. A classic and formal survey of law enforcement units at all levels of government.

State-Local Relations in the Criminal Justice System. Washington: GPO, 1971. Y 3.Ad9/8: 2C 86. Detailed analysis of proposals, conditions, and issues, with informative tables.

Task Force Report: The Police. Washington: GPO, 1967. Pr 36.8: L41/P75. Administrative problems, coordination, personnel, standards, and community relations.

Terry v. Ohio, 392 U.S. 1, 88 S.Ct. 1868 (1968). Stop and frisk permitted on reasonable suspicion during street investigation.

United States v. Wade, 388 U.S. 218, 87 S.Ct. 1926 (1967). Right to counsel during line-up following formal accusation.

Westley, William A., "Violence and the Police," *American Sociological Review* 59 (1953): 34–41. Police duties and concepts, use and legitimation of force.

Wilson, James Q. *Varieties of Police Behavior*. New York: Atheneum, 1970. Law enforcement policies and styles in eight selected communities.

Wilson, O. W. and McLaren, Roy Clinton. *Police Administration*. New York: McGraw-Hill, 1972. Third edition of a leading text by two noted authorities.

Wong Sun v. United States, 371 U.S. 471, 83 S.Ct. 407 (1963). Evidence indirectly obtained through illegal search is subject to exclusion as "fruit of the poisonous tree."

Part III: The Courts

Abraham, Henry J. *The Judicial Process*. New York: Oxford University Press, 1968. Thorough introduction to courts and judges, with an exceptional and extensive bibliography.

Argersinger v. Hamlin, 407 U.S. 25, 92 S.Ct. 2006 (1972). No imprisonment, for either major or minor crime, without full rights of defense counsel.

Baldwin v. New York, 399 U.S. 66, 90 S.Ct. 1886 (1970). Right to jury trial assured whenever imprisonment for more than six months may result.

Blumberg, Abraham S. *Criminal Justice*. New York: Quadrangle, 1967. A careful analysis and discussion of actual procedures in urban court systems.

Carter, Robert M. and Wilkins, Leslie T., "Some Factors in Sentencing Policy," *Journal of Criminal Law, Criminology and Police Science* 58 (1967): 503–514. An excellent short study of relationships between presentence recommendations and final dispositions.

Courts. Washington: GPO, 1973. Y 3.C86: 2C83. Controversial recommendations by the National Advisory Commission on Criminal Justice.

SUGGESTED READINGS

Downie, Leonard. *Justice Denied: The Case for Reform of the Courts.* Baltimore: Penguin, 1971. A popular examination of practical problems relating to mass judicial processing.

Hall, Jerome. *General Principles of Criminal Law.* Indianapolis: Bobbs-Merrill, 1960. Lucid and provocative inquiry into basic principles, doctrines, and theories of penal law.

In re Gault, 387 U.S. 1, 87 S.Ct. 1428 (1967). Basic protections of due process are extended to include coverage of juvenile delinquency hearings.

Johnson v. Louisiana, 406 U.S. 356, 92 S.Ct. 1620 (1972). The Constitution does not prohibit states from allowing less than unanimous findings of criminal guilt.

Juvenile Court Statistics. Washington: National Center for Social Statistics, published annually. HE 17.23: 95. Statistical summaries of delinquency, dependency, and neglect cases.

Kalven, Harry and Zeisel, Hans. *The American Jury.* Boston: Little, Brown, 1966. Extensive analysis of functions, members, attitudes, and performance.

Karlen, Delmar. *Anglo-American Criminal Justice.* New York: Oxford University Press, 1967. A comparison of U.S. and English legal processes.

Lewis, Anthony. *Gideon's Trumpet.* New York: Vintage, 1964. Well-told story of the landmark decision of Gideon v. Wainwright, 372 U.S. 335, 83 S.Ct. 792 (1963).

Mallory v. United States, 354 U.S. 449, 77 S.Ct. 1356 (1957). After arrest, judicial hearings are required without unnecessary delay under federal rules of procedure.

Malloy v. Hogan, 378 U.S. 1, 84 S.Ct. 1489 (1964). Amendment V protections against required self-incrimination are applied to the states.

Manual for Courts-Martial. Washington: GPO, 1969. D 1.15: 69. Official criminal code, with extended commentary, for the armed forces.

Mayers, Lewis. *The American Legal System.* New York: Harper & Row, 1964. Comprehensive survey of civil and criminal justice in the United States.

Modern Court Management. Washington: GPO, 1970. J 1.36/2: 70-3. Brief but significant discussion of methods for improvements in processing.

O'Callahan v. Parker, 395 U.S. 258, 89 S.Ct. 1683 (1969). Courts-martial restricted to cases directly involving the armed services.

Puttkammer, Ernst W. *Administration of Criminal Law.* Chicago: University of Chicago Press, 1953. Concise discussion of procedures from arrest through sentencing.

Task Force Report: The Courts. Washington: GPO, 1967. Pr 36.8: L41/C83. Generalized survey of negotiated pleas, procedures, and officers of justice.

Trebach, Arnold S. *The Rationing of Justice.* New Brunswick, N.J.: Rutgers University Press, 1964. Constitutional rights and realities of police and court processing.

Tumey v. Ohio, 273 U.S. 510, 47 S.Ct. 437 (1927). Trial by magistrate receiving fees for convictions held invalid.

United States v. Tempia, 16 U.S.C.M.A. 629 (1967). Court of Military Appeals requires warnings prior to interrogation and the application of constitutional rights in the armed forces.

Part IV: Corrections

di Beccaria, Marchese (Cesare Bonesana). *On Crimes and Punishments*. Indianapolis: Bobbs-Merrill, 1963. Since 1761, the classic work on the purpose of penal law.

Barnes, Harry Elmer. *The Story of Punishment*. Montclair, N.J.: Patterson Smith, 1972. History and development of concepts relating to legal penalties and correction.

Clark, Ramsey. *Crime in America*. New York: Simon & Schuster, 1970. Controversial but significant commentary by a former attorney general.

Clemmer, Donald. *The Prison Community*. New York: Holt, Rinehart & Winston, 1958. Objective study of life within adult correctional institutions.

Conrad, John P. *Crime and Its Correction*. Berkeley: University of California Press, 1967. International study of practices involving punishment and rehabilitation.

Dressler, David. *Practice and Theory of Probation and Parole*. New York: Columbia University Press, 1969. Sound exposition of the duties and responsibilities of community treatment.

Furman v. Georgia, 408 U.S. 238, 92 S.Ct. 2726 (1972). Imposition of the death penalty is in violation of constitutional rights.

Gibbons, Don C. *Changing the Lawbreaker*. Englewood Cliffs, N.J.: Prentice-Hall, 1965. Objective study of programs and policies of rehabilitation.

Glaser, Daniel. *The Effectiveness of a Prison and Parole System*. Indianapolis: Bobbs-Merrill, 1964. Results of very extensive research on imprisonment, release, and recidivism.

Instead of Court. Washington: GPO, 1971. HE 20.2420/2: C83. Means of diverting and reforming juveniles outside of formal judicial procedures.

Manual on Jail Administration. Washington: National Sheriff's Association, 1970. Detailed and formal discussion on diverse aspects of local confinement facilities.

Mempa v. Rhay, 389 U.S. 128, 88 S.Ct. 254 (1967). Rights to counsel are applied to hearings on probation revocation.

Menninger, Karl. *The Crime of Punishment*. New York: Viking, 1969. Impassioned but stimulating discussion of the overt failures of American justice.

National Jail Census 1970. Washington: GPO, 1971. J 1.37/2: 1. Comprehensive and original statistical survey on local confinement facilities in all parts of the United States.

National Prisoner Statistics: Prisoners in State and Federal Institutions for Adult Felons. Washington: Bureau of Prisons, 1972. J 16.23: 47. Bulletin on recent inmate populations, commitments, and forms of release.

National Survey of Youth Service Bureaus. Washington: GPO, 1973. HE

17.802: Y8/4. Explanation and evaluation of central agencies for prevention and control of juvenile delinquency.

Rubin, Sol. *The Law of Criminal Correction*. St. Paul: West, 1963. Valuable examination of the formal rules applicable to sentenced persons.

Schur, Edwin M. *Crimes Without Victims*. Englewood Cliffs, N.J.: Prentice-Hall, 1965. Public policy toward abortion, homosexuality, and drug addiction.

Sellin, Thorsten. *The Death Penalty*. Philadelphia: American Law Institute, 1959. Comprehensive volume on the controversial issue of capital punishment.

Shaw, George Bernard. *The Crime of Imprisonment*. New York: Philosophical Library, 1946. Sharp and provocative criticism of traditional penal methods.

Standards Relating to Probation. N.p.: American Bar Association, 1970. General principles and recommendations on use, conditions, revocation, and administration.

Statistics on Public Institutions for Delinquent Children, 1970. Washington: National Center for Social Statistics, 1971. HE 17.23: 96. Statistical summaries on training schools, camps, ranches, and reception centers.

Sykes, Gresham M. *The Society of Captives*. New York: Atheneum, 1970. Relations among inmates and guards in a maximum security prison.

Task Force Report: Corrections. Washington: GPO, 1967. Pr 36.8: L41/C83. Singularly impressive study of various forms of probation, confinement, and parole.

Tate v. Short, 401 U.S. 395, 91 S.Ct. 668 (1971). Equal protection prevents jail sentences for those unable, as opposed to those unwilling, to pay fines.

Index

Abandoned cars, 70
Abraham, Henry J., 247
Abrahamsen, David, 244
Absence without leave, 170
Accidents, 26, 71, 77, 80, 81, 109, 149
Accusation, 97, 118, 135–137, 146, 149, 153, 171
Accusatory stage, 95
Acquinas, St. Thomas, 7
Acquittals, 122, 129, 152, 153, 154, 159, 229
Addiction, 39, 40, 41, 43, 47, 53, 56, 180, 189, 193, 210, 218, 228, 231
Administrative agencies, 15, 21, 110, 119, 155, 162–164, 173
Adult probation, 197, 202–204, 205
Adversary practice, 118, 122–133, 151–152, 238
Advisory councils, 85
Aftercare, 177, 184, 188, 189, 190, 194, 213, 224–226, 233, 238
Agency supervision, 196–200
Aggravated assaults. *See* Assault
Air Force, 171, 172
Alcohol, 3, 42, 48, 50, 56, 105, 109. *See also* Liquor
Alcohol, Tobacco, and Firearms Division (Internal Revenue Service), 62
Alcoholics Anonymous, 193
Alcoholism, 42, 180, 193, 228. *See also* Drunkenness
American revolution, 7, 102
Amnesty, 222, 238
Amphetamines, 40
Anarchy, 2, 113, 179
Angles, 10
Appeal, 119, 158–160, 163, 167
Appointed judges, 142, 146
Arbuthnot, John, 4
Argersinger v. Hamlin, 247
Aristotle, 7
Armed forces, 170–173
Army, 171, 172
Arraignment, 148, 149, 151, 156, 160, 238

Arrests, 23, 28, 35, 41, 46, 51, 56, 60, 61, 76, 78, 84, 88–92, 96, 99, 112, 117, 119–133, 135, 138, 148, 149, 154, 156, 160, 163, 164, 168, 171, 180, 181, 183, 196, 198, 228, 229, 230, 232, 238
Arson, 22, 90
Artists, 98
Asia, 9
Assault, 22, 23, 24, 25, 32, 35, 42, 77, 79, 90, 122, 130, 152, 156, 180, 208, 213, 219
Assembly, freedom of, 111, 114
Assigned counsel, 128, 133, 149
Atlanta, 32
Attorney general, 64
Augustus, John, 176
Austin, John, 7
Automobile patrol, 76
Automobiles, 80–81, 92, 105, 109, 138, 141, 149, 166. *See also* Traffic
Autopsies, 136
Auto theft, 23, 24, 35, 46, 78, 90, 91, 229

Babylonia, 9
Bad checks, 51, 78, 125
Bail, 117, 118, 120–122, 128, 132, 148, 157, 198, 214, 238
Bailiffs, 142.
Bail schedule, 120
Baldwin v. New York, 247
Baltimore, 169
Bar associations, 124
Barbiturates, 40
Barnes, Harry Elmer, 249
Bartolus (Bartolo da Sassoferrato), 10
di Beccaria, Marchese (Cesare Bonesana), 176, 249
Becker, Howard S., 244
Bentham, Jeremy S., 7, 244
Bill of Rights, 61, 102–114, 144
Bisovereignty, 139, 146, 154
Black, Hugo L., 111, 246
Black market, 52–53

251

252 INDEX

Black police officers, 84
Blacks, 26, 27, 28, 29, 30–33, 39, 45–48, 56, 84, 86, 89, 119, 186, 187, 189, 219, 230
Blackstone, William, 11
Blumberg Abraham S., 247
Boats, 76
Bonaparte, Napoleon, 10, 11
Bondsman, 118, 121
Booking, 89, 90, 97, 120
Bookmaking, 38
Bootlegging, 37, 38
Border Patrol (Immigration and Naturalization Service), 63, 64
Boston, 68
de Bracton, Henry, 10
Brandeis, Louis D., 107
Brant, Irving, 246
Briar, Scott, 246
Bribery, 53, 54, 126, 189
Brockway, Zebulon R., 177, 226
Broken homes, 3, 31, 48–50, 56
Brown v. Mississippi, 246
Brutality, 49, 122, 183, 208, 210
Buckle, Henry T., 45
Buffalo, New York, 38
Burden of proof, 137, 145, 152, 167
Bureaucracy, 54, 129, 132, 155, 163, 164, 194, 200
Bureau of Customs, 63
Burglary, 22, 23, 24, 25, 35, 39, 46, 73, 78, 90, 91, 108, 141, 154, 213, 222, 229
Burke, Edmund, 192
Business, 50–53, 73, 162
Byzantine Empire, 9

California, 26, 38, 65, 66, 67, 155, 212, 216, 217
California Highway Patrol, 65
Canon law, 10, 238
Canons of ethics, 124
Capital punishment. *See* Death penalty
Capote, Truman, 244
Card games, 38
Carter, Robert M., 247
Caseloads, 197, 198, 200, 202, 225, 227, 228, 232
Casting away arms, 170
Causation, 28, 46–50, 55–56, 180
Celts, 10
Censorship, 112–113, 210
Centralization, 83, 209
Certification of cases, 159
Certiorari, 159, 238
Chain of custody, 98
Challenge for cause, 145
Chambers (judicial), 142
Chambers of commerce, 53
Champions, 122, 128
Change of venue, 138

Chevigny, Paul, 246
Chicago, 38, 68
Child abuse, 82
Child molesting, 49, 156, 214
Child neglect, 165
Child support, 19, 214
Chimel v. California, 246
Chinese-Americans, 28
Cities, 26, 27, 31–33, 39, 47, 53, 60, 68, 69, 76, 77, 83, 84, 85, 125, 138, 144, 156, 165, 210, 214, 219, 225. *See also* Urbanization
Civil demonstrations, 111–112
Civil (continental) law, 10, 11, 17, 104, 238
Civil (private) law, 18–19, 238
Civil service, 70, 85, 125
Civil suits, 18–19, 81, 89, 123, 139, 141, 149, 165, 172, 189
Civil War, 60, 103, 212
Civilian clothes, 78
Civilian review boards, 85
Clark, Ramsey, 249
Classification, prisoner, 209, 211
Clemmer, Donald, 249
Closed institution, 238
Cocaine, 39
Code of Twelve Tables, 9
Codex Justinianus, 9
Coercion, 95
Commissioners, 139, 142
Common law, 10, 17, 22, 94, 102, 104, 118, 123, 137, 144, 146, 152, 164, 238
Communications, 61, 78, 82–83, 86, 182
Community, 27, 29, 32, 53, 68, 75, 127, 144, 145, 146, 154, 155, 172, 176, 179, 198, 199, 204, 211, 221, 224, 225, 233
Community relations, 61, 80, 84–85, 182
Community treatment, 177, 188, 189, 190, 192–205, 224–229, 231, 232
Commutation, 222, 227
Compensation of victims, 181
Complaints, 19, 85, 126
Computers, 81
Concurrent jurisdiction, 137
Conduct bringing discredit, 170
Confessions, 94–96, 100, 103, 107, 109
Confidence games, 78
Confinement, 153, 157, 166, 167, 169, 176, 177, 183, 187, 192, 193, 197, 198, 199, 202, 204, 207–210, 214, 221–224, 225, 226, 229, 230. *See also* Imprisonment
Conjugal visits, 218, 238
Connecticut, 215
Conrad, John P., 249
Consecutive sentences, 155
Consolidation, 67
Constables, 60, 67

INDEX 253

Constantinople, 9
Constitution of the United States, 14, 102–114, 160, 170, 186
  Amendment I, 111–113, 114
  Amendment IV, 88, 92, 106
  Amendment V, 94, 103, 108–111, 154
  Amendment VI, 128, 144
  Amendment VIII, 121, 183
  Amendment XIV, 103–104
  Article I, 105
  Article III, 16
Contempt, 158, 163
Conviction, 91, 129, 130, 143, 168, 181, 183, 187, 188, 189, 198, 228–232
Coordination, 66, 68, 83
Coroner, 136
Corporal punishment, 213
Corporate crime, 52–53
Corpus delicti, 151, 239
Corrections, 59, 91, 153, 164, 166, 169, 175–234, 235, 236, 237
Corruption, 3, 36–37, 43, 53–55, 56, 76, 79, 126, 143, 158, 164, 183, 208, 215
Cosa Nostra, 38
Cotgrave, Randle, 135
Cottage supervisors, 212
Counseling, 42, 82, 179, 185, 193, 202, 209, 211, 215, 218, 223
Counterfeiting, 22, 63, 138
County line provisions, 137
Court of Military Appeals, 173
Courts, 5, 10, 18, 21, 34, 41, 43, 56, 79, 82, 94, 98, 99, 103, 104, 110, 113, 114, 117–173, 176, 177, 178, 180, 181, 183, 188, 189, 190, 193, 196, 197, 200, 201, 203, 207, 210, 212, 214, 225, 229, 232, 235, 236
Courts-martial, 119, 170–173
Courts of Appeal, U.S. "circuit," 139
Courts of military review, 173
Courts of record, 159
Cowardly conduct, 173
Craps, 38
Cressey, Donald R., 244
Crime, 1–57, 59, 60, 63, 69, 73, 75, 76, 77, 81, 86, 88–92, 94, 95, 99, 106, 117, 120, 125, 126, 138, 144, 145, 146, 154, 162, 165, 166, 176, 178–181, 185, 186, 187, 190, 197, 209, 216, 225, 226, 229–232, 235, 239
Criminal investigation, 61, 77–78, 82–86, 91, 94, 171, 182, 183, 189
Criminal law, 2, 18–29, 59, 106, 111, 143, 183, 187, 239
Criminal procedure, 15, 104, 108, 118–119, 140, 151–154, 235
Criminalistics, 83–84, 86, 98, 239
Criminals. *See* Offenders
Crisis intervention, 182, 239
Cross-examination, 151, 166

Crowds, 111–113
Cruel and unusual punishment, 183
Cultural law, 7–8, 16
Culture, 3, 45–57
Curfew, 34, 35, 90, 213
Custom, 8, 9, 13, 17, 117, 124, 136, 141, 151, 156

Danger, 65, 76, 85, 86, 93, 208
Dangerous drugs, 39, 40, 43, 239. *See also* Drugs; Narcotics
Dark Ages, 9
Data processing, 66, 83
Death penalty, 19, 184, 185, 186, 190, 222
Decemviri, 9
Decentralization, 66–68
Defective goods, 189
Defendants, 96, 105, 106, 110, 113, 118, 123, 128, 130, 132, 141, 143, 144, 148, 149, 152, 153, 155, 157, 158, 159, 235
Defense counsel, 97, 112, 118, 121–124, 127–133, 141, 143, 144, 145, 149, 151, 152, 153, 156, 160, 166, 172, 173, 189, 204
Deferred conviction, 169, 204
Deferred prosecution, 169
Deferred sentencing, 204
Delaware, 215
Delay, 120, 122, 127, 144, 148, 156, 157, 159, 160
Democracy, 20, 21, 60, 61, 107, 111, 112, 114, 158, 178, 190
Department of Justice, 62, 215
Department of the Treasury, 62
Deportation, 177, 184
Depressants, 39, 40
Desertion, 170
Detached workers, 179
Detectives, 77–78, 79, 86, 171
Detention center personnel, 211
Detention centers, 164, 177, 188, 190, 200, 201, 207, 210–212, 214, 219, 221
Deterrence, 81, 154, 177, 182, 183, 185, 186, 190, 202, 210
Detoxification centers, 42
Detroit, 32, 38
Diagnostic release, 223
Diagnostic sentencing, 155
Dictatorship, 6, 13. *See also* Tyranny
Differential treatment, 156, 198, 200, 228, 231
Direct discharge, 229
Direct examination, 151
Dirksen, Everett, 52
Disciplinary punishment, 210
Discovery, 123–124
Discretion, 54, 59, 76, 112, 118, 126, 132, 154, 156, 158, 159, 160, 163

Dishonorable discharge, 172
Dismissal of charges, 126, 130, 132, 139, 151, 153, 166
Disorderly conduct, 22, 24, 35, 41, 89, 90, 96, 111, 112, 122, 136, 141, 149, 213, 216
Disparity of sentences, 156, 160
Dispatching, police, 67, 83
District attorneys, 119, 125–127, 130, 132, 133. *See also* Prosecution
District of Columbia, 26, 32, 39, 62, 68, 84, 139
Disturbing the peace. *See* Disorderly conduct
Diversion, 176, 196
Divorce, 48, 49
Dockets, 139
Dogs, 70, 76
Double jeopardy, 154
Downie, Leonard, 248
Draftees, 171
Dragnet, 97–98
Dressler, David, 249
Driving while intoxicated, 24, 26, 41, 42, 90, 99
Dropout, 47, 181
Drug Enforcement Administration, 63
Drug rehabilitation centers, 209
Drugs, 38–41, 43, 48, 49, 50, 55, 63, 64, 162, 193, 199. *See also* Dangerous drugs; Narcotics
Drunkenness, 3, 9, 22, 24, 41–43, 89, 90, 96, 136, 141, 149, 180, 216, 228. *See also* Alcoholism
Drunk tank, 214
Due process, 61, 102–104, 106, 113, 160, 166, 172, 182, 204, 239

Early release, 185–221
Eavesdropping, 93–94, 100, 239
Economic loss, 25, 28, 37, 51, 52, 55
Economy, 188, 194, 203, 225
Education, 28, 31, 33, 46, 47, 54, 66, 69, 121, 143, 155, 179, 181, 185, 190, 194, 196, 202, 208, 209, 211, 213, 215, 217, 218, 219, 227. *See also* Training; Schools
Elected judges, 142, 146
Electorate, 20, 223
Elmira, New York, 177
Embezzlement, 22, 26, 51, 73, 90, 214, 229
Emergency telephone numbers, 82–83
Employment, 31, 46, 194, 198, 227
Encouragement, 79
England, 10, 11, 60, 102, 105, 108, 118, 129, 144, 157, 177, 226
Entrapment, 79, 239
Escapes, 213, 217
Espionage, 63
Europe, 9, 39, 123

Evidence, 15, 19, 61, 77, 79, 83, 84, 86, 91–96, 98, 100, 106–110, 113, 123, 124, 127, 130, 144, 145, 151, 152, 157–160, 163, 166
Examining trial, 149, 156
Exclusionary rule, 106–108, 113, 239
Exclusive jurisdiction, 137
Ex-convicts, 221–224, 226–229, 231
Execution. *See* Death penalty
Executive clemency, 222
Exile, 19, 184
Expenditures, 56, 64, 65, 68, 69, 78, 79, 94, 125, 128, 188, 194, 200, 203, 212, 213
Expert witnesses, 152, 157
Ex post facto, 105, 239
Extortion, 38, 55, 122, 126
Extradition, 138, 146

Failure to obey an order, 170
False advertising, 52
False pretenses, 52
False reporting, 54
Family, 27, 28, 38, 46, 48–50, 56, 75, 90, 122, 125, 126, 166, 179, 180, 182, 190, 196, 202, 203, 217, 218, 223, 225, 228
Federal Bureau of Investigation, 23–25, 63, 66
Federal courts, 139–140, 146, 160
Federal police agencies, 62–64, 73
Federal prisons, 216
Federal probation, 197
Fee system, 143
Felonies, 22, 23, 29, 89, 122, 125, 128, 130, 136, 141, 144, 149, 152–156, 168, 201, 203, 205, 214, 216, 221, 223, 226, 228, 239
Females, 26, 67, 71, 82, 212, 214, 216, 219, 224
von Feuerbach, Paul J., 104
Financial manipulation, 52
Fines, 19, 80, 137, 144, 156, 163, 175, 185, 186, 187, 192
Fingerprints, 66, 83, 98, 99, 100
Firearms, 3, 42–43, 45, 73, 77, 109
First offenders, 216
Fixed shifts, 77
Florida, 38
Foot patrol, 76
Footprints, 83, 98
Force, 85, 89, 92, 95, 208, 209. *See also* Violence
Forestry camps, 212
Forfeiture of pay, 170, 172
Forfeiture of property, 22
Forgery, 90
Foster homes, 193, 201
France, 10, 39
Fraud, 25, 26, 52, 90
Frisk, 92–93

"Fruit of the poisonous tree," 93, 108
Furman v. Georgia, 249

Gambling, 3, 22, 25, 36, 37, 38, 42, 43, 63, 79, 90, 92, 94, 109
Gangs, 35, 89
General court-martial, 172, 173
General jurisdiction, 137, 139, 159
Gibbons, Don C., 249
Gideon v. Wainwright, 248
Gilbert, William S., 75
Glaser, Daniel, 249
Glorious revolution, 108
"Good time," 221, 222, 227, 228
Government, 3, 36, 43, 50, 52, 53–56, 57, 67, 69, 102–109, 111, 113, 119, 123, 128, 129, 133, 164, 165, 181, 183, 188, 190, 200, 201, 215, 217, 235
Grand juries. *See* Juries
Greece, 9
Group therapy, 185, 194, 232
Guards, 122, 212, 217, 218, 219
Guilt, 91, 93, 95, 96, 106, 107, 110, 118, 119, 121, 122, 123, 127–130, 132, 136, 137, 141, 142, 144, 145, 148, 149, 151–154, 159, 169, 171, 175, 184, 198, 204, 219, 222, 229

Habeas corpus, 105–106, 141, 239
Habitual offenders, 154
Halfway houses, 194, 209, 223, 239
Hall, Jerome, 248
Hallucinogens, 39, 40
Hard labor, 154
Hart, H. L. A., 245
Hawaii, 64–65, 66, 155
Hawkins, Gordon, 246
Helicopters, 76
Henry II, 10
Heroin, 39, 40, 43, 63
Highway patrols, 64, 65
Hoebel, E. Adamson, 245
Holmes, Oliver Wendell, Jr., 5–6, 245
Home release, 223
Homes. *See* Family; Housing
Homicide, 22, 23, 24, 35, 42, 78, 80, 90, 136, 155, 221. *See also* Manslaughter; Murder
Homosexuality, 122, 215, 218, 219
Honorary police, 72, 73
Hoover, J. Edgar, 63
Horses, 76
Hot pursuit, 138
Housing, 28, 31, 33, 42, 46, 47, 54
"Hue and cry," 60
"Hung" jury, 146, 154

Identification, 61, 66, 78–79, 96–99, 100, 230
Illinois, 39
Imbued fraud, 52

Immigration and Naturalization Service, 63
Immunity statutes, 96, 110
Impeachment, 143
Imprisonment, 19, 113, 128, 154, 155, 156, 163–172, 184, 185, 186, 207–220. *See also* Confinement
Incapacitation, 176, 184, 186, 190
Incest, 22
Indefinite sentences, 222, 239
Indeterminate sentences, 222, 239
Index crimes, 23–25
Indian, American, 9, 28, 45, 47, 62, 63
Indictment, 149, 152, 156, 239
Indigents, 128, 129, 133, 159
Industrial espionage, 52
Information, 136, 146, 149, 239
Informers, 79, 219
Infractions, 23, 118, 127, 136, 139, 149, 165, 166
Initial hearing, 148, 149, 156, 160
Inner cities, 3, 28, 29, 31–33, 40, 43, 47, 76, 84, 89, 179, 239
Innocence, 119, 121, 122, 127, 132, 137, 149, 151, 152
Inquisitorial system, 137
In re Gault, 248
Insanity, 141, 145
Insurance, 25, 81, 232, 236
Intake, 196
Intelligence, 78, 94
Intelligence Division (Internal Revenue Service), 62
Intensive counseling, 198
Intermediate courts of appeal, 159
Internal Revenue Service, 62
Interrogation, 76, 94–96, 109
Interstate flight, 63
Interviews, 95
Irish-Americans, 48
Italian-Americans, 38, 48

Jail, 22, 23, 27, 42, 43, 82, 89, 118, 119, 120–122, 128, 132, 143, 144, 164, 177, 184, 185, 188, 189, 190, 192, 193, 194, 198, 202, 203, 207, 208, 210, 214–216, 219, 221, 223, 224, 226
Johnson v. Louisiana, 248
Judge advocates, 172
Judges, 1, 4, 21, 37, 42, 53, 54, 61, 92, 94, 110, 112, 118, 119, 123, 124, 129, 130, 132, 137–139, 141, 142–144, 145, 146, 148, 149, 151–158, 160, 162, 165, 169, 171, 173, 198, 202, 203, 211, 222, 224, 232, 236. *See also* Magistrates
Juries, 10, 21, 110, 118, 119, 123, 126, 127, 136, 138, 139, 141, 144–146, 152, 155, 157, 160, 166, 167, 172–173

Jurisdiction, 118, 125, 137–139, 146, 168, 170, 171, 239
Justice, 13, 17, 56, 79, 104, 106, 118, 123, 176, 190
Justices of the peace, 143, 159
Justice under law, 3, 4–17, 61
Justinian, 9, 10, 11
Jutes, 10
Juvenile courts, 34, 90, 119, 164–169, 173
Juvenile delinquency, 3, 33–35, 41, 43, 48–50, 56, 164–169, 173, 175, 177, 179, 188, 210–214, 235, 240
Juvenile detention, 210–212, 219
Juvenile probation, 197, 200–202, 205
Juveniles, 67, 82, 91, 122, 135, 164–169, 173, 177, 187, 188, 190, 193, 200, 207, 210–214, 219, 224–225, 233. *See also* Youth

Kalven, Harry, 248
Kangaroo courts, 215
Kansas, 155, 226
Kantorowicz, Hermann, 5, 245
Kaplan, John, 243
Karlen, Delmar, 248
Kidnapping, 22, 63

Labeling, 56, 169, 185, 196
Labor, 51–52, 53, 55, 65, 80, 124
Laboratories, 61, 66, 83–84
Landor, Walter S., 120
Larceny, 22, 23, 24, 35, 46, 51, 78, 90, 91, 240. *See also* Theft
Latin Americans, 45, 47–48
Law, 2, 3, 4–17, 102, 159, 240
Law of the land, 102
Leadership, 3, 55, 71, 73, 78, 158, 173, 179, 236
Legal aid, 128, 129
Legal history, 8–13
Legislatures, 20, 37, 38, 54, 55, 65, 95, 109, 110, 142, 163, 164, 169, 187, 236
Lewis, Anthony, 248
Licensing, 19, 45, 54, 65, 70
Life sentences, 154, 172, 221
Lighting, 179
Limited jurisdiction, 137, 141, 146
Line operations, 61
Line-up, 97, 100
Liquor, 35, 36, 41, 64, 79, 90. *See also* Alcohol
Livestock inspectors, 72
Loan-sharking, 36, 37
Local courts, 141, 146, 159
Local ordinances, 14, 21, 125
Local police, 66–71, 73, 209
Locks, 179
Lockups, 214
Loitering, 35, 90, 213

London, 60
Los Angeles, 32, 68
Louisiana, 11, 38
Lysergic acid diethylamide (LSD), 40, 63

Machiavelli, Niccolo, 18
McLaren, Roy C., 247
Mafia, 38
Magistrates, 89, 93, 106, 121, 139, 141, 143, 144, 148, 157, 158, 165. *See also* Judges
Magna Carta, 10, 102, 103
Maiming, 184
Make sheet, 141
Males, 2, 26, 28, 29, 33, 41, 89, 187, 212, 219, 230
Malfeasance, 54
Mallory v. United States, 248
Malloy v. Hogan, 248
Manslaughter, 23, 42. *See also* Homicide
Mapp v. Ohio, 246
Marijuana, 39, 40, 43, 63
Marine Corps, 171, 172
Marshals (U.S.), 62
Maryland, 39, 64
Massachusetts, 38, 176, 196
Mass processing, 119, 136–137, 141, 157, 172
Maximum security, 217
Maximum sentences, 154, 155, 160, 172
Mayers, Lewis, 248
Medical care, 33, 122, 208, 211
Medical examiners, 136
Medium security, 217
Men. *See* Males
Menninger, Karl, 249
Mental health clinics, 201
Mental illness, 180, 193, 201, 209, 222
Mentally retarded, 217, 219
Metropolitan Police Act (London), 60
Mexico, 40
Michigan, 39
Middle Ages, 10
Midwest, 228
Migration, 47
Military, 9, 16, 54, 57, 62, 63, 119, 168, 169, 170–173
Military judges, 172, 173
Military police, 171
Mills, C. Wright, 53
Minimum security, 217
Minimum sentences, 154, 160, 224
Minorities, 3, 26, 45–48, 53, 84, 217
Miranda v. Arizona, 246
Misbranding livestock, 8
Misdemeanant probation, 203–204, 205
Misdemeanor, 22, 23, 29, 118, 128, 136, 137, 141, 144, 149, 152, 153, 155, 168, 192, 203, 205, 214, 215, 216, 221, 226, 240

Missing persons, 75, 82
Mississippi, 26
Missouri, 38
Missouri plan, 142
Mistrial, 146, 153
Moonlighting, 69
Monopolies, 19, 52
Morale, 65, 85
Morality, 36, 76, 78, 90, 127, 181, 202, 221
Morris, Norval, 246
Moses, 10
Municipal planning, 201
Murder, 8, 23, 29, 38, 42, 43, 121, 122, 125, 141, 152, 170, 171, 185, 189, 202, 213, 214, 215. See also Homicide
Mutilation, 19, 184
Mutiny, 170

Narcotics, 3, 36–39, 43, 64, 78, 79, 90, 92, 94, 99, 108, 109, 218, 221, 240. See also Dangerous drugs; Drugs
National Advisory Commission on Civil Disorders 31
National Crime Information Center, 66
National Park Rangers, 62
Natural law, 7, 16
Navy, 171, 172
Neglect, 49, 82, 165, 208
Negotiated pleas, 129–133, 144, 149, 157, 158. See also Plea-bargaining
Negroes. See Blacks
Neighborhood police officers, 85
Nepotism, 54
Nevada, 38, 65
New England, 197, 210, 216, 226
New Hampshire, 217, 226
New Jersey, 38, 39
New York City, 32, 38, 39, 68, 169
New York State, 26, 65, 67, 217, 226
Niederhoffer, Arthur, 246
No bill, 136
"No knock" statutes, 92
Nolle prosequi, 126, 240
Nolo contendere, 149, 240
Nonjudicial punishment, 170, 172, 173, 240
Norman conquest, 10
North Dakota, 26, 65, 217
Northeast, 212
Nulla poena sine lege, 104–105, 240
Numbers, 38

O'Callahan v. Parker, 248
Offenders, 2, 26–29, 50, 55, 79, 96, 121, 124, 135, 158, 175–177, 189, 209, 210, 231, 235
Oklahoma, 226
Omaha, 68

Open charge, 90
Open community, 217, 240
Opium, 39, 40
Organization, police, 62–73
Organized crime, 3, 35–38, 43, 78, 121, 126, 240
Original jurisdiction, 139
Overcharging, 130
Overcrowding, 122, 213

Pardons, 222, 227, 240
Parens patriae, 165, 166–167, 173, 240
Parks, 76
Parole, 155, 163, 177, 184, 188, 189, 190, 194, 203, 207, 216, 222, 223, 224, 225, 226–229, 230, 233, 240
Parole boards, 224, 227
Parole officers, 227–228
Parole revocation, 228
Partial release, 215, 223
Patrol, 61, 75–77, 78, 79, 82, 85, 182
Pawnbroker reports, 70
Peel, Robert, 60
Penal law. See Criminal law
Penalties. See Punishment
Penitentiaries, 216–219
Pennsylvania, 39, 65, 177
Peremptory challenge, 145
Personality, 48–50
Personal recognizance, 120, 215, 240
Petition, freedom of, 111, 114
Petitions, juvenile, 165, 166
Philadelphia, 38, 68
Photographs, 98, 100
Piliavin, Irving, 246
Pitt, William, 6
Plea-bargaining, 118, 128, 129–133, 144, 149, 153, 157, 166, 173, 183, 240. See also Negotiated pleas
Police, 4, 20, 23, 25, 34, 35, 37, 42–45, 53, 56, 59–114, 117–120, 122, 124, 127, 130, 135, 136, 138, 143, 148, 152, 153, 163, 164, 167, 169, 171, 173, 176, 177, 178, 180, 181, 183, 188, 189, 190, 198, 199, 201, 211, 224, 228, 229, 230, 232, 235, 236, 237
Police administration, 69–71, 73, 82, 235
Police auxiliary, 71–72, 73
Police operations, 75–86
Police personnel, 62, 64, 68, 69–71, 73, 75–86, 182, 236–237
Police ratio, 68, 69, 240
Police reserve, 71–72, 73
Policewomen, 67, 71, 82
Politics, 55, 63, 65, 71, 118, 125, 126–127, 133, 135, 136, 142, 143, 146, 190, 209, 216, 217, 236
Pollution, 54, 162
Polygraph, 72, 84, 240

Poor, the, 2, 26, 28, 29, 31–33, 46–47, 56, 84, 86, 121, 129, 166, 179, 186, 187, 189, 217, 219
Poppies, 39
Pornography, 113
Positive law, 7, 16
Post Office Inspectors, 62
Poverty. *See* Poor
Powell v. Texas, 245
Precedent, 6, 240
Prejudice, 3, 47, 56, 84, 156, 179
Preliminary hearings, 119, 141, 148–151
Pre-parole studies, 227
Pre-release guidance, 223
Pre-release investigation, 225
Pre-release planning, 228
Presentence investigation, 155, 197, 203, 241
Presentence recommendation, 198
President, 63, 125, 139
Press, freedom of, 111, 112–113, 114
Presumption of innocence, 153
Pretrial motions, 127, 141
Prevention, 53, 176, 178–190, 201, 210
Preventive detention, 121, 182, 241
Price administration, 52–53
Prison, 22, 23, 25, 27, 128, 143, 163, 175, 177, 184, 185, 188, 189, 190, 192, 193, 194, 196, 198, 207, 208, 212, 214–229
Prison agriculture, 217
Prison industry, 217
Prison rules, 218
Prison subculture, 218
Private investigators, 72
Private police, 72–73
Private training schools, 213
Probable cause, 88–89, 91, 92, 94, 98, 99, 148, 230, 241
Probation, 130, 154, 155, 156, 163, 165, 169, 176–177, 184, 185, 188, 189, 190, 192, 193, 194, 196–205, 207, 210, 216, 226, 227, 229, 230, 241
Probation officers, 142, 155, 156, 165, 166, 173, 197, 199, 200, 202, 211, 225
Probation rules, 199, 204
Procedure, legal, 15–17, 118–119, 151–154
Prohibition, 41, 43, 55
Promotion, 70, 78, 217
Property crimes, 22, 34, 39, 55, 180, 187, 198, 216
Prosecution, 50, 52, 53, 55, 56, 91, 93, 96, 97, 110–112, 118, 122–133, 135–137, 139, 142–146, 149, 151–154, 156, 157, 159, 160, 163, 169, 172, 173, 183, 187, 189, 219, 231, 232. *See also* District attorneys
Prostitution, 22, 36, 37, 39, 47, 79, 90, 121, 199

Protective Service (General Services Administration), 62
Proverbs, Book of, 221
Psychiatric care, 156, 180
Psychiatric examination, 185
Psychopathic personality, 49
Public defenders, 128, 135
Public relations, 81, 82, 84–85, 86, 124
Puerto Ricans, 45
Punishment, 19, 20, 21, 22, 40, 52, 56, 91, 106, 118, 119, 123, 124, 141, 142, 145, 153, 155, 156, 160, 163, 164, 170–173, 175, 176, 183–187, 190, 192–196, 198, 203, 209, 210, 211, 222, 223, 229
Puttkammer, Ernst W., 248

Quakers, 177
Questioning, 61, 94–96, 109
"Quota" of tickets, 80

Race, 32, 45–47, 145, 155, 210
Radar, 81
Radio, 67, 72, 82, 83, 93, 94
Radzinowicz, Leon, 243
Railroad detectives, 72
Rangers, 60, 62
Rape, 22, 23, 24, 25, 35, 90, 122, 141, 202, 213, 221, 229
Rebuttal, 152
Reception center discharge, 223
Recidivism, 169, 177, 229–233, 241
Records, 61, 66, 78, 79, 81, 82, 83, 86, 98, 167, 182, 230
Recreation, 181, 182, 211, 215, 218
Re-cross examination, 152
Recruits, police, 64, 66, 69, 70, 167
Redirect examination, 152
Reduced charge, 126, 130, 132, 136
Reduction in pay, 170
Referral, 82, 196
Reformation, 176, 181–183, 185, 186, 190, 192, 193, 197, 199, 210, 212, 224, 226, 229. *See also* Rehabilitation
Reformatories. *See* Training schools
Rehabilitation, 56, 154, 169, 185, 193, 198, 201, 208, 209, 216, 219, 224, 226, 231, 232, 236. *See also* Reformation
Reiss, Albert J., 246
Release, 221–233
Religion, 7, 9, 16, 50, 111, 114, 181, 190, 196, 219
Reprieve, 222
Residential communities, 212
Residential treatment, 194, 209
Restitution, 202
Retribution, 176, 184, 186, 190
Retroactivity, 105, 113

INDEX 259

Revenge. See Retribution
Reversal, 149, 153, 160
Revocation hearings, 204, 228
Revocation of parole, 228, 230
Revocation of probation, 199, 204, 230
Rhode Island, 215
Riots, 1, 32, 84, 106, 112, 158, 208, 209
Road camps, 216
Robbery, 22, 23, 24, 35, 38, 39, 43, 46, 51, 63, 90, 91, 141, 155, 170, 213, 221
Robinson v. California, 245
Rome, 7, 9, 10
Rotating shifts, 77
Rowan, Charles, 60
Rubin, Sol, 250
Rule of law, 104–106, 113
Runaways, 35, 90, 122, 210, 213, 214

Salaries, 64, 65, 68, 69, 125, 143, 208
San Antonio, 68
San Diego, 68
von Savigny, Friedrich K., 8
Saxons, 10
Schafer, Stephen, 245
Schmerber v. California, 246
Schools, 180, 181, 182, 201. See also Education; Training
Schur, Edwin M., 245, 250
Search, 61, 76, 79, 88, 91–94, 98, 99, 106, 107, 108, 113
Secret Service (U.S.), 63
Security police, 171
Segregation, 31, 33, 47
Self-incrimination, 94–96, 108–111, 113–114
Sellin, Thorsten, 250
Senate, 139
Sentence adjustment, 160, 173
Sentence recommendations, 130, 132, 198
Sentencing, 119, 122, 141, 144, 145, 148, 149, 154–157, 160, 173, 178, 182, 185, 187, 189, 197, 207, 215, 216, 219, 221, 222, 223, 229, 230
Sentencing hearings, 156
Shaw, George Bernard, 207, 250
Sheriff, 60, 65
Shoplifting, 51, 73
Shore patrol, 171
Show-up, 97, 100
Skid rows, 41
Skolnick, Jerome H., 247
Slander, 112
Slot machines, 38
Smith, Bruce, 247
Smuggling, 63, 64, 99
Social welfare. See Welfare
Sociopath, 49, 56, 241
Solitary confinement, 177
South, 26, 216, 226

South Carolina, 226
Space exploration, 188
Special court-martial, 172, 173
Special courts, 162–173
Special police, 72–73, 241
Speech, freedom of, 61, 111, 112–113, 114
Speed traps, 80
Spencer, Herbert, 62
Spontaneous admissions, 95
Staff functions, 82–84
Standing, 108, 241
State courts, 140–141, 146
State police, 64–66, 73, 209
Status of forces agreements, 170
Statutes, 14, 21, 55, 59, 124, 137, 138, 141, 156, 164, 181, 187, 202
Stephen, James, 178
Stigmatization. See Labeling
Stimulants, 39, 40
Stolen property, 38, 63, 90
Strict construction, 105, 113
Structural immorality, 53
Study release, 223
Substance, legal, 15–17
Suburbs, 26, 31, 35, 67
Suicide, 122, 215
Summary court-martial, 172, 173
Summary probation, 203
Summation, 152, 160
Supportive therapy, 193
Supreme Court of the United States, 5, 103, 106, 139, 143, 160
Suspects, 61, 91, 97, 99, 100, 120, 122, 135, 141
Suspended sentences, 196, 203, 241
Suspicious persons, 77, 90, 92, 99
Sutherland, Edwin H., 51, 245
Swindling, 138
Sykes, Gresham M., 250
Syndicate, 36
Syrus, Publilius, 162

Table of maximum punishments, 172
Tate v. Short, 250
Taxes, 19, 26, 45, 54, 55, 68, 109, 124, 164, 232, 236
Television, 83
Ten Commandments, 10
Terry v. Ohio, 247
Texas, 39, 64, 217
Theft, 25, 26, 32, 38, 39, 51, 63, 90, 125, 141, 155, 166, 170, 213, 218. See also Larceny
Thrasher, Frederick M., 245
Tickets of leave, 226
Torture, 19, 94, 95, 103, 110
Traffic, 8, 20, 22, 23, 41, 45, 61, 65, 80–81, 82, 89, 90, 118, 119, 127, 136, 139, 149, 165, 166. See also Automobiles

Training, 70, 71, 72, 78, 80, 82, 85, 143, 197, 208, 211, 218. *See also* Education; Schools
Training schools, 177, 188, 190, 194, 207, 212–214, 219, 221, 224, 225, 229
Transportation, 226
Treason, 16, 22
Treatment teams, 217
Trebach, Arnold S., 248
Trial, 110, 112, 113, 117, 118, 119, 122, 127, 130, 141, 144, 145, 148–160, 163, 168, 169, 170–173, 207, 214, 215, 230
Trial *de novo*, 159, 241
Trial juries. *See* Juries
Truancy, 34, 35, 166
True bills, 136
Trustees, 221, 228
Tumey v. Ohio, 248
Tyranny, 106, 112, 113, 144, 171, 179. *See also* Dictatorship

Uniform Code of Military Justice, 170–173
United States v. Tempia, 249
United States v. Wade, 247
Unreported crime, 25, 29
Urbanization, 26, 31, 50, 77, 144, 162. *See also* Cities

Vagrancy, 41, 90
Vagueness, 105
Vandalism, 25, 32, 35, 90, 106, 213
Venue, 137, 138, 146
Verdict, 119, 146, 151, 152, 160
Vice, 31, 36, 38, 45, 53, 78, 79, 107, 126, 187
Victims, 2, 19, 26–29, 32, 36, 79, 97, 123
Violence, 3, 22, 31, 34, 42, 50, 53, 76, 77, 88, 96, 106, 111, 113, 168, 179, 198, 208, 216, 218, 224. *See also* Force
Vocational training, 185, 209
Voiceprints, 99
Voir dire, 145, 241
Voluntariness test, 95, 109
Voluntary declarations, 95
Voluntary defenders, 129, 133
Voting, 20, 223

Waiver, 110, 144, 146, 149, 157
Wardens, 217
Warnings, 92, 94–96, 97, 100
Warrants, 92, 93, 107, 141, 204, 241
Washington (D. C.). *See* District of Columbia
Washington (state), 226
"Watch and ward," 60
Wayward minors, 169
Weapons, 22, 42–43, 60, 90, 93, 99, 199
Weber, Max, 6
Weight of evidence, 152
Welfare, 47, 60, 82, 164, 165, 166, 179, 180, 196, 197, 200, 201, 225
West, 26
Westley, William A., 247
West Virginia, 26
White collar crime, 51–52, 56–57, 189, 241
Whites, 26, 29, 32–33, 46, 47, 56
Wilkes, John, 148
Wilkins, Leslie T., 247
Wilson, James Q., 247
Wilson, O. W., 247
Wiretapping, 93–94
Witnesses, 19, 59, 94, 95, 96, 97, 98, 110, 113, 128, 143, 149, 151–152, 157, 166, 214
Wolfgang, Marvin E., 243, 245
Women. *See* Females
Wong Sun v. United States, 247
Work camps, 217
Work release, 223
Workhouses, 215, 224
Working mothers, 50
World War I, 65
World War II, 65, 226
Wormser, Rene A., 246
Wyoming, 65, 217, 226

Youth, 2, 28, 29, 33–35, 48–50, 53, 82, 84, 86, 89, 119, 164–169, 187, 200–202, 210–214, 216, 224–226, 230. *See also* Juveniles
Youth athletic leagues, 182
Youth centers, 212
Youth corrections acts, 169
Youthful offenders, 119, 164–169, 201
Youth services bureaus, 180

Zeisel, Hans, 248